Dreamweaver® MX 2004
Complete Course

Joyce J. Evans

D1370506

WILEY
Wiley Publishing, Inc.

Dreamweaver® MX 2004 Complete Course

Published by:

Wiley Publishing, Inc.
111 River Street
Hoboken, NJ 07030
www.wiley.com/compbooks

Published simultaneously in Canada

For general information on our other products and services or to obtain technical support please contact our Customer Care Department within the U.S. at 800-762-2974, outside the U.S. at 317-572-3993 or fax 317-572-4002.

Library of Congress Cataloging-in-Publication Data: 2003116747

ISBN: 0-7645-4304-0

Manufactured in the United States of America

10 9 8 7 6 5 4 3 2

» Credits

Publisher: Barry Pruett
Project Editor: Katharine Dvorak
Acquisitions Editor: Michael Roney
Editorial Manager: Robyn B. Siesky
Technical Editor: Mary Rich
Copy Editor: Gwenette Gaddis Goshert
Production Coordinator: Maridee Ennis
Layout and Graphics: Beth Brooks, Joyce Haughey, Jennifer Heleine, LeAndra Hosier, Lynsey Osborn, Heather Pope
Quality Control: John Tyler Connoley, Brian H. Walls
Indexer: Ty Koontz
Proofreader: Vicki Broyles
Special Help: Cricket Krengel, Adrienne Porter

» Dedication

To my loving and wonderful family.
I couldn't have done it without you.

» Acknowledgements

I'd like to thank my acquisitions editor, Mike Roney, for giving me the opportunity to write this book. I'd also like to thank my project editor, Katharine Dvorak, as well as the in-house folks at Wiley, including Rev Mengle, Robyn Siesky, Cricket Krengel, Adrienne Porter, and Maridee Ennis. I'd like to thank to Jacquelin Vanderwood for her wonderful illustrations she let me use in the Frames chapter. I'd also like to acknowledge that Donna Casey wrote the last two chapters in the first version of this book. I updated them to reflect Dreamweaver 2004 changes. Much appreciation goes to Macromedia and their top-shelf team of engineers and support staff for producing such a great program as Dreamweaver. Thanks also go to the hard-working guys and gals who write the extensions for Dreamweaver that extend its capabilities so greatly.

» About the Author

Joyce J. Evans is a training veteran with over 10 years' experience in educational teaching, tutorial development, and Web design. She has been asked to speak at conferences such as Macromedia MAX 2003 and TODCON. Joyce received Editors' Choice Awards for her book, *Fireworks 4 F/X and Design*, and has authored several computer books including *Dreamweaver MX Complete Course*, *Web Design Complete Course*, and *Fireworks MX: Zero to Hero*. Joyce is a Team Macromedia Volunteer and her work is also featured in the Macromedia Design/ Developer Center and the *MX Developers Journal* magazine. She can be reached at Joyce@ JoyceJEvans.com. Her Web site is www. JoyceJEvans.com and she maintains the Idea Design Web site at www.je-ideadesign.com.

» Table of Contents

Introduction	**1**
Confidence Builder	**5**
Part I Course Setup	**19**
Dreamweaver Basics	**21**
Project Overview	**25**
Part II Getting Started	**29**

Session 1 Laying the Foundation — 30

Session Introduction	31
Laying the Foundation	32
Setting Up and Viewing the Workspace	35
Customizing the Workspace	38
Customizing Keyboard Shortcuts	40
Defining a Site	42
Using the Files Panel	44
Using the Assets Panel	46
Using the Start Page	47
Session Review	48
Other Projects	48

Session 2 Building the Site's Framework — 50

Session Introduction	51
Transitional Design	52
About Browser Modes	53
DOCTYPES	53
XHTML versus HTML	54
Advantages of CSS	54
The Home Page and Design Notes	55
Opening and Saving a Document	58
Choosing a Design View	60
Setting Browser Preferences	62
Setting Accessibility Preferences	63
Setting Page Properties	64
Adding Meta Tags	66
Session Review	68

Session 3 Working with Tables — **70**

Session Introduction	71
Learning Table Basics	72
Selecting Table Elements	76
Changing Colors in a Table	78
Adding Custom Borders	80
Using Fixed Tables to Build the Home Page	82
Build the Interior Pages	88
Adding the Navigation Table	90
Adding the Content Table	92
Exploring the Layout View	93
Session Review	96

Session 4 Working with Images — **98**

Session Introduction	99
Inserting the Masthead Images	100
Inserting the Navigation Images	104
Replacing Images	106
Making a Rounded Table Using Images	109
Using Background Images	113
Session Review	114

Session 5 Adding Text   116

Session Introduction   117
Adding Text   118
Importing Text   120
Adding Structural Formatting   122
Wrapping Text around an Image   125
Making a List   127
Adding Flash Text   128
Session Review   130

Session 6 Adding Navigational Links   132

Session Introduction   133
Adding Links   134
Adding Rollovers   136
Making an Image Map   138
Adding a Flash Button   140
Session Review   142

Part III Automating the Design Process   145

Session 7 Using Cascading Style Sheets (CSS)   146

Session Introduction   147
Removing Embedded Styles   148
Attaching a Style Sheet   150
Editing the BODY Tag   152
Grouping Selector Tags   154
Applying Custom Classes   155
Using Pseudo-Class Selectors   158
Assigning a Class Name to the Footer Area   160
Using a Contextual Selector to Add a Style   161
Adding Space Using CSS   164
Session Review   166

Session 8 Using Templates and Libraries   168

Session Introduction   169
Using an Existing Document as a Template   170

Applying a Template   172
Editing a Template   175
Detaching a Template   177
Making a Library Item   178
Inserting Library Items   179
Editing Library Items   180
Session Review   182

Session 9 Adding Forms and Behaviors   184

Session Introduction   185
Building a Basic Form   186
Adding Submit and Clear Buttons   190
Inserting Radio Buttons   191
Inserting Check Boxes   194
Inserting a Text Area and a List   196
Using Jump Menus   198
Session Review   200
Other Projects   200

Part IV Publishing the Site   203

Session 10 Editing Images with or without an Image Editor   204

Session Introduction   205
Cropping Images in Dreamweaver   206
Resampling an Image   208
Adding Brightness, Contrast, and Sharpening in Dreamweaver   209
Using External Image Editors   210
Optimizing Images in Fireworks   211
Editing a Source Image in Fireworks from Dreamweaver   213
Session Review   216

Session 11 Performing Site Checks   218

Session Introduction   219
Running a Site Report for Links   220
Checking Site Reports   222

Using Find and Replace   225
Doing Browser Checks   227
Session Review   228

Session 12 Getting Your Web Site Online   230

Session Introduction   231
Finding a Host   232
Setting FTP Preferences   235
FTPing Files to Your Host   237
Synchronizing the Local and Root Folders   238
Session Review   240

Part V Working with a Data Source 243

Session 13 Setting Up a Database Connection   244

Session Introduction   245
Installing a Personal Web Server (Windows 98)   246
Installing IIS   247
Defining a Dynamic Web Site   249
Setting Up a DSN Name   255
Setting Up a Local DSN Connection   258
Setting Up a Remote DSN Connection   259
Setting Up a Connection String (DSN-less)   261
Using the MapPath Method   263
Session Review   264

Session 14 Building a Web Application   266

Session Introduction   267
Adding a Recordset   268
Using Repeating Regions   271
Using Insert Record on Forms   273
Validating Your Forms   275
Building Update Pages   276
Inserting a Recordset Navigation Bar   281
Building Delete Pages   283
Making Master Detail Pages   285
Session Review   288

Part VI Extra Features   291

Session 15 Making a Pop-Up Menu   292

Session Introduction   293
Adding the Show Pop-Up Menu Behavior   294
Setting the Menu's Appearance   295
Setting the Advanced Settings   296
Setting the Menu's Position   298
Adding the Rest of the Menus   300
Making a New Template Page   303
Session Review   306
Other Projects   306

Session 16 Building a Frame-Based Site   308

Session Introduction   309
Building the Frameset   310
Naming the Frames   312
Adding a Nested Frame and Saving the Frameset   313
Adding Content to the Frames   314
Linking the Navigation   316
Adding Multiple Links   318
Coding for Search Engines   320
Adding a Specialized Jump Menu   321
Session Review   324
Other Projects   324

Appendix A What's on the CD-ROM 327

Appendix B Resources   333

Index   341

Introduction

Understanding the Process

Dreamweaver MX 2004 Complete Course is designed to walk you through all the design stages from the basic planning of a Web site to connecting to a database. Each session builds upon the others to develop the fictitious *Palmetto Design Group* Web site. While building this site, you learn techniques that can be applied to your own Web site. You can also use this design and simply trade these images, logos, and so on for your own.

Dreamweaver MX 2004 Complete Course is divided into manageable sessions that are also topic related, so you can use this book as a reference when you need to refresh your memory. The instructions are succinct. The sessions are taught in a way that beginners can understand, but they are also laced with intermediate skills right from the start.

Is This Book for You?

Absolutely, if you are serious about designing Web pages. Although it is a beginner's book, it is not for the faint of heart. Dreamweaver is a complex, full-featured, professional-level application. It's very easy to skim an instruction and make a mistake. If you are willing to follow the instructions carefully and repeat them if you make a mistake, you'll be amazed at how fast you learn by doing. This book is written for today's new Web designers. You create a dynamic site using a database and other interactivity.

What's in This Book?

Dreamweaver MX 2004 Complete Course is divided into parts, sessions, and tutorials. The parts are subject categories that contain sessions, which in turn contain tutorials and discussions. Each tutorial focuses on a specific topic. These tutorials walk you through the steps for using specific features to create a portion of the Palmetto Design Group Web site, which you develop throughout the book.

Each tutorial builds on the previous tutorials and assumes that you have performed the previous tutorials and learned the skills taught in them. Each session has a starter file, so you can jump in anywhere, but the text assumes that you have learned all previous lessons. Some sessions are bonuses with additional information that this site didn't need but is important for a new designer to know and learn. You can easily skip these if you want to do so; they are marked as such in the introduction of the session.

I have found that most people I teach and help on a daily basis learn best by actually performing a project. It's a great way to get hands-on experience using the various tools, and it's more interesting than reading about what each tool does and how to use it.

Here is an overview of what you find in each part.

Stepping through the Project Stages

Part I: Course Setup

Dreamweaver Basics gives you enough information to get started—not too much and not too little.

Project Overview reviews the process used in this book, as well as system requirements and Windows and Macintosh differences.

Part II: Getting Started

Session 1—Laying the Foundation explains the key questions to ask when planning a site. You meet the Dreamweaver authoring environment, learn how to define a site, and learn to use the Site and Assets panels to manage your site's files.

Session 2—Building the Site's Framework begins to build the structure of your Web site. You delve into setting the page properties, such as background and text color. You also learn how to use Design notes to communicate with co-workers or as a reminder to yourself. In this session, you also add the `<head>` content of metatags and descriptions to your Web page.

Session 3—Working with Tables shows you how to insert and test your table structure in different browsers. You learn how to develop fixed-width tables as well as a fluid table design that changes with the size of the user's browser.

Session 4—Working with Images teaches you how to add images such as photos, buttons, and logos to your document. You also learn how to align them and use an image as a background.

Session 5—Adding Text shows you that adding text is quite easy in Dreamweaver. You learn some of your options and how to change fonts and their attributes. You also add some Flash text.

Session 6—Adding Navigational Links helps you become comfortable using the many techniques of adding links. You also learn how to make rollover images and use the Behaviors panel.

Part III: Automating the Design Process

Session 7—Using Cascading Style Sheets (CSS) teaches you how to control your text using style sheets. You learn how to embed a style sheet and how to use an external one. You also learn how to use CSS for page layout and to control background images.

Session 8—Using Templates and Libraries helps you automate your workflow. You learn how to set up a template and add editable and repeating regions, and you learn how to attach, edit, and update pages using templates. You make a library item and use it as well.

Session 9—Adding Forms and Behaviors teaches you how to add and use various styles of forms and attach behaviors to do things such as validate the form after it's been submitted.

Part IV: Publishing the Site

Session 10—Editing Images with or without an Image Editor teaches you how to edit images from within Dreamweaver and directly in Fireworks and how to return to Dreamweaver again. You also use some of the new editing tools which don't require that any image editor be installed.

Session 11—**Performing Site Checks** shows you how to run various reports and how to make repairs.

Session 12—**Getting Your Web Site Online** walks you through the procedures to upload your files to a remote server and to secure a domain name if you choose to get one. Several free servers are recommended if you want to practice on one before purchasing space on an ad-free server.

Part V: Working with a Data Source

Session 13—**Setting Up a Database Connection** teaches you the steps to take to connect your Web site to an ASP database. The methods are taught for Windows users, but tips are given for Macintosh users as well.

Session 14—**Building a Web Application** teaches you the basics of manipulating a data source (the database) to provide dynamic Web content.

Part VI: Extra Features

Session 15—**Making a Pop-Up Menu** teaches you how to use the new pop-up menu behavior in Dreamweaver. You not only learn the basics, but you also see how to edit the menu and perform complex positioning.

Session 16—**Building a Frame-Based Site** shows you how to set up a frames site and how to work with and save a frameset. The site you build in this book does not use frames, so this is a bonus session to teach you the fundamentals of using frames.

Appendix A—**What's on the CD-ROM** tells you how to access the program files and bonus software on the CD included inside the back cover of this book.

Appendix B—**Resources** provides lots of wonderful resources for you to check out. It includes demo software offers and mini reviews of products that I've personally used and found helpful in Web site design.

Confidence Builder

In this lesson, you construct an entire Web page very quickly. You get some hands-on experience that gives you a feel for the Dreamweaver interface and some of its capabilities. By constructing a simple Web design, you can discover how powerful and easy it is to develop a Web site using Dreamweaver. You add images, text, and links to your first Web page. You'll even be using CSS (Cascading Style Sheets).

One of the issues touched upon in this book is accessibility for the disabled. You add text links and alternative text to your pages to comply with Section 508 of the accessibility laws, enabling disabled users to access your site.

TOOLS YOU'LL USE
Property inspector, Page Properties dialog box, Insert menu, Main menu

MATERIALS NEEDED
The ConfidenceBuilder folder from the accompanying CD-ROM

TIME REQUIRED
30 minutes

Tutorial
» Setting Up Your First Web Page

You can lay out a Web page in Dreamweaver in many ways. You can choose from several different design views, you can use tables for positioning, or you can format using CSS (Cascading Style Sheets). You learn each of these techniques in this book, but in this lesson, you make a simple Web page to familiarize yourself with the Dreamweaver interface.

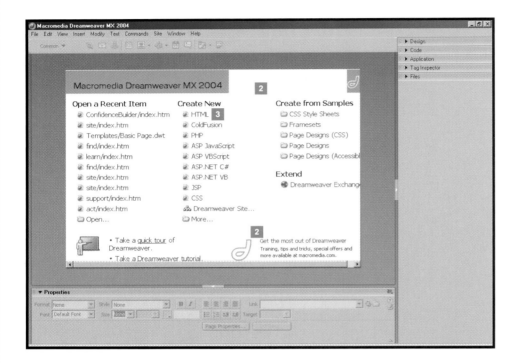

1. **Copy the ConfidenceBuilder folder from this book's companion CD-ROM onto your hard drive. Windows users need to right-click the folder, select Properties, uncheck Read-only, and click OK to unlock the files.**
   All the images you need for this lesson are included in this folder.

2. **Open Dreamweaver.**
   The Welcome screen opens by default.

   <NOTE>
   The bottom-right corner will show what you see here only if you have an online connection.

3. **In the Welcome screen in the center column (Create New), click HTML.**
   This opens a new HTML document.

   <NOTE>
   Windows saves the document with the default extension of .htm, and Macintosh saves with the default extension of .html. There is no difference in the actual HTML file.

   <NOTE>
   You look at the other options in the Properties dialog box in a tutorial later in this book

4. **In the Title field of the toolbar, enter the text** My first Web page.
To enter the text, click in the Title field to place your cursor and then type the text.

5. **Choose File→Save As from the menu bar.**
Save the file into the ConfidenceBuilder folder, and name it index.htm.

<NOTE>
Every Web site has either an index.htm or a default.htm file. Often, it's your preference of which to use, but your ISP host or administrator may specify that you must use one or the other.

6. **Choose Modify→Page Properties from the menu bar.**

<NOTE>
You can also click the Page Properties button in the Property inspector.

7. **Select Appearance in the Category column.**

8. **Click the color box next to the Background field.**
Your cursor turns into an eyedropper. Hold the cursor over the first green swatch from the left on the top row, and click it.

The hexadecimal number for this color is #006600, and it is automatically added to the Background color field in the Properties dialog box.

9. **Click OK.**
You just made the background color of the Web page dark green.

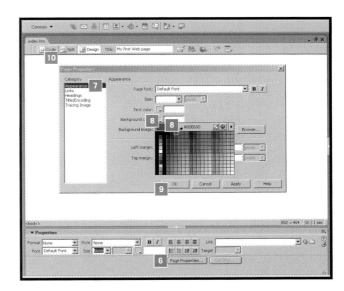

10. **Click the Code View icon.**
You just added an embedded CSS style which looks like this:

```
<style type="text/css"><!—
body {
    background-color: #006600;
}
—>
</style>
```

<NOTE>
The background color information was added as a CSS style for you in the head of the document. You learn all about this as the book progresses. But you just added a CSS style painlessly!

Tutorial
» Inserting Images

Inserting images into Dreamweaver is extremely easy. You can't actually make the images in Dreamweaver, so you need to produce them from an image editor, such as Fireworks, or obtain them from the client. For this tutorial, the images have been placed in the ConfidenceBuilder folder for you.

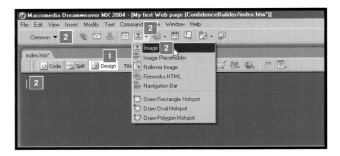

1. **Click the Show Design View icon.**

2. **In the Common category of the Insert bar, click the Images icon arrow and select Image.**
   The image inserts in the location of your cursor. The cursor placement is in the upper-left corner by default.

3. **Navigate to the Images folder inside the ConfidenceBuilder folder, select the** `logo.gif` **file, and then click Open.**
   This places the image in your document in the default location of top left.

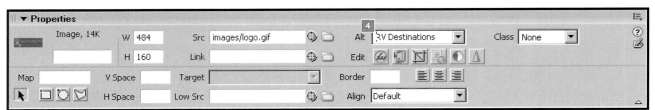

4. **In the Property Inspector, locate the Alt field, click in it to place the cursor there, and type** RV Destinations**.**
   The image has to be selected for the Alt field to show in the Property inspector. You can tell that an image is selected by the black squares surrounding it.

<NOTE>
The Alt field is important for users who browse with images turned off. It's also important for users who rely on accessibility readers. These readers use the text that you enter into the Alt field.

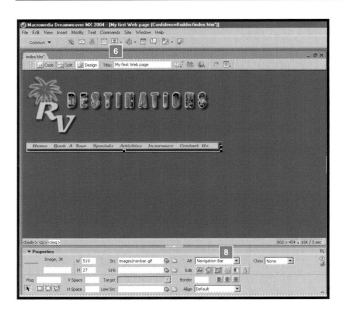

5. **Click to the right of the logo image to deselect it, and press Enter/Return to add a paragraph space.**
   Be sure that the cursor is in the space below the logo image.

6. **Click the Image icon from the Insert bar.**

7. **Navigate to the Images folder in the ConfidenceBuilder folder, select the** `navbar.gif` **file, and click Open.** You now have two images inserted into the Web page, one on top of the other.

8. **Add the alternate text of** Navigation Bar **into the Alt field.**

9. **Click to the right of the Nav bar to deselect it, and press Enter/Return.**

10. **Choose Insert→Image Objects→Fireworks HTML from the menu bar.**
    The Insert Fireworks HTML dialog box opens.

11. **Click the Browse button, navigate to the ConfidenceBuilder folder, and open the Navigation folder.**

12. **Select navigation.htm, and click Open. Click OK to close the Insert Fireworks HTML dialog box.**
    The birdhouse navigation image appears. Note that there are green table markings above the birdhouse. This is actually a table which assemblies all the images made in Fireworks.

13. **Choose File→Save.**
    Remember to save your work frequently.

<N O T E>

These images and HTML code were exported from a Fireworks document. The document is actually a small table containing all the images and code needed to reconstruct the navigational element.

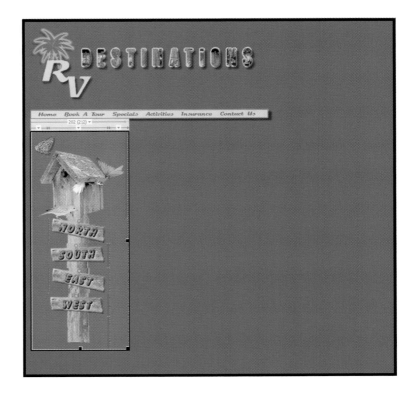

Tutorial
» Making an Image Map

In this tutorial, you add hotspots to the nav bar image that you inserted. You then add hyperlinks to each area of the nav bar.

1. **Select the nav bar image.**
   It's not technically a nav bar until you add links, but it will be soon.

2. **In the Property inspector, locate the Rectangular Hotspot tool and click it.**

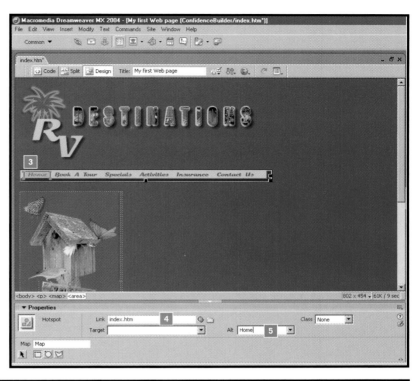

3. **Click and drag a rectangle shape around the word** Home.
   The rectangle shape appears blue. It is a representation only of the hotspot, which is a clickable area, and not visible in a browser.

4. **In the Link field of the Property inspector, select the pound sign (#) to highlight it and type** index.htm.
   When users click this link, they are returned to the home page.

5. **Add the alternative text of** Home **in the Alt field of the Property inspector.**

6. **Repeat Steps 2 through 5, adding the following text:**
   » Book a Tour, booking.htm (link), Book a Tour (alt)
   » Specials, specials.htm (link), Specials (alt)
   » Activities, activities.htm (link), Activities (alt)
   » Insurance, insurance.htm (link), Insurance (alt)

7. **Add a hotspot for Contact Us, but in the Link area type** mailto: tours@rvdestinations.com, **with alternative text of** Contact Us.

Tutorial
» Adding and Formatting Text

In this tutorial, you add text for links for those who can't see images. You style and position the text using a CSS style.

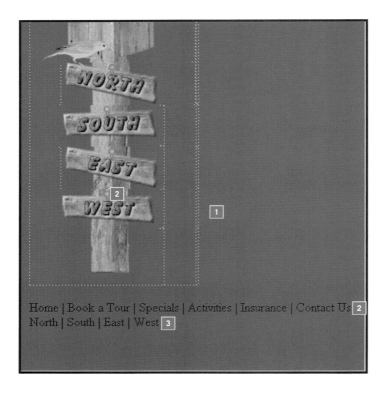

1. **Click your cursor to the right of the birdhouse navigation image, and press Enter/Return to place the cursor below the navigation.** Next you add text to your document. The text you add is actually used for navigation. So far, all the navigation used in this Web page relies on images. You need to provide an alternative way to navigate your site when users cannot view your images.

2. **Type the following text:** Home | Book a Tour | Specials | Activities | Insurance | Contact Us.

3. **Press Shift+Enter to add a <br> tag (one space), and then type** North | South | East | West.

4. **Press Shift+F11 to open the CSS Styles panel.**
   This panel is on the right of your screen in the panel group area.

5. **Click the plus sign (+) at the bottom of the panel to add a new style.**

6. **In the Selector Type area, select Tag (redefines the look of a specific tag).**

7. **In the Tag field, type** p.
   The p is to format the paragraph tag. When you pressed Enter/Return, you added a paragraph tag (<p>) to the document.

8. **In the Define In field, select This Document Only.**

9. **Click OK.**
   The CSS Style Definition for p dialog box opens. The Type category is selected by default.

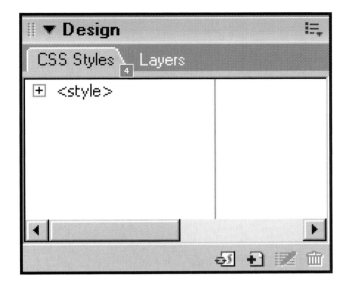

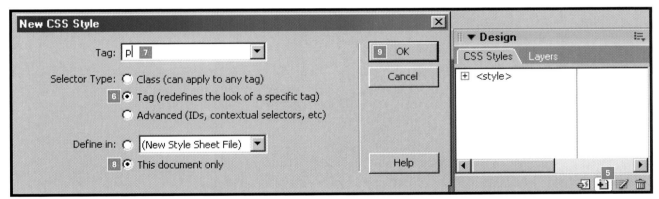

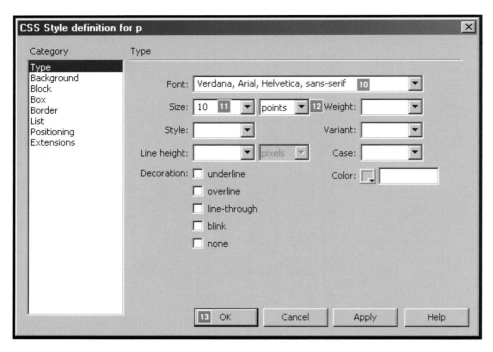

10. **Click the down arrow for the Font field, and select Verdana, Arial, Helvetica, sans serif from the drop-down list.**

11. **From the Size drop-down list, select 10.**

12. **To the right of the Size field, click the arrow for the next field and select Points.**

13. **Click OK, and look at your document.**

    The text has been styled automatically because you formatted the paragraph tag. Each time you pressed Enter/Return you added a paragraph tag. The images aren't affected but your text gets changed.

Tutorial
» Linking the Text

You'll add links to the text pretty much the same way you did for the nav bar.

<NOTE>
If this were a real site, you'd have a file for each of the files you are linking to. When developing this book's project site, you'll do just that.

1. **Click and drag over the word Home to select it.**

2. **In the Link field of the Property inspector, type** index.htm**.**

3. **Use Table CB-1 as a reference for the rest of the links.**

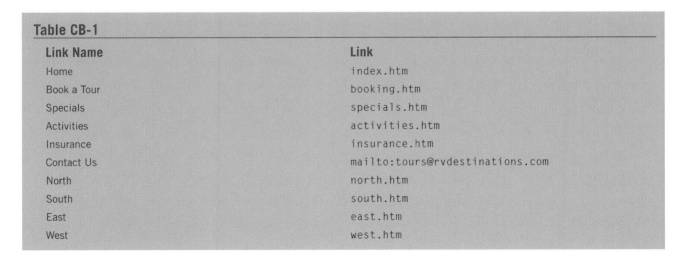

Table CB-1

Link Name	Link
Home	index.htm
Book a Tour	booking.htm
Specials	specials.htm
Activities	activities.htm
Insurance	insurance.htm
Contact Us	mailto:tours@rvdestinations.com
North	north.htm
South	south.htm
East	east.htm
West	west.htm

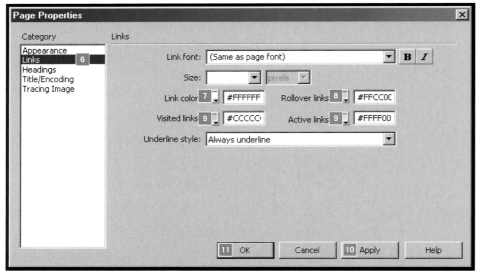

4. **Press Shift+Enter after the word** West, **and in the Insert bar, Common category, click the Email Link icon.**

5. **In the Text field, type** tours@rvdestinations.com, **and in the Email field, type** tours@rvdestinations.com. **Click OK.**

<N O T E>
You typed the link into the text area so that users who don't have their e-mail clients set to work with their browsers can copy and paste your e-mail address into their e-mail programs.

6. **Choose Modify→Page Properties, and select the Links category.**

7. **Click the color box next to the Link Color name, and using the eyedropper, select the white color swatch.**

8. **Click in the Rollover Links color box, and select a gold color swatch.**

9. **For the Active color select a light yellow and for Visited, select a light gray.**

10. **Click the Apply button to see the change in your document.**
    When you click the Apply button you are supposed to see the change in your document before you commit to it. As of this first release of Dreamweaver MX 2004, the Apply does not always work.

11. **Click OK to close the Page Properties dialog box.**
    Save and Preview your document. Pass your cursor over the links to see the rollover effect.

12. Select the <body> tag in the Tag Selector.

13. In the Property inspector, select the Align Center icon.
Everything on the page is now centered.

14. Save your file. Preview in a browser to see the final Web page.

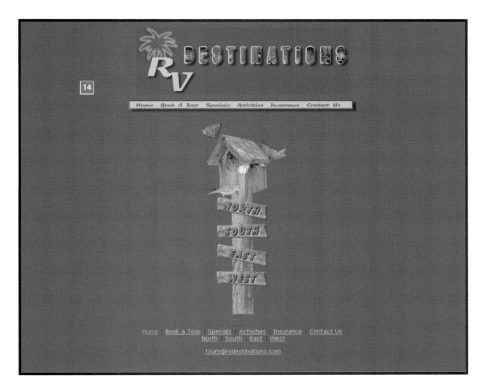

Part I:
Course Setup

In this part of the book you get a glance at what Dreamweaver MX 2004 is good for and its strong features. You also learn a few of the basic HTML terms and tags. From there you get a description of how this course works and how it benefits you, followed by brief descriptions of each session. A few computer specifics are discussed, such as requirements needed to run Dreamweaver MX 2004 and some differences in the Windows and Macintosh versions of Dreamweaver.

Dreamweaver Basics

Dreamweaver and HTML

HTML (HyperText Markup Language) is a markup language containing a series of tags that define the structure of a Web page. This markup tells a browser how to present the content of your page. In order to write HTML, you simply need a text editor; even Notepad will suffice. Because many developers want to save time, they use visual editors such as Dreamweaver to help speed up the process of marking up a Web page. In this course, we use Dreamweaver MX.

Dreamweaver is a deceptively easy tool, but it's also an industrial-strength application, making it a favorite among Web design professionals. With Dreamweaver, you can develop one page or a huge site. You can also open pages from co-workers or even pages produced in other editors, just to edit and clean up the code. You can add JavaScript, forms, tables, and more without writing or viewing a piece of code. As your skills develop, you might want more access to the code; Dreamweaver has this built-in functionality. It is as easy or as complex as you desire.

Dreamweaver utilizes Web technologies and HTML standards, and it also provides backward compatibility for older browsers. It was designed for the professional Web developer, so it can accommodate a designer's workflow. Basically, two kinds of Web developers exist: the coders and the designers. The designers typically want to design in a visual environment, so Dreamweaver provides the Design View or the "WYSIWYG" (or almost) environment. For the coders, Dreamweaver provides the Code View. Dreamweaver also has the Design and Code View for those who want it all. The illustrations here show the three design view types of the Web page that you develop in this course.

Basic HTML

You can actually design in Dreamweaver without knowing any HTML code. But you're better off learning at least the basics. HTML isn't nearly as intimidating as it looks. Learning the basics is easy. This book introduces you to bits of code here and there. Before you know it, you'll be recognizing HTML code and understanding it.

The World Wide Web Consortium (W3C) is a standards body that oversees and promulgates the standards for HTML code. Although compliance is voluntary, most Web browsers (especially the newer ones) support the standards consistently. Find out more about this organization at www.w3c.org.

HTML Tags

HTML uses tags to indicate how things should appear in a browser. Certain tags are required in every HTML page for a Web page to display properly. For a browser to know that a file contains HTML, the document must declare itself with an `<html>` opening tag and end with a closing tag of `</html>`. An opening tag declares what type of content follows. The ending tag declares the end of that particular type of content. Opening and closing tags act as a container for the content that they surround. Every HTML document requires `<head>`, `<body>`, and `<title>` tags. Dreamweaver generates these tags automatically whenever you open or add a new document. When you choose File→New, Dreamweaver generates a basic page that contains the required code and tags as seen in the illustration. Later in the book you'll learn how to change the title from Untitled Document to a meaningful name.

```
1  <!DOCTYPE HTML PUBLIC "-//W3C//DTD HTML 4.01 Transitional//EN"
2  "http://www.w3.org/TR/html4/loose.dtd">
3  <html>
4  <head>
5  <title>Untitled Document</title>
6  <meta http-equiv="Content-Type" content="text/html; charset=iso-8859-1">
7  </head>
8
9  <body>
10 </body>
11 </html>
12
```

Some Other Basic Tags

A handful of other tags appear in the `<body>` section of a Web page that you use every time you build a Web page, whether you see the code or not. This section shows some of them. Don't worry if you don't remember them; you see and use these tags throughout this course.

Paragraph tags are extremely common; they begin with $\langle p \rangle$ and close with $\langle /p \rangle$. This tag places an empty line of white space around each block of text contained within the tag container. The container consists of the opening and closing paragraph tags.

Anchor tags are used for linking from one page to another or to another spot within a page. A typical anchor tag looks like this:

```
<a href="linknamehere.htm"> Click on this text </a>
```

When the user clicks the text, he is taken to the page referenced in the anchor tag container.

Image tags are included with every image that you insert into your document. Dreamweaver automatically adds the height and width dimensions of the image into the tag and the alternative (alt) text if you've entered it into the Property inspector. An image tag appears like this:

```
<img src="images/logo.gif" width="300" height="100"
    alt="Palmetto Design Group">
```

The image tag has no ending tags.

Another set of tags you see frequently are **table** tags. The container is $\langle table \rangle \langle /table \rangle$. Within this container, you'll see $\langle tr \rangle$, which is the tag for a specific row, and $\langle td \rangle$, which is the tag for a specific cell.

New Standards

The final version of HTML is HTML 4.01 transitional. The new standard set by the W3C is XHTML. Although XHTML is officially the new standard, we are still waiting for better browser support. Don't worry; you don't have to jump into it just yet, but you should start thinking about it and read up on it when you get a chance. Because we made the decision for this book to continue supporting Netscape 4, we do not use XHTML coding.

Project Overview

The Dreamweaver MX 2004 Complete Course Project

Dreamweaver MX 2004 Complete Course is written for the aspiring Web designer. The goal of the book is to discuss and teach the techniques of building a Web site while developing an actual site.

Dreamweaver MX 2004 Complete Course is designed to walk you through all the design stages from planning a Web site to connecting to a database. Each session builds upon the others while you develop the Palmetto Design Group Web site. This company is a fictitious design firm that also specializes in custom corporate training courses. You may discover that the needs of this Web site may be very similar to your own personal goals if you are a new Web designer/developer.

Dreamweaver MX 2004 Complete Course is broken into manageable sessions that are also topic related so that you can use this book as a reference when you need to refresh your memory. It is taught in a way that beginners can understand, but it is also laced with intermediate skills right from the start. The focus is on productivity as well as training. For instance, most Dreamweaver books teach you how to insert text and images, and then they show you how to use tables to control your layout. It makes more sense from a workflow perspective to insert the tables and learn how to control them prior to adding content and images. That sort of logic is used in this training course.

Dreamweaver is a complex program that offers many ways to achieve the same results. For example, adding links to images and text can be accomplished in several ways. Instead of being presented with a boring list of different options, you will try each technique at different times so you get a feel for using each one, and then you can choose which method fits the way you work best.

As the course progresses, it gets considerably more complex. By the time you complete this course, you will have firsthand experience developing a business Web site that's interactive and contains dynamic content. Because of the complexity of this version of Dreamweaver, its many capabilities cannot be covered in one book. Dreamweaver supports several server models such as ASP, ColdFusion, PHP, and ASP.NET. We will use only ASP in this course. If, after learning how to develop a Web site, you want to dig deeper into the nitty gritty of every tool and function of Dreamweaver, I recommend that you also obtain a good Dreamweaver reference book such as *Macromedia Dreamweaver MX Bible* from Wiley Technology Publishing.

The browsers that are used for testing in this project include Netscape 4.79, Internet Explorer 6, and Netscape 7.

The directions are succinct and to the point. If any section is difficult for you to grasp, simply repeat it. Although the directions are easy to follow, Dreamweaver is a complex and professional-level piece of software. The learning curve requires plenty of practice.

This course uses the following software:

» **Dreamweaver MX 2004** is a professional layout editor that you'll use to assemble your Web site. A 30-day fully functional trial version is included on the book's companion CD-ROM, along with installation instructions.

» **Fireworks 2004** is an image editor used for creating Web graphics. All of the images used in the Palmetto Design Group Web site were made, sliced, and optimized in Fireworks. Although you won't do those things in Dreamweaver, you will learn how to do minimal image editing from Dreamweaver if you have Fireworks installed. A 30-day fully functional trial version is included on the book's companion CD-ROM, along with installation instructions.

General Work Tips and Computer Instructions

The following sections provide information about using the files on the accompanying CD-ROM and the minimum requirements that your computer will need in order to complete this course.

Organizing Your Files

On the CD that accompanies this book, you'll find a DWCC folder. Copy this to your hard drive. Windows users need to right-click the folder and select Properties. Then click to uncheck Read-Only and close the dialog box. From here, you can access new files used in each session from the session's folder on the CD when you need them.

Each session has a starter_files folder. In it is the html folder of the site. Inside the html folder, you'll find the images folder and site files. You can use these starter files at any time by dropping them into your defined root folder (stockimagenation). If you'd rather not overwrite your working folder but want to use a starter file (to troubleshoot), you can copy the starter file to your hard drive and define a new site. (Session 1 tells you how to define a site.) The DWCC_final folder contains the completed site files. The site is also live online at www.palmettodesigngroup.com. Some of the links in the menus are working links.

Copying Files from the CD

When a session instructs you to copy files from the CD-ROM to your hard drive, you will have to unlock the files if you are a Windows user. By default, Windows makes files copied from a CD to your hard drive read-only, which means that you can't edit or change these files. After you copy them to your hard drive, you can right-click and select Properties. Uncheck the read-only option.

System Requirements

System requirements for Microsoft Windows are as follows:

» An Intel Pentium III processor or equivalent, 600 MHz or faster, running Windows 98 SE, Windows 2000, or Windows XP

» Netscape Navigator 4.0 or later, or Microsoft Internet Explorer 4.0 or later

» 256MB of random-access memory (RAM) (512MB recommended)

» 800MB of available disk space

» A 256-color monitor capable of 800x600 pixel resolution or better (millions of colors and 1024x768 pixel resolution recommended)

» Dreamweaver and Fireworks must be activated over the Internet or phone prior to use

System requirements for Apple Macintosh are as follows:

» A 500 MHz PowerPC G3 processor

» Mac OS 10.2.6

» Netscape Navigator 4.0 or later, or Microsoft Internet Explorer 4.0 or later

» 256MB of random-access memory (RAM) (512MB recommended)

» 500MB available disk space

» Dreamweaver and Fireworks must be activated over the Internet or phone prior to use

Macintosh and Windows Differences

For the most part, Dreamweaver looks and works the same for the Windows and Macintosh operating systems. Macintosh users will be pleased to know that Dreamweaver for the Mac was written for the Macintosh, not for Windows and ported over. Here are the differences:

» The counterpart of the Windows Control (Ctrl) key is the Macintosh Command key (the Apple "propeller" key).

» The counterpart of the Windows Alt key is the Macintosh Option (Opt) key; it is marked as ALT on all newer Mac-compatible keyboards. I believe that it is on all keyboards since the Macintosh Enhanced keyboard (the one with the power key along the top edge in the middle and no "F" keys). When opening files, the Windows selection button is named Select; on the Macintosh, it's named Open.

» Windows on the PC close by clicking the close box in the upper-right corner. The close box on a Macintosh is in the upper-left corner.

Part II:
Getting Started

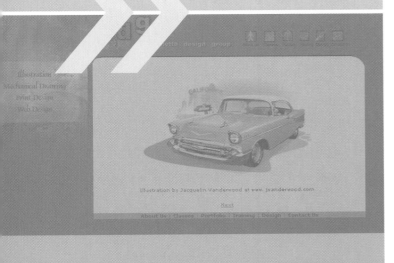

Session 1 **Laying the Foundation**

Session 2 **Building the Site's Framework**

Session 3 **Working with Tables**

Session 4 **Working with Images**

Session 5 **Adding Text**

Session 6 **Adding Navigational Links**

Session 1
Laying the Foundation

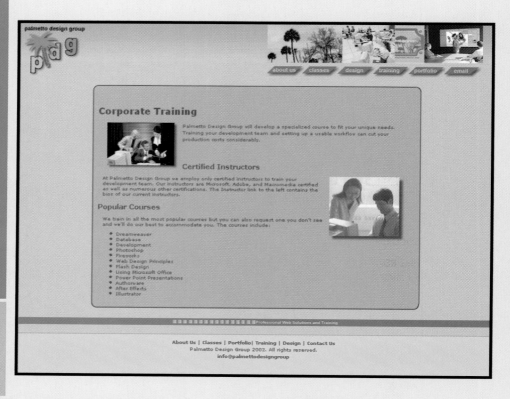

Discussion: **Laying the Foundation**

Tutorial: **Setting Up and Viewing the Workspace**

Tutorial: **Customizing the Workspace**

Tutorial: **Customizing Keyboard Shortcuts**

Tutorial: **Defining a Site**

Tutorial: **Using the Files Panel**

Tutorial: **Using the Assets Panel**

Tutorial: **Using the Start Page**

Session Introduction

Becoming comfortable with your design tools increases your productivity and shortens the learning curve. This session helps you explore the major menu and panel areas in the Dreamweaver workspace and shows you how to customize it for the way you work best. You won't look at every panel and every tool in this session—that would be really boring. Besides, the manual that ships with Dreamweaver and the help files are more than sufficient for tool recognition. What you do in this session is explore the major areas you use all the time, plus a couple of the panels that you use while developing a Web site. So instead of boring you to death with the details of every panel and tool, this session delves into the various panels as needs arise throughout the development of the Palmetto Design Group Web site.

You set up a local root folder in which to develop your site. Later in the book, you set up a remote folder and learn how to upload your Web site to a server.

TOOLS YOU'LL USE
A little bit of everything as you get familiar with the Dreamweaver workspace

MATERIALS NEEDED
DWCC folder on the CD-ROM

TIME REQUIRED
60 minutes

Discussion

Laying the Foundation

In this discussion, you see some of the things you need to think about and decide when planning a Web site. Some questions only the client can answer, and some can be determined only by testing. The planning stage is vital to a Web site's success. You can find additional questions to consider on a questionnaire I developed at www.je-ideadesign.com/question.htm.

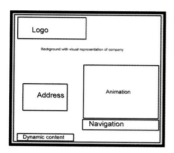

Consider, for example, the following questions when planning your site:

» What is your objective?

Putting a Web site up on the Internet for the sake of establishing a presence isn't a good reason for a Web site; you need to gain an understanding of the site's purpose. Is the site going to sell something, train, entertain, or perhaps disperse information? You need to determine the site's primary objectives.

» Who is your audience?

Palmetto Design Group determined that its audience would most likely be business-owners who want a Web site developed and corporations that need a Web development team trained in the use of Web tools. The audience would probably be using both Netscape and Internet Explorer browsers and perhaps even Opera. They also determined that users would access the Web site by both modem and high-speed connections.

» Who is your competition?

For the Palmetto Design Group Web site, the competition is worldwide, but any local competition should also be checked out. See what the Web sites look like, what works, what doesn't work, and what their clients like or dislike about the competition's site.

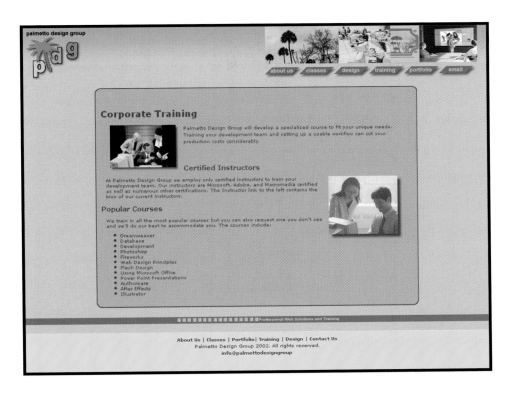

After you have answered these questions, consider the following initial steps to planning the new Web site:

» Make a mock up to determine the visual look and feel.

You might develop a site that causes the users to stare in awe, but then they might discover the content has nothing to do with the look of the site. Or the site could be so poorly designed that great content gets lost. You need to get the correct look and content to evoke the intended emotional response from the users.

The mock up may contain actual graphics, placeholders, or just outlines of where different components will be placed. The mock up assists you and the client in determining the user experience. Is it logical? Is there a consistent look and feel throughout the site? Can the users find what they are looking for?

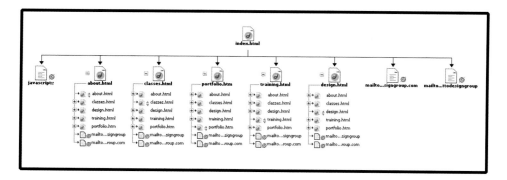

» Evaluate navigational options.

According to recent studies, top and left side navigation are the most widely used. That's not to say that other navigation isn't right for your site. The main thing to consider is whether the users can find their way around your site without frustration. Users must understand where they are in relation to everything else. Links should be identifiable by text, or at least by text that appears as the mouse passes over the link.

» Determine the available assets.

Is the client providing images, text, logo, and so on? If not, are you responsible for developing it? If the client is providing you with assets, when are they due?

» Set up the site structure.

From your planning session with the client and answers to the questions you've asked, you can develop a preliminary mock up of the Web site. You now know what your links will be and the pages needed to contain the necessary information.

Tutorial
» Setting Up and Viewing the Workspace

Your work environment is an important one. You set it up in this tutorial, and you get a feel for where all the tools are in your workspace.

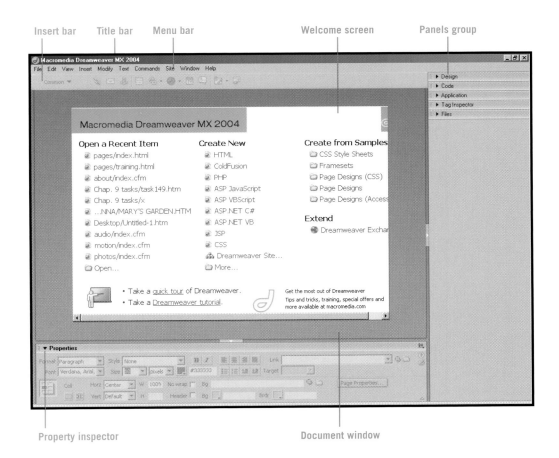

1. **Open the Dreamweaver application.**

   In Windows, click the Start button and then choose Programs→Macromedia Dreamweaver MX. Macintosh users, double-click the hard drive icon and then the Macromedia Dreamweaver MX folder, and then double-click the Dreamweaver MX program icon. The Start Page opens by default. If this is your first time running Dreamweaver MX, a dialog box opens.

2. **Click OK if the Designer option is selected (it should be selected by default).**

   This book assumes that you are using the MX Designer workspace. The HomeSite/Coder style is used by the folks who primarily hand code and is beyond the scope of this book.

   <NOTE>
   The integrated workspace using MDI (Multiple Document Interface) isn't supported on the Macintosh so the windows and panels are floating.

<NOTE>
If you add or edit anything on the page, prior to saving, you'll notice an asterisk (*) next to the title indicating that changes have been made since you last saved.

Changing Workspaces

If you have previously chosen to work in HomeSite/Coder workspace, choose Edit→Preferences. Click General, and then click the Change Workspace button. Click the Design workspace option. You can always change it back when you finish this book if you find that you prefer to work in the HomeSite/Coder workspace. You have to restart Dreamweaver to change the workspace.

3. **Look at the title bar.**
   The program name and document name are displayed in the title bar. Untitled Document (Untitled-1) is the default name until you name and save it.

4. **Look at the menu bar.**
   The menu bar contains menus with various commands. Many of the menu items can be accessed using shortcut keys or by using various panels.

5. **Look at the Insert bar.**
   The Common tab, selected by default, shows the most commonly used functions. It contains 10 buttons with categories to insert objects into your document. Click the arrow next to the Common button to change categories.

6. **Look at the Document toolbar.**
   The Document toolbar has buttons and pop-up menus with options for different views of the Document window, as listed in Table 1-1.

Table 1-1: The Functions Accessed from the Document Toolbar

Name	Function
Code View	Provides a view of just code for those who want to hand-code or edit any other type of code, such as JavaScript or ColdFusion.
Split View	Provides a split working environment with the code on top and your visual work area below.
Design View	Provides a visual working environment.
Title	Where you type the title of your page.
Browser Check	The ability to check cross-browser compatibility.
File Management	Displays file management options.
Preview/Debug in Browser	Gives you the choice of browser to use for a preview.
Refresh Design View	Forces the browser to reread the page to view any changes you made.
View Options	Activates the Options menu.
Browser Target Check	Provides options to check browser incompatibilities. Red squiggly lines are added in Code View. Use this menu to check the errors if any are present.

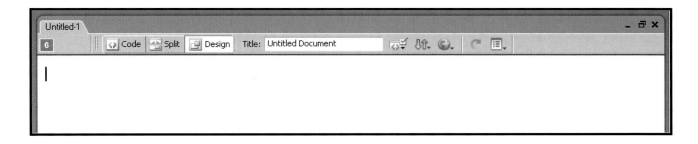

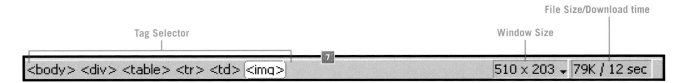

7. **Look at the status bar.**
The status bar at the bottom of the Document window contains information about your document.

» The **Tag selector** shows the hierarchy of tags that surround the current selection in your document.

» If your document window is maximized, the window sizes are grayed out. Click the Restore Down icon (in the title bar), and then choose the window size you'd like from the **Window Size pop-up menu**.

» **Document size** and **estimated download time** for the page are shown in the status bar.

8. **Look at the Property inspector.**
The Property inspector is context-sensitive. If the inspector is closed, simply click the name to open it. The options displayed depend on which element you have selected. To see all the properties of a selected element, click the expander arrow in the lower-right corner.

9. **Look at the Panels group.**
To access the various panels, click the panel names or the expander arrows and then click a specific panel name. If a panel isn't open by default, you can open it by choosing Window→Panel name. You can also customize the panel area for the way you work, as shown in the next tutorial.

Tutorial
» Customizing the Workspace

Everyone works differently, and Dreamweaver is such a complex program that you might be using advanced portions such as ColdFusion, PHP, and other programming languages. The panels to which you need easy access depend on your workflow. This tutorial shows you how to rearrange your workspace.

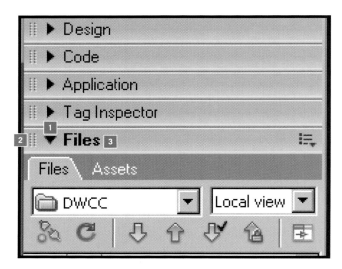

1. **To expand (or collapse) the Files panel group, click the expander arrow in the Files panel group.**

<NOTE>
To activate a panel within a panel group, click the name of the panel that you want to activate. The selected panel then appears as a tab; unselected panels appear as text only.

2. **Click and drag the Files panel's gripper (small gray dots on the left) onto the document.**
You have just undocked the panel group. You can use this floating panel group as it is or rearrange it in a custom configuration. If you have a large monitor, you might want to place some of the most used panels on the right and left edges.

3. **Click the Files name.**
You have to be slightly tricky to separate the panels from within a panel group. You first must select the tab or name of the panel that you want to remove or move from a panel group.

4. **Click the Files Options menu, and click Group Site with→New Panel Group.**
This removes the Files panel (or the selected panel) from its current group. You can move it independently, or you can choose to place it in another panel group. Notice that the Files panel group name changes to Assets after you move the Files panel out as a new panel.

5. **If desired, put these two panels back together using one of the following methods:**

   » Clicking the Files panel Options menu

   » Clicking Group Files With Assets

   » Clicking the Options menu again

   » Clicking Rename Panel Group, and naming it Files again

<NOTE>

If you remove a panel and put it back again, it is not in the same order. For example, when you move the Files panel and then put it back with the Assets panel, it appears as the second panel in the group. Personally, I like it to be first. To rearrange, you have to then put the Assets panel in a New group and then regroup it with the Files panel.

6. **Click and drag the gripper bar to drag the panel group back in the docked panel area.**
   When you see a solid black line, release the mouse button to dock the panel group again.

7. **Click the gripper of the Property inspector, and drag it below your document area (if you want).**
   Some people using smaller monitors may prefer to move the Property inspector off the document window to give more design space or move it to another monitor.

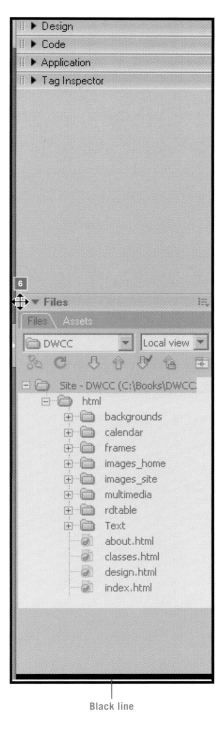

Black line

Tutorial
» Customizing Keyboard Shortcuts

If you are used to using certain keyboard shortcuts and Dreamweaver doesn't have them by default, you can customize them to work the way you want.

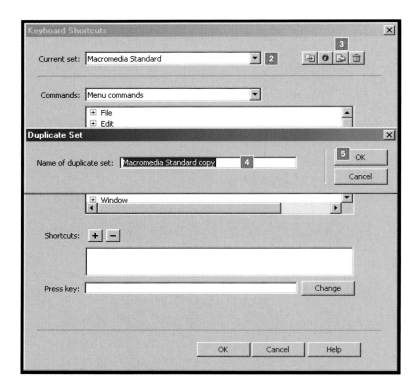

1. **Choose Edit→Keyboard Shortcuts to edit or add your own keyboard shortcuts.**
   In the Current Set field, you see the default Macromedia Standard set of keyboard shortcuts.

2. **Click the down arrow in the Current Set field to use shortcuts for BBEdit, HomeSite, or Dreamweaver 3 if you are more comfortable with those.**

3. **Click the Duplicate Set icon.**
   You need to make a duplicate so you don't overwrite the original. Choose a set that is the closest to what you want.

4. **In the Duplicate Set dialog box, type a new name.**

5. **Click OK to close the dialog box.**
   You made a duplicate set of shortcuts so that you make changes without overwriting the original file.

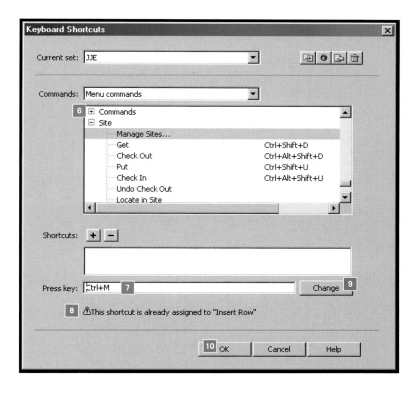

6. **Click a plus (+) sign to expand the category in which you are interested.**
   Functions with keyboard shortcuts already assigned are shown. The blank features have no preset shortcut assigned, but you can add one yourself or change the ones that are predefined.

7. **Type a new key combination in the Press Key field.**
   For PC users, the key combination must contain the Control (Ctrl) key; for Macintosh users, the key combination must contain the Command (⌘) key. Many combinations are taken, but you can override an existing shortcut.

8. **If you type in a combination already in use you'll see a warning. Type in a new combination.**

9. **Click Change when you have an acceptable combination.**

10. **Click OK to close the Keyboard Shortcuts dialog box when you are finished.**

Tutorial
» Defining a Site

In Dreamweaver, defining your site is extremely important, so don't even be tempted to skip this part. Believe me, you are not utilizing the full power of Dreamweaver if you don't define each site that you make. Defining every site you work with allows Dreamweaver to track your assets and links and to provide you with a lot of other functions as well.

1. **Copy the DWCC folder from this book's CD-ROM onto your hard drive.**

2. **In Dreamweaver, choose Site→Manage Sites from the main menu bar.**

3. **Click the New button and then select Site.**
   The Site Definition dialog box opens to the Basic tab. Select the Advanced tab—the Category of Local Info should be highlighted.

<NOTE>
Don't be intimidated because you are using the Advanced tab. I like the fact that most of what you need to define the site is all in one window. You can then switch to other categories when you need to. When you edit a site's definition, it's much easier to do it in the Advanced tab, so you may as well get used to it now.

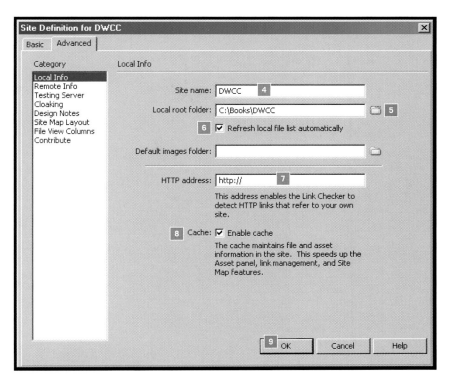

4. **In the Site Name field, highlight the default name (Unamed Site1) and type** DWCC.

   You don't have to be concerned about long names here; this name in no way affects any of your files. You can use spaces between words if you'd like.

5. **Click the yellow folder icon in the Local Root Folder area, navigate to where you have the DWCC folder saved, select it, and click Select.**

   The local folder is your working directory for all your Web site's files. You need to make a local folder for every Web site that you design.

6. **Click Refresh Local File List Automatically if it is unchecked.**

   This option shows you any changes made to your site structure and files in the Files and Assets panels.

7. **If you already have a hosting service and want to add the HTTP address, add it now.**

   You need this information later in the book if you want to utilize Dreamweaver's FTP capabilities for uploading your site's files to an Internet server.

8. **Leave Enable Cache checked if you want quick access to your links and site assets.**

   This is up to you. I always leave the Enable Cache option checked, but if your computer's RAM (memory) is low, you might want to uncheck this option.

9. **Click OK to finish defining your site.**

   I'm sure that you noticed lots of other categories in the Site Definition dialog box. You use most of them as you progress through the Palmetto Design Group Web site design.

   < N O T E >

   You can also use the Basic tab, which contains a wizard, to set up your Site definition.

   < N O T E >

   If you encounter a situation where you didn't set up a local folder ahead of time as you did for this tutorial, you can add the new folder after you click the Browse for Folder icon in the Site Definition dialog box, by browsing to the partition or area in which you'd like to set up your site. I use drive C with a folder named DWCC. Just click the Create New Folder icon in the Choose Local Root Folder for Site DWCC dialog box.

Tutorial

» Using the Files Panel

The Site panel is one that many beginners avoid or never use. You begin using it right away because it is a great timesaver and is not nearly as intimidating as it appears. The Files panel is in the Files panel group. The Files panel is where you can view a list of files, rename files, add files and folders, and refresh the view when changes have been made.

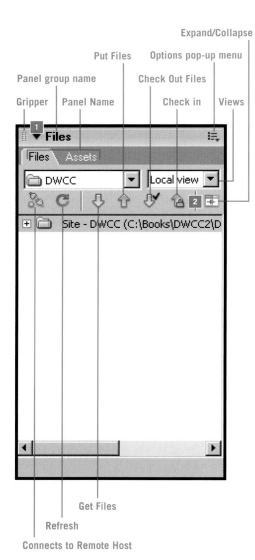

Expand/Collapse

Put Files   Options pop-up menu

Panel group name   Check Out Files

Gripper   Panel Name   Check in   Views

Get Files

Refresh

Connects to Remote Host

1. **Click the Files panel group expander arrow or name, and click the Files name if it isn't already active.**
   As you can see from the labels in the image, you can manage a lot of functions in this panel. You can check your files in and out in a shared work environment, define your sites, upload and download files, and much more.

2. **Click the Expand/Collapse icon.**
   Notice the additional icons in the expanded and split view. Use this portion of the Files panel when you get to the section of this book in which you connect your site to a database.

<NOTE>
You can rename any file or folder by choosing the File menu in the Files panel Options pop-up menu [Files➜New File (or Folder)], selecting Rename, and typing the new name. You can also right-click for the contextual menu and choose Rename. On a Macintosh, choose Site➜Rename or Ctrl+click for the contextual menu and choose Rename. Type the new name.

3. **Click the Expand/Collapse icon to return the Files panel to the normal size in the panel group area.**

4. **In the Files panel, right-click (Macintosh: Ctrl+click) on the html folder and choose New File from the menu that appears.**
   A new untitled file is added, and the name is highlighted.

<NOTE>
Alternatively, click on any folder to which you want to add a file or folder, and the new file or folder is added to the one that you have selected.

5. **Type** index.html.
   The default file extension for Windows is .HTM and for Macintosh it's .HTML. But you can change the default by typing it in.

6. **Repeat Steps 4 and 5, and add the remaining files you need for this Web site, naming them as follows:**

   » about.html

   » portfolio.html

   » training.html

   » design.html

   » classes.html

7. **Right-click (Macintosh: Ctrl+click) the site name, and choose New Folder.**
   If you prefer not to right-click (Macintosh: Ctrl+click), you can also choose the File menu from the Files Options pop-up menu and choose File→New Folder. Either way, a new, untitled folder is added.

8. **Type** multimedia.
   You can add as many files and folders as you'd like. You add more as you progress through the project.

<NOTE>
You may wonder why I didn't have you open a new file from the Start Page. Adding files the way you just did automatically saves the files in your root folder. You see how to use the Start Page in the last tutorial in this session.

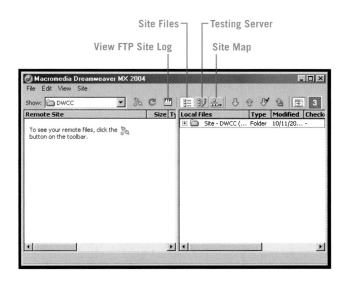

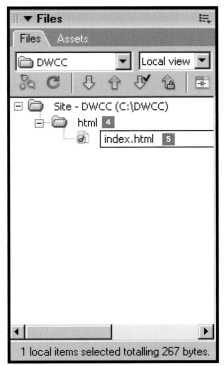

Tutorial
» Using the Assets Panel

The Assets panel is your control center for all the media that you use in your Web site. It includes the images, sound files, Flash movies, custom scripts, and more.

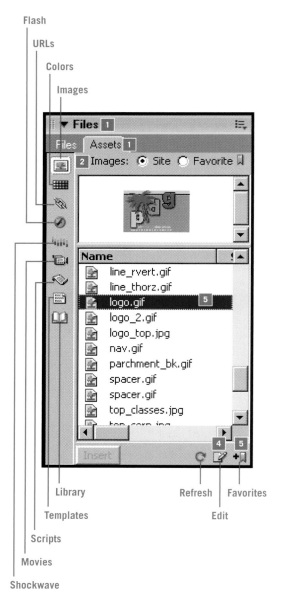

Flash
URLs
Colors
Images

Library
Templates
Scripts
Movies
Shockwave

Refresh
Favorites
Edit

1. **Click the Files panel group expander arrow, and click the Assets name, if it isn't already active.**
   The Assets tab opens with a list of available files.

2. **Click the top icon (Images) on the left side of the panel.**
   If you have a site defined (Files panel) that has images in its root or local directory, you see the filenames in this panel. You also see an icon representation in the top portion of the panel.

3. **Select one of the images.**

4. **Click the Edit button.**
   The appropriate application—Fireworks for images, Flash for a Flash movie—launches.

5. **Select logo.gif, and then click the Favorites icon in the lower-right corner to add one of the assets to a list of assets that you use frequently.**
   A warning dialog box opens, stating that the assets have been added to the Favorites list. You can check the Don't Show Message Again option so this dialog box won't open each time you add an asset to the Favorites list. To view the Favorites list, choose Favorites at the top of the Assets panel.

< N O T E >

By adding something to the Favorites list, you simply make a short-cut to it so you can access the asset faster. The asset isn't removed from its original location. This is extremely helpful when you are developing a large site with lots of assets to scroll through.

6. **Select an image, and then click the Insert button to add it to your Dreamweaver layout.**
   This is just for practice, so delete the image after you insert it.

Tutorial
» Using the Start Page

The Start Page is a new addition to Dreamweaver MX 2004 and opens by default when you first launch the program.

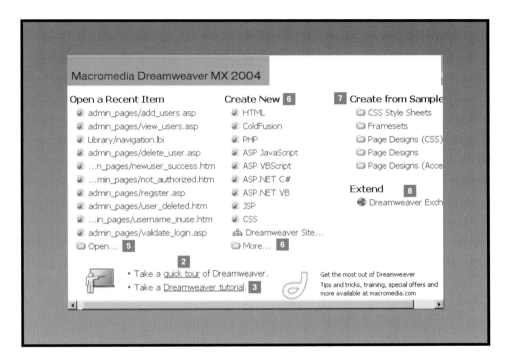

1. **Close any open documents so you can see the Start Page.**

2. **Click the Quick Tour link, and check out the available tutorials.**
   You have to be connected to the internet for this feature since the link takes you to Macromedia.

   <N O T E>
   The Start Page is available only when you first launch Dreamweaver or if all documents are closed.

3. **Click the Take a Dreamweaver Tutorial link, and check it out.**
   You don't have to have an online connection for the tutorial, it is part of the Help system.

4. **Notice the shortcuts to many functions in the main part of the window.**

5. **Click Open in the Open a Recent Item category.**
   The Open dialog box appears, enabling you to navigate to any file in your root. This category also contains a list of files that you've recently opened. Click on any one of the file names to open it.

6. **Check out the Create New category.**
   Here you find links to file types as well as a link to define a site, or set up a server connection. The More link opens the same New Document dialog box that you can open with File→New.

7. **Click on any of the links in the Create from Samples dialog box to check them out.**
   These are premade templates.

8. **Click on Dreamweaver Exchange in the Extend category if you want to go there.**
   You must be connected to the Internet for that link to work.

» Session Review

In this session, you fired up Dreamweaver and made it your friend while visiting its diverse workspace. You then got down to the business of preparing a Web site by setting up a local root folder and using the Site and Assets panels to manage your content.

You took a look at some of the planning stages that you need to go through prior to designing a Web site. You then familiarized yourself with the Dreamweaver workspace. You learned how you can customize the panel groups to your liking and how to use the Site and the Assets panels. You then prepared to begin your Web site by defining the DWCC root folder.

Answer the questions below to review the information in this session. The answer to each question can be found in the tutorial noted in parentheses.

1. Can you change your chosen workspace? (See "Tutorial: Setting Up and Viewing the Workspace.")

2. How do you dock a panel? (See "Tutorial: Customizing the Workspace.")

3. How do you move a panel group? (See "Tutorial: Customizing the Workspace.")

4. How do you change or add a keyboard shortcut? (See "Tutorial: Customizing Keyboard Shortcuts.")

5. How do you add files or folders to your site? (See "Tutorial: Using the Files Panel.")

6. Why is it best to add new files using the Files panel? (See "Tutorial: Using the Files Panel.")

7. Why should you define your site? (See "Tutorial: Defining a Site.")

8. Name several types of assets accessed through the Assets panel. (See "Tutorial: Using the Assets Panel.")

9. What is the quickest way to open a recently opened document? (See "Tutorial: Using the Start Page.")

10. What type of files are in the Create from Samples category of the Start Page? (See "Tutorial: Using the Start Page.")

» Other Projects

This project enables you to expand your new skills learned in this session. Challenge yourself to plan a new Web site, perhaps one with a different theme than the one you are currently building. Then determine the look and feel and the type of navigation that you want to use.

Suppose that a new client has approached you to design a site for its new bed-and-breakfast business. It is a quaint home with four luxurious rooms, set in the mountains of Colorado. Much of their business comes from winter skiers. Your challenge is to make the first mock-up showing the client how the site encourages potential customers to explore the various areas of content and how the navigation is easy to understand.

pdg

palmetto design group

Professional Web Solutions and Training

about us   design   classes   training   portfolio   email

About Us | Classes | Portfolio| Training | Design | Contact Us
Palmetto Design Group 2002. All rights reserved.
info@palmettodesigngroup

Building the Site's Framework

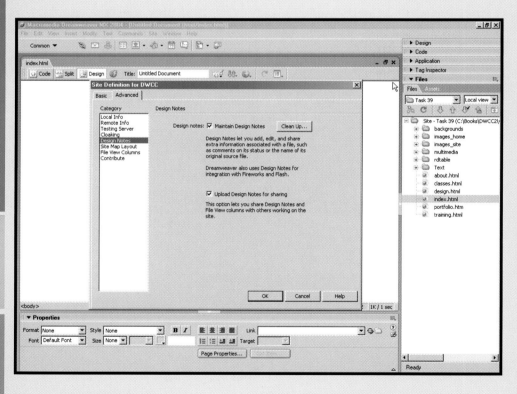

Discussion: **Transitional Design**

Tutorial: **The Home Page and Design Notes**

Tutorial: **Opening and Saving a Document**

Tutorial: **Choosing a Design View**

Tutorial: **Setting Browser Preferences**

Tutorial: **Setting Accessibility Preferences**

Tutorial: **Setting Page Properties**

Tutorial: **Adding Meta Tags**

Session Introduction

In this session, you set your home page for the Palmetto Design Group Web site and learn how to insert Design notes to yourself and others. You then begin to set the page properties such as the title, background color, text color, and margins. All these elements are present in the entire Web page. Dreamweaver automatically generates the code for the page properties for you.

Another part of the `<head>` code is the meta tags, which contain the keywords and description for each page. Many search engines use the content in the meta tags. They send out spiders and robots, which gather the information from the meta tags to help index and categorize your Web pages.

A Web page contains two very specific areas—the head and the body. The body contains the code, which enables the user to view your Web page. Although the head contains elements invisible to the viewer, the information that you enter in this area takes a visitor to your site.

Elements—such as the page title, the background color and/or image, text and link colors, as well as margins—apply to an entire page rather than to an individual object. Dreamweaver automatically adds the HTML code for these elements to the head section when you use the Page Properties dialog box, which you do in just a bit.

You need to make some important decisions before you even begin building your Web site. Planning saves you numerous hours of work and countless headaches. You need to decide not only the navigation and layout of the site, but also elements such as the background color (which fills the entire browser) or image.

TOOLS YOU'LL USE
Files window, Property inspector, Code view, Design view and Split view, Page Properties dialog box, Insert menu, and Preferences

MATERIALS NEEDED
Your DWCC root directory from session 1. You may start this session using the session2_starterfiles (on the CD-ROM).

TIME REQUIRED
90 minutes

Discussion

Transitional Design

The world of Web design and development is one that moves quickly. There have been major changes to the Standards for Web design (www.w3.org.com). The biggest change involves moving to cascading style sheet (CSS) styles for not only text formating but also for positioning of all page elements. The browser support for this has improved tremendously but is still not fully functional. Because of this most designers still use a moderate amount of tables for layout but are designing with the future in mind. Since CSS isn't totally ready for all designers to adapt, I made the decision to use a transitional design in this book. The next version will most likely be completely CSS-oriented if the browser support keeps improving, as I suspect it will.

As a warning, you'll see discussions by some CSS experts that you must make the change now. As with most topics involving Web design there is always conflicting information. Tables will still be around for quite some time to come, so don't let the purists scare you.

Designing for Tomorrow

The Web site you're building is made using a transitional method. What this means is that you will be using a combination of CSS styles and tables. According to the newest standards recommendations, a standards-based sites structure is built using only CSS for presentation, and no tables. Because a great majority of designers still need to use tables, we use a nominal amount of tables in this design. Many of the presentational elements, such as formatting the text and backgrounds, is done using CSS styles. The best use of CSS styles is to create a separate style sheet, but you'll also learn how Dreamweaver embeds styles into the page automatically, depending on the methods you use. This is pointed out as we proceed.

Another step toward a standards-based page is to use XHTML instead of HTML. Read the XHTML sidebar to learn the differences. To summarize, XHTML is stricter code, but we are using transitional XHTML, which is a bit more forgiving. The newer browsers, version 6 and up, have very good support at this time for CSS1 and CSS2 (www.w3.org), but the older browsers do not. Using the transitional design, as you do in this book, makes the site accessible to more browsers.

The Web standards of using CSS for presentational design is finally entering main-stream. ESPN.com has converted its huge commercial site, which gets 10 million readers a day, to a CSS-designed layout. When highly visible commercial sites prove that it is possible to deliver visually appealing and highly accessible content using the Web standards, more will follow.

<NOTE>
By the time this book was completed there was an announcement that there will no longer be new ver-sions of Netscape. This design still supports Netscape 4.79 but this browser by the time you receive this book will almost be in the past—finally! Be sure to check your company's log records to see if you still need to support the old and outdated browser.

About Browser Modes

Browsers use two different modes to read and render your CSS: full standards mode and quirks mode. In quirks mode, layout emulates nonstandard markup that is required to prevent existing content from breaking. In full standards mode, the behavior is described by the HTML and CSS specifications. The mode used is determined by the DOCTYPE in your page. You read more about DOCTYPES in the next section. The older browsers prior to version 6 allow all kinds of broken or improper code to render properly. But this practice does you more harm than good, because the newer browsers are stricter and will continue to be so. You should learn now how to code your pages with a view toward the future and full standards compliancy. Purists insist that you must do it now, but browsers aren't quite yet able to comply completely. Even with the support that the browsers cur-rently have, you can produce a visually stunning site using transitional methods.

DOCTYPES

DOCTYPES declare to the browser what type of page needs to be loaded and which rules to apply to it. DOCTYPES appear at the top of your HTML pages. These are the DOCTYPES for XHTML:

» Transitional: The closest to HTML. It forgives presentational markup (such as tables), as well as deprecated (being phased out) elements and attributes (such as cell background colors).

» Strict: Does not allow presentational markup elements or attributes.

» Frameset: Use if you are building a framed site.

XHTML versus HTML

XHTML is very similar to HTML, but it's a bit stricter. However, you should be aware of several differences, especially if you get handed an old HTML site to remake. When creating new XHTML, Dreamweaver obeys these differences and codes the HTML properly for you. You'll understand some of the things mentioned in the following list when you get to the session dealing with them. Just remember where to find this information for reference.

 » Declare your DOCTYPE and Content Type: Dreamweaver does this for you. Later in this session, you look at the code and see where the DOCTYPE and content are added to the page.

 » Tags in lowercase: All tags must be lowercase. For instance `<TITLE>` is `<title>`. Other tags such as behaviors also need to be lowercase. For example, onMouseOver is the way Dreamweaver would normally write this tag, but for XHTML, it is onmouseover—which Dreamweaver gets right when you start with an XHTML page.

 » Element and attribute names must be lowercase, but not the values.

 » Values and attributes need to be quoted. For example, HTML allows `size=4`, but XHTML requires `size="4"`. Many designers already code this way.

 » Close all tags, even empty ones. Typically, tags such as `<p>` don't require the closing `</p>` tag. Empty tags such as `<img>` don't either, but they do in XHTML. For tags such as `<p>`, the `</p>` closing tag is added. Empty tags such as `<img>` and `<br>` are closed by adding a space and a forward slash, like this: `<img />` or `<br />`.

 » Comments can contain double dashes only at the beginning and end of an XHTML comment.

Advantages of CSS

To keep it short, the biggest advantage of a standards-compliant site is that it uses CSS to separate presentation from content. Using this method makes updating large sites much easier and faster because you change the style sheet, which then affects all the pages using the style sheets. CSS is also more accessible. It can also cut your file size in half, sometimes more. CSS removes the font tags, table positioning tags such as top, center, cell padding and so on, plus all the table tags if you go with CSS for positioning. All this adds up to slim pages that are much easier to update and edit. You can use one style sheet for all browsers without using any browser detection methods.

Tutorial

» The Home Page and Design Notes

The home page is the starting point to the rest of your site. You must specify the home page in Dreamweaver for some of its functions, such as the site map, to work properly. Design Notes help you remember important information.

1. **Open Dreamweaver.**

2. **Click the Files panel group name or extender arrow.**

3. **Click the Files name/tab if it isn't active.**

4. **Click index.html to select it.**

5. Open the Files Options Pop-up menus, and select Site→Set As Home Page.
   The index.htm page is now set as the home page.

6. **Double-click the filename index.html to open it.**

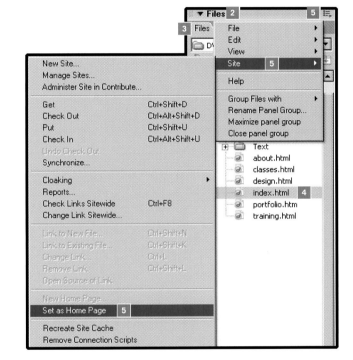

7. **Click the down arrow of the Site Definition box (where you see DWCC).**

8. **Click the Manage Sites option.**
   The Manage Sites dialog box opens. Be sure that you highlight the DWCC site.

9. **Click the Edit button.**

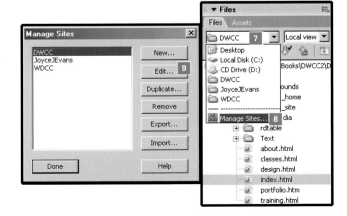

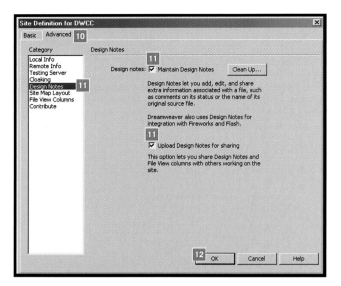

10. **Click on the Advanced tab if it isn't selected already.**

11. **In the Category column, click Design Notes.**
    Be sure that check marks appear in the Maintain Design Notes and the Upload Design Notes for Sharing check boxes.

12. **Click OK, and then click Done in the Manage Sites dialog box.**

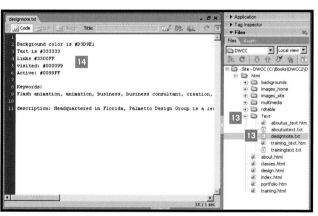

13. **Expand the Text folder and double-click on designnote.txt to open it.**
    You may notice that because it's a text file it automatically opens in the Code view and no other view option is available.

14. **Select all the text and copy it (Ctrl/Command+C).**

15. **Close the file.**
    You'll be pasting this text into your design note.

16. **Right-click (Control-click) index.htm in the Files window, and select Design Notes.**

    The Design Notes dialog box opens with the Basic Info tab selected.

17. **Click the arrow for the drop-down menu for the Status Field, and select revision1.**

    This list contains different stages of the page development cycle.

18. **In the Notes field, paste using either Edit→Paste or the keyboard shortcut of Ctrl/Command+V.**

19. **Click the Insert Date icon to insert today's date.**

20. **Click the Show When File Is Opened check box, and then click OK.**

21. **Close the index.html page. Now double-click the index.html file name in the Files panel to reopen it.**

    You'll notice that the note opens every time you open index.html. Simply click OK to close the note. If you'd rather not have the note open with the file, uncheck this option. I am unchecking this option now so future instructions will not tell you to close the file when it opens.

22. **You can close the index page now.**

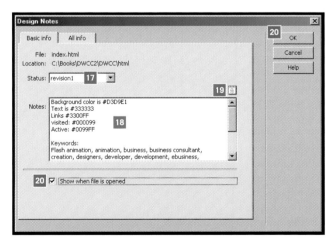

Tutorial
» Opening and Saving a Document

In this tutorial, you open a new document, make a new folder, and save the new file in the new folder. Opening and saving documents in Dreamweaver is easy.

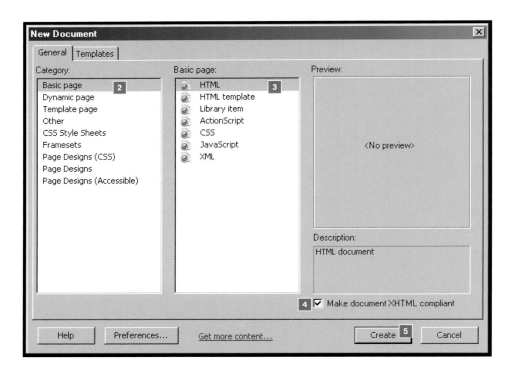

1. **Click File→New in the Main menu bar.**

2. **In the Category column select Basic Page.**

3. **In the Basic Page column, select HTML.**
   Notice how many different file formats you can open from the New Document dialog box.

4. **Click on the Make Document XHTML Compliant option.**

5. **Click the Create button.**
   You now have a blank HTML page. It's best to save the page before you add content. You use this page later in this course.

6. **Click File→Save As.**

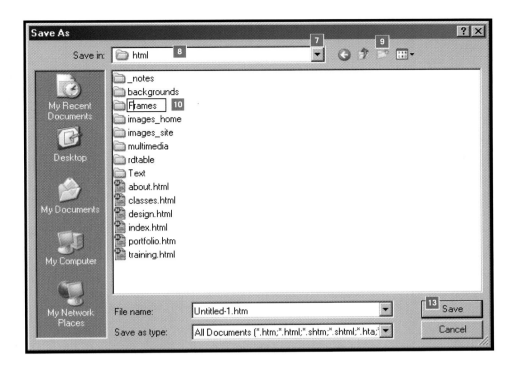

7. **Click the Save In list arrow. Choose the drive in which you saved the DWCC folder, and then double-click DWCC to open it.**

8. **Open the html folder.**

9. **Click the Create New Folder icon.**
   The folder will be named New Folder by default

10. **Type** frames **on top of the New Folder name and press Enter.**
    A new folder is added inside the html folder and can be seen in the Files panel.

11. **Double-click the new frames folder to open it.**

12. **Type** frames **in the File Name/Name field to name the page.**

<NOTE>
Some platforms such as UNIX are case-sensitive. Using all lower-case characters for filenames is a good convention to use to ensure that all your files can be loaded in all platforms.

13. **Click Save.**
    The file named frames.htm is now saved in the frames folder.

<NOTE>
After you save a file, you can save any changes by simply clicking File➔Save or Ctrl/Command+S.

14. **Close the new file now; you'll use it in another session.**

Tutorial
» Choosing a Design View

Dreamweaver allows you to work the way you are most comfortable. If you write code, you may fine the Code view helpful. You can design in a total visual environment by using the Design view. You can also have the best of both in the Split view.

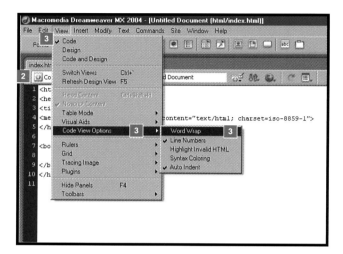

1. **Double-click on the** `index.html` **file in the Files panel to open it.**

2. **Click the Code view icon in the Document toolbar.**
   You now see just the code in the document window.
   To help find code when you need it, you change a code view preference.

3. **Click View in the Menu toolbar, and pass your cursor over Code View Options. Click Word Wrap.**

4. **Click View in the Menu toolbar, and pass your cursor over Code View Options. Click Line Numbers.**

5. **Click the Design view icon in the toolbar again.**
   The document window shows only the working area.

6. **Click the Split view icon.**
   Notice that you have both code and the visual design in the same area. You can adjust how much code you see by dragging the gray line between the Code view and the Design view up or down.

7. **Click the Window Size pop-up menu, and choose the 760x420 option.**

8. **If the options are grayed out, click the Restore Down button (Minimize/Maximize) for the document page.**
   If you need to view the page at a certain resolution to make sure that it works within those constraints, you cannot have the document window maximized.

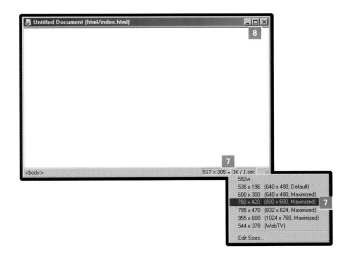

9. **Click the Minimize/Maximize icon to maximize the document. You'll see two small squares**
   When the document is maximized to use the available work-space, you'll see tabs for all the open files in the workspace making it easy to navigate between open files.

Screen Size

You need to be aware of how your site appears on the user's screen and what resolution users might have. Normally, designers try to design Web pages to fit the majority of the users' browser windows without scrolling horizontally. The former recommendation was for designers to develop sites for a 640x480 resolution, because many users browse with this setting. However, the standard recommendation has increased to 800x600. In this course, you create a fluid Web page design, which means that your design adjusts to the size of the user's browser window.

Tutorial
» Setting Browser Preferences

As you design your Web page, you should continually review your design in different browsers to assure that your page displays the way you want it to. In order to do so, you need to have recent versions of Netscape and Internet Explorer (or Mozilla and Opera). In this course, you check your pages in Internet Explorer 6, Netscape 7, and Netscape 4.79. (You may use whatever browsers you want to test, but this book assumes these three.)

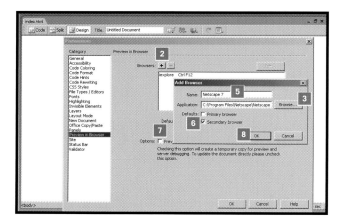

<NOTE>
I had you name the file after selecting the file because once you select the file, the name changes to the file name.

<NOTE>
You can install multiple versions of Netscape. To have multiple versions of Internet Explorer, you must install dual operating systems, each with a different version of Internet Explorer or test on different machines.

11. **Preview in a browser by choosing one of these options:**
    » Press icon in the Document toolbar.
    » Press F12 to access the primary browser.
    » Press Ctrl+F12/⌘+F12 for the secondary browser.
    » Choose File➔Preview in Browser from the pop-up menu and select the browser.

12. **Close any open pages.**

1. **Click the Preview/Debug in Browser icon in the Document toolbar, and click Edit Browser List.**
   The Preview in Browser category of the Preferences dialog box is selected. Your default browser most likely is shown in the browser window area.

2. **Click the plus sign next to Browsers.**

3. **Click the Browse button next to the Application field, and find the browser that you want to add.**
   Your browsers will normally be installed in the Program Files folder on a PC.

4. **Locate the browser application's executable file. Select it, and click Open.**
   If you don't have file extensions visible, you can usually find the executable file in the applications root folder with an icon next to it. Following the example, you use an icon with an N in it for Netscape.

5. **Type a name for the browser that you are adding in the Add Browser dialog box.**
   Consider naming your browsers with actual browser names. The example uses Netscape 7.

6. **Click Secondary Browser to select it, or check Primary if you are adding a primary browser.**
   If you see a check mark, the option is selected. This example uses Internet Explorer as the primary browser because it has the largest user base. If you have Web statistics for your site and your users more frequently use another browser, consider selecting it as the primary.

7. **Select Preview Using Temporary File.**
   Don't select if you'd rather not use a temporary file. If you are low on computer resources don't select it.

8. **Click OK.**

9. **Repeat Steps 1 through 7 to add other browsers.**
   For this book's purposes, I am testing and commenting on Internet Explorer 6, Netscape 4.79, and Netscape 7.

10. **Click OK to close the dialog box when you are done.**

Tutorial

» Setting Accessibility Preferences

Making your site accessible to as many people as possible is not only the right thing to do, but it's also the law for many types of organizations. Dreamweaver has a built-in system that helps you add the appropriate tags and labels to various elements.

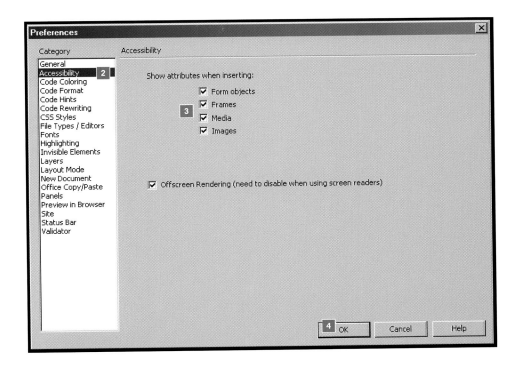

1. **Click Edit→Preferences.**

2. **In the Category field, select Accessibility.**

3. **Check all the options.**

4. **Click OK.**
   Now, whenever you insert one of the checked elements, a dialog box opens into which you can enter data. Each dialog box is discussed as it appears in your workflow.

<NOTE>
The Accessibility standards are set by the World Wide Web Consortium (W3C). To view an extensive study of the standards, you can go to their Web site at www.w3c.org. It's pretty heavy reading but very informative. You just use a few of the very basic accessibility standards. For more information on accessibility issues, refer to the Using Dreamweaver manual's chapter on Accessibility and the Help files.

Tutorial

» Setting Page Properties

A Web page contains two very specific areas, the head and the body. The head contains invisible elements, and the body contains the code that makes your Web page visible to the viewer. What you do first is set the attributes of the <body> tag.

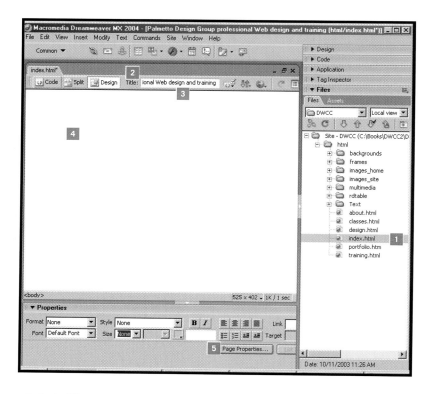

1. **In the Files panel, double-click on** `index.html` **to open it.**

2. **Select the Untitled Document text in the Title field.**

3. **Type:** Palmetto Design Group professional Web design and training.
   Some search engines use the title to rank your site higher in a search. Try to use some of your most important keywords in the title. The title appears at the top of a browser window; it is not the filename.

<NOTE>
If you forget to change the title name, Dreamweaver does not prompt you to do so. It calls your page "Untitled Document."

4. **Click anywhere inside the document window of index.html to set the cursor.**

5. **In the Property inspector, click the Page Properties button.**
   You can also choose Modify➜Page Properties or use the keyboard shortcut of Ctrl/Commandl+J. The General category is open by default.

<NOTE>
If the Page Properties option is grayed out or you don't see the button in the Property inspector, you may not have your cursor in the document window.

6. **The Appearance category is selected by default. If you've changed it, select it now.**

7. **Click the arrow for the Page font field, and select Verdana, Arial, Helvetica, sans-serif.**

8. **Click the arrow for the Size field, and select 12 pixels.**

9. **Type the hex code #333333 (near black) in the Text field for the text color.**

10. **Type the hex code #D8DEE5 in the Background field.**

11. **Type 0 in all four Margin fields.**
    This aligns all your elements to the edge.

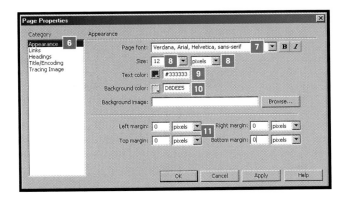

<NOTE>
Internet Explorer reads the Left Margin and the Top Margin entries, but Netscape reads the Margin Width and the Margin Height entries. To be compatible with both of the major browsers, enter your values into all four fields.

12. **Click on the Links Category.**

13. **Type the hex code #000099 in the Link Color field.**
    The link text appears in this color on the page in the browser.

14. **Type the hex code #0066FF in the Visited Links field.**
    The link text appears in this color to indicate that a user has already visited the link.

15. **Type the hex code #00BB00 in the Rollover Links field.**

16. **Type the hex code #000066 in the Active Links field.**
    The link text appears in this color when a user clicks the mouse on it.

17. **Click OK when you are finished.**
    These are all the properties that you set for now.

18. **Click the Code view icon.**

19. **Scroll to the top and notice the area starting with <style>.**
    This is an embedded style sheet. These are CSS styles that define your background color and text colors. Later in this book, you see how to get these out of the document and into an external style sheet to which you can link every page in your site.

20. **Save the page.**

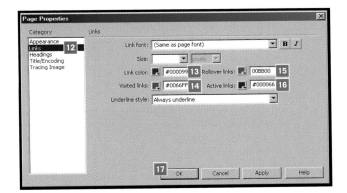

<NOTE>
When you set your link and text colors, be aware that color-blind people may have a hard time reading low contrast text. The colors used here should work well since it is dark blue against a gold background—a high contrast choice.

<NOTE>
You won't need to use the Page Properties at all to set these properties after you are more comfortable using CSS styles. But for now, I thought a beginner would prefer this method. I show you later in the book how to move these settings to an external style sheet.

Tutorial
» Adding Meta Tags

If you want users to find your Web site, you must list the site with the various engines and insert keywords and descriptions into your Web page. These keywords and descriptions help the search engine categorize your Web site. This tutorial shows you how to enter meta tags with specific attributes, making your Web page more user-friendly to search engines.

1. **Open** `index.html` **if you've closed it.**

2. **Expand the Text folder in the Files panel and double-click on the** `designnotes.txt` **file to open it. Copy all the keyword text.** Leave the file open for now.

3. **Click on the** `index.html` **name in the document to make it the active document.**

4. **Select the HTML category in the Insert bar.**

5. **Click the Head icon, and select Keywords.**
   The head content is invisible to users; they can't see what you enter, but what you enter can determine whether search engines find your site.

<NOTE>
The icons in the Insert bar with multiple selections will change to the last used selection. For instance, once you select Keywords, the icon now seen in the Insert bar for the head category will be the key.

6. **Paste (Ctrl/Command+V) into the Keyword dialog box:** Flash animation, animation, business, business consultant, creation, designers, developer, development, ebusiness, e-business, graphic design, information design, interactive design, internet, multimedia, website, webpage, corporate training, Dreamweaver, Fireworks, Flash, training, classes.

   Or, type any keywords you'd like to use.
   Type the words according to their importance—what you think users may enter into a search engine that will bring them to your site. Separate keywords with commas.

7. **Click OK.**

Keyword Usage

About 90 percent of Web hits are generated from a major search site. Knowing this, choosing your keywords wisely is important. The frequency of the keywords in a particular document can also influence your search rankings. Try to use some of your important keywords in the title of your page as well as in the document itself. Some engines even check the `<alt>` tag text, so use it wisely as well. For more information on coding your meta tag information, visit these sites:

» Search Engine Watch at www.searchenginewatch.com

» Web Developer at www.webdeveloper.com/html/
   html_metatag_res.html

8. **Click on the designnote.txt file name and copy the text for the description.**
   Choosed Edit➔Copy or easier yet, use the keyboard shortcut of Ctrl/Command+C.

9. **Close the designnote.txt file.**

10. **In the Insert bar, click the arrow next to the Head:keywords icon to access the menu, and select Description.**
    The Description dialog box opens.

11. **Paste (Ctrl/Command+V) in the description area. The description is:**
    Headquartered in Florida, Palmetto Design Group is a leading Web solution developer specializing in Ebusiness, Web Design and Corporate training.
    Use as many keywords as possible. This is the description that appears in many search engine listings.

12. **Click OK.**

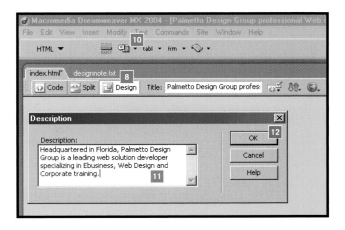

<**WARNING**>
Do not use a certain word multiple times. This is considered spamming the search engine. Many search engines do not index your site if you do this. Another trick that keyword spammers try, which is considered in poor taste within the industry, involves adding keywords to the top of the document, but making the text the same color as the background. Spiders or robots think that the document contains more relevant keywords in it, but users can't see the superfluous words. The search sites caught on to this trick, and if they find text the same color as the background, they do not list your site.

13. **Click on the Code view icon.**

14. **Scroll down until you see** `<meta name="keywords"`...
    The meta tags appear below the styles.

15. **Click inside the part that says** `<meta name="keywords"`.
    Notice the Property inspector. You can see the keywords there. This is where you make any modifications. You can also directly edit the code if you are comfortable doing so.

16. **Click inside the part of the code that says**
    `<meta name="description"`.
    The description also appears in the Property inspector where you can easily modify it.

17. **Click File➔Save (or Save As) to save your work.**
    A copy of everything up through this session is included in the Session3_exercise folder on the CD-ROM.

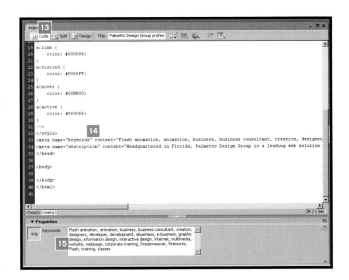

<**NOTE**>
Do not click the keyword or description icons again to modify keywords or descriptions. This adds another set of keywords and descriptions to the `<head>` of the document. If you were to add another set, search engines might consider this spamming and might not list your site.

» Session Review

Answer the questions below to review the information in this session. The answer to each question can be found in the tutorial noted in parentheses.

1. How do you access a design note? (See "Tutorial: The Home Page and Design Notes.")

2. What are the differences among Code view, Design view, and Code and Design view? (See "Tutorial: Choosing a Design View.")

3. List two ways in which you can preview a Dreamweaver document in a browser. (See "Tutorial: Setting Browser Preferences.")

4. How do you set page margins? (See "Tutorial: Setting Page Properties.")

5. What part of the document code stores the meta tags? (See "Tutorial: Adding Meta tags.")

6. What should you never do when adding keywords? (See "Tutorial: Adding Meta tags.")

7. Why is it important to use meaningful keywords? (See "Tutorial: Adding Meta tags.")

Working with Tables

Tutorial: **Learning Table Basics**

Tutorial: **Selecting Table Elements**

Tutorial: **Changing Colors in a Table**

Tutorial: **Adding Custom Borders**

Tutorial: **Using Fixed Tables to Build the Home Page**

Tutorial: **Build the Interior Pages**

Tutorial: **Adding the Navigation Table**

Tutorial: **Adding the Content Table**

Tutorial: **Exploring the Layout View**

Session Introduction

In this session, you learn the ins and outs of building tables. A table in Dreamweaver is a container with rows, columns, and cells. Tables were originally made to hold data, but Web designers discovered that they were great containers to aid in the placement of images. You can also place tables inside of tables, but if you want to be more compliant with Web standards, you should avoid nesting tables. You may do it, but it'll take you longer to make the transition at a later date (which means more editing).

Tables come in three varieties: a fixed table, which is a specific size no matter what size a browser window is, and an autostretch table, which is also called a fluid or stretchy table. The autostretch table expands to fill the browser window. And the best of both—the hybrid, which uses both fixed and autostretch features. By designating certain columns to be a fixed width and one column to autostretch, you can control how the fixed areas appear in all browsers. The column that is set to autostretch fills whatever space is left in a browser window after the fixed columns are in place.

Tables have a hierarchy—cell values have the highest priority. If a value in a row, column, or even a table contradicts the cell's value, the cell value overrides the others.

Tables are frequently the backbone of your layout, offering you lots of control. Later in this course, you learn how to do some positioning of tables using Cascading Style Sheets. But standard tables are still the most widely used method of page layout. You encounter plenty of frustrating little details, such as selecting cells that collapse, while building tables in Dreamweaver. In this session, you learn how to overcome these small obstacles. You also learn some quirks about different browsers and what to do to make your tables look the same in Netscape and Internet Explorer.

TOOLS YOU'LL USE
Property inspector, Commands menu, Standard view, layout view, Table tools

MATERIALS NEEDED
The session3_starterfiles if you've skipped any previous sessions; the Xtras folder in the session3 folder (you don't have to copy it to your hard drive)

TIME REQUIRED
120 minutes

Tutorial
» Learning Table Basics

In this tutorial, you learn how to insert a table and add some quick formatting to see the difference in cell padding and cell spacing. Then you learn how to make modifications to the table. This table is used later in this session for a calendar. This page is not used in the site design, so you can skip this tutorial if you are in a hurry. However, it does help you get familiar with additional tools and options not used in this particular site design.

1. **Open the Files panel.**

2. **Right-click (Ctrl-click) on the html folder, select New Folder, and name it Calendar. Press Enter (Return) to accept the name.**

3. **Right-click (Ctrl-click) the Calendar folder name, and click New File.**

4. **Name the file** `calendar.html`**, and double-click to open it.**

5. **Click on Design view if it isn't selected already.**
   You make the calendar on its own page.

6. **In the Insert bar, select the Common category.**

7. **Click the Table icon.**

8. **Enter these values into the Table dialog box:**
   » Rows: **6**
   » Columns: **6**
   » Width: **400 pixels**
   » Border: **1**
   » Cell Padding: **0**
   » Cell Spacing: **0**

   If pixels aren't showing in the Width area, click the down arrow to access them. The choices are percent or pixels. Pixels are used to set an exact size for a table.

9. **In the Summary area type** layout table**.**
   You do this to help make the site more accessible. Screen Readers can read this.

10. **Click OK to close the Table dialog box and add the table to your document.**

< N O T E >
The Cell Padding and Cell Spacing options in the Table dialog box are blank by default. However, blank does not mean zero. Most browsers have a default cell padding of 1 pixel and a default cell spacing of 2 pixels. To get zero, you have to type it in.

11. **In the document, click on a little arrow below one of the columns. Don't select anything.**

    By clicking on the arrow, you select the entire column. You also see a menu of options.

<**NOTE**>

You add lots of layout tables in this chapter, so you repeat this action of adding layout table to the summary of each table.

12. **Choose Commands→Format Table from the main menu.**

    The Format Table dialog box opens.

13. **Select AltRows:Blue&Yellow from the list of options.**

14. **You can click in any of the color boxes and change the colors of the columns if you so choose.**

15. **You can also change the Alternate settings by selecting a different one from the drop-down list.**

    For instance, you can change the coloring of every two rows instead of every other row.

16. **In the Top Row area, click the arrow next to Align and select Center.**

17. **In the Left Column area, click the arrow next to Align and select Center.**

18. **Type 1 in the Border field.**

19. **Click OK to close the dialog box and apply the new formatting to the table already in your document.**

20. **Click to place your cursor inside the top-left cell, and type** Sunday. **Then click outside the table.**

    Notice that the remaining cells collapse. You can probably still see the cells to insert your cursor into but sometimes the cells will collapse so far that you can't tell where to click. You'll see a couple of workarounds for that shortly.

<**NOTE**>

To accept changes such as values and attributes or even text, you simply click anywhere in the document. You can also press Enter (Return), but use this action carefully because pressing Enter/Return will add a paragraph tag to your document.

21. **Press the Tab key to get to the next cell, and type** Monday.

    Pressing the Tab key navigates you through the columns. If you need to go backward, press Shift+Tab.

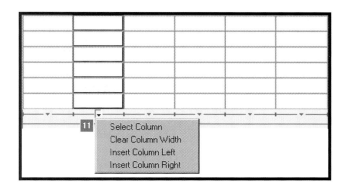

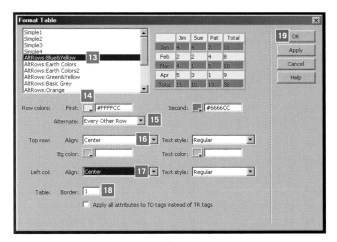

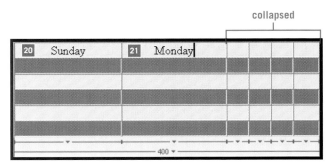

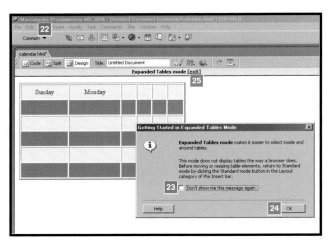

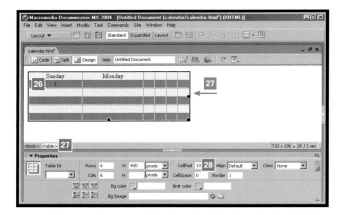

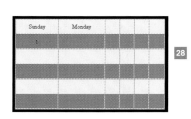

22. **To make cells even easier to select, choose View→Table Mode→Expanded Tables Mode.**
A warning dialog box opens that tells you this is not the way your table will view in a browser.

23. **Select: Don't show me this message again.**

24. **Click OK to close.**
Notice the gray border and extra space around your table. If you prefer this method of navigating table cells, use it. But Tab works great and is my preferred method so I'll show you how to revert back to Standard view.

25. **Click the Exit text to return to Standard view.**

< N O T E >
The warning dialog box said to switch to Standard view use the Layout category of the Insert bar and select Standard. You can do that, or use the View→Table Mode menu as well. There are frequently multiple ways to do things in Dreamweaver.

26. **Click to place your cursor inside the first cell in the second row, and type** 1.
This content is being entered only so you can better see the effects of cell padding and cell spacing which you'll add shortly.

27. **Select the table using one of these methods:**
» Click outside the table; then drag towards the table border.
» Click anywhere in the table and select the <table> tag from the Tag Selector.

28. **Change the CellPad to** 10 **in the Property inspector, and then click in the document or press the Enter (Return) key to apply the change.**
Notice the 10-pixel padding around the words and the number.

29. **Click Edit→Undo Set Attribute.**

30. **Change the CellSpace to** 10 **in the Property inspector, and press Enter (Return).**
The white borders are the background showing through. A cell space does not take on the color that you add to your table.

31. **Type** 10 **for the CellPad in the Property inspector.**
You are adding the cell padding back in.

32. **Highlight the CellSpace number of 10 and type** 0. **Press Enter (Return).**
You use this table for the next tutorial, so save it now.

< N O T E >
If you have an image in the cell and you want to see its properties, select the image and tap the right-arrow key once. This places your cursor in the cell, and the properties appear in the Property inspector.

33. **Place your cursor inside the top-right cell of the first row.**
You can see in the corresponding image, marked with 33, where you should click.

34. **Right-click (Ctrl+click) and when the contextual menu appears, hold the cursor over Table and choose Insert Rows or Columns.**
The Insert Rows or Columns dialog box opens.

<NOTE>
You could also choose Insert Column, but there are no options; the column is inserted to the right of the selected column. You can also access the table options via the Modify→Table menu.

35. **Click the Columns radio button if it isn't already selected. Change the Number of Columns to 2, click After Current Column if it isn't selected, and click OK.**
Two additional columns are added; your table now has eight columns instead of six. The table has one more column than is needed for a calendar, but that is taken care of in just a while.

36. **Click inside any cell on the top row, and right-click (Ctrl+click). When the contextual menu appears, hover over Table and choose Insert Row.**
With the Insert Row command, a row is added above the row in which the cursor is located. Because you added the row, the row colors no longer alternate (two yellow lines are together). In the next tutorial, you fix and change the colors.

37. **Click inside any cell of the new top row, and right-click (Ctrl+click). When the contextual menu appears, hold the cursor over Table and choose Split Cell.**
The Split Cell dialog box opens. You have the choice of splitting the cell into rows or columns. If you choose columns, columns are added to the selected cell. If you choose rows, rows are added to the cell.

38. **Choose Rows, type 2, and click OK.**
Notice that the selected cell now has two rows in it. Leave this file open; in the next tutorial, you learn several ways to make selections in tables.

39. **Save the file but leave it open.**
Choose File→Save.

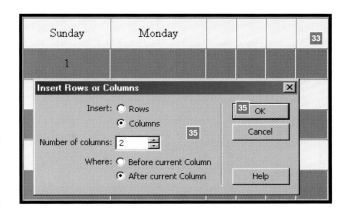

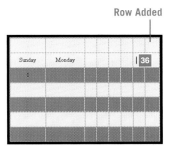

Row Added

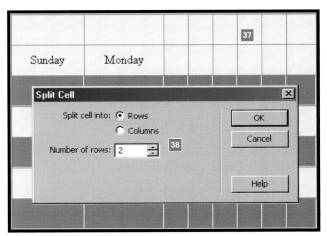

Tutorial
» Selecting Table Elements

It is sometimes difficult to select exactly what you want in a table, especially if a cell or column has no content and it collapses. You've already seen how to use the Expanded tables mode, now you'll see other ways to select various parts of a table.

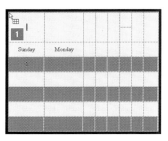

1. **With the** `calendar.html` **file open, hold your cursor over the upper-left corner of the table to select it. When you see the little table icon, click to select the table.**
   When selected, the table will be surrounded by a thick border. You'll also see the `<table>` tag in the Tag Selected highlighted.

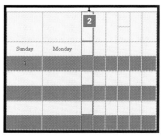

2. **You can select a column in a similar manner. Place the cursor pointing down above the column, and click when you see the dark arrow.**

3. **To select a row, place the cursor over a row on the right side until you see a right-pointing arrow, then click to select.**

4. **Select the** `<table>` **tag in the Tag Selector to select a table, or the** `<tr>` **tag to select a row, or the** `<td>` **tag to select a column.**
   This is the most precise and easiest way to make a difficult selection. However, you choose the selection option that works best for you.

Selecting a Cell

You may select one or more cells in these ways:

» **Turn the Expanded Table Mode on, and then click in the cell that you want.**

» **Click in any cell within the row that you want to select. From the status bar, click the** `<td>` **(Table Data) tag.**

» **Ctrl+click each cell that you want to select, even discontinuous cells.**

» **Click inside the cell, and drag across and/or down to select multiple continuous cells.**

Selecting a Row

Notice that all the cells in the first row have a black border around them, indicating that the entire row is selected. You can select a row in these additional ways:

>> Turn the Expanded Table Mode on.

>> Click in any cell within the row that you want to select. From the status bar, click the `<tr>` (Table Row) tag.

>> Ctrl+click (⌘+click) to the left of a row. When you see the horizontal arrow, click the row. Repeat to select multiple rows, even non-continuous rows.

>> Click inside the first cell of a row, and drag across to select the entire row.

5. Place your cursor in a cell, and press Ctrl+A (⌘+A).

6. Select the entire top row. Right-click (Ctrl+click), and when the contextual menu appears, hold the cursor over Table and choose **Merge Cells.**
   The entire row is now one large cell that spans the entire table. You can span just two cells if you want. You can span cells across rows, columns, or both.

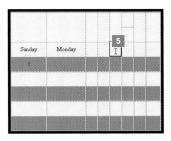

<NOTE>
When you select the entire top row, the split cell you did earlier is selected as well. This is fine since it was added simply for practice.

<CAUTION>
Merging Cells is not something you should do if you can avoid it. It makes your table load slower. Many designers use this feature, but as you'll see in this book's site design, you can easily live without it. A better solution is to add a one-row table.

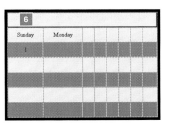

7. Save the `calendar.html` page but leave it open for the next tutorial.

Selecting a Column

You may select columns in these additional ways:

>> Turn the Expanded Table Mode on, and select the column with one of the following methods.

>> Use the Table Width column arrows to open the Column Header menu.

>> Ctrl+click (⌘+click) the top of a column. When you see the vertical arrow, click the column. Repeat to select multiple columns, even discontinuous columns.

>> Click inside the first cell of a column, and drag down to select the entire column.

Selecting a Table

Use any of these options to select a table:

>> Turn the Expanded Table Mode on.

>> Use the Table Width arrows to open the Table Header menu.

>> Click outside the table, and drag the cursor over the edge of the table.

>> Click anywhere inside the table, and then select the `<table>` tag from the status bar.

>> Choose Modify→Table→Select Table.

>> Right-click (Ctrl+click) the table, and when the contextual menu appears, hover over Table and click Select Table.

>> Press Ctrl+A (⌘+A) twice.

Tutorial

» Changing Colors in a Table

Adding or changing colors in Dreamweaver is easy. You need to make selections, of course, and then you can find the color options in the Property inspector. You saw how you could dictate color in the Table Format dialog box, but you can change the color of individual rows and/or cells as well.

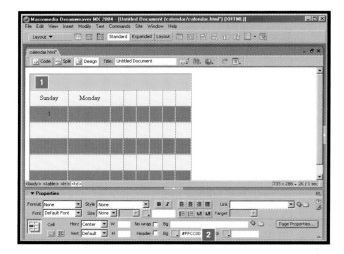

1. **With the calendar.html page open, place the cursor inside the top row that you merged into one cell in the preceding tutorial.**

2. **In the Property inspector, highlight the color #FFFFCC in the Bg field (background color) and type** #FFCC00 **for a deep gold color.**

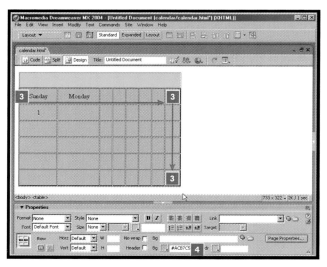

3. **Place the cursor inside the first left cell in the second row. Press the left mouse button, and drag across and down to select all the remaining cells.**

4. **Type the Hexadecimal number** #ACB7C5 **into the Bg color field.** Your table now has a gold bar across the top, and the remaining cells are a light blue color.

5. **Select the table. In the Property inspector, type #003399 into the Brdr color (Border) field.**
   Your borders are now dark blue instead of the default gray.

6. **Preview your work in different browsers.**
   You can press F12 for your primary browser, or you can select a browser from the Preview/Debug in Browser icon.

   In Internet Explorer, the borders are dark blue; in Netscape 4.7 and 7, the borders aren't colored. This is why it's important to always check your work in various browsers. This way, you can see how it will be rendered on a viewer's screen. The next tutorial shows my preferred method for making a table with borders.

7. **Save the file as** mycalendar.html **(File➔Save As).**

8. **You can close this practice file.**

Choosing Colors

The background image, text, and links all have a small color box. When you select a color, such as the background, which is white by default, you see the hexadecimal code to the right of the color box. In the case of the background, the number is #FFFFFF.

You can change the color by clicking the square color box. This opens the color picker, where you can select a color either from a color palette, or from anywhere on your desktop. You can pick colors from an open document, which is a great way to coordinate your color scheme.

If you want different colors available in the palette, use the Options pop-up menu (in the top-right corner). You can select

Color Cubes (default), Continuous Tone (these two are Web safe), Windows OS, Mac OS, and Grayscale.

You can make any palette Web safe by choosing Snap to Web Safe from the Options pop-up menu. Be aware that this option shifts your selected color to the nearest Web safe color, which can result in a different color than selected. If you select a color and notice that it does not appear as you intended it, or if you want to use a non-Web safe color, make sure that you uncheck the Snap to Web safe option.

Tutorial

» Adding Custom Borders

In this tutorial, you apply color formatting manually, not with the Format Table command as you did in the Learning Table Basics tutorial. Doing it this way offers much more control over what is colored. You make a new table for a calendar for the Palmetto Design Group Web page. Once this is completed, you can choose which method you prefer—the automatic borders or a custom border with no dimension.

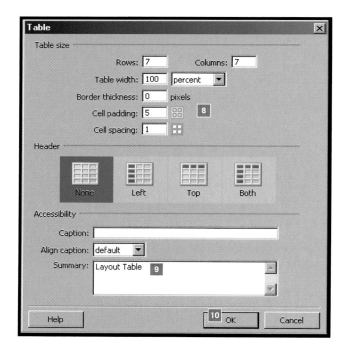

1. **Double-click the** `calendar.html` **file in the Files panel to open it.**

2. **Select the entire table, and delete it.**
   You make a new one in the next step. You can delete this table because you saved it with a different name in the preceding tutorial.

3. **Click the Insert Table icon in the Common tab of the Insert menu, and enter these values:**
   » Rows: **1**
   » Width: **400**
   » Cell Padding: **0**
   » Columns: **1**
   » Border: **0**
   » Cell Spacing: **0**

4. **Type** Layout Table **in the summary box.**

5. **Click OK.**

6. **Type** #003399 **in the Bg color field in the Property inspector while the table is still selected, and then press Enter (Return).**

7. **Click inside the table that now appears in your document.**

8. **Click the Insert Table icon (from the Common category or the Layout category), and enter these values:**
   » Rows: **7**
   » Width: **100 percent**
   » Cell Padding: **5**
   » Columns: **7**
   » Border: **0**
   » Cell Spacing: **1**

9. **Type** Layout Table **in the Summary box.**

10. **Click OK.**
    By placing a table within a table, you nest the second table. Use this judiciously because nested tables take longer to render. If you need borders, the preferred way is to add them using CSS. You'll learn how to add CSS styles in Session 7.

<NOTE>

A small table with a nested table won't affect your download speed much but it does add to the complexity of the site design. Remember, simple is better and will be easier to update in the future. But like anything, it's a technique and not evil in itself. There may be times that nesting tables is the only way to achieve what you need to accomplish.

11. **Click and drag your cursor to select all the cells.**

12. **Type** #ACB7C5 **in the Bg field, and then press Enter (Return).**
    You now have a 1-pixel flat border of the dark blue color that renders properly in all the browsers.

13. **Preview your work in different browsers.**
    The border is now 1 pixel and flat without the extra dimension that the Border option adds.

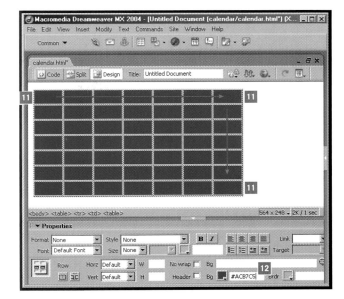

14. **Place your cursor in the top-left cell, and drag horizontally to select the row or select the** <td> **tag from the Tag Selector.**

15. **Click the Merge Cells icon in the Property inspector.**
    Refer to the illustration to locate the icon. It's in the Cell area.

16. **Place the cursor in the merged cell, type** #FFFFCC **in the Bg field in the Property inspector, and then press Enter (Return).**

17. **Preview your work in different browsers.**

18. **Save this file for use as a calendar.**

19. **Close the file.**

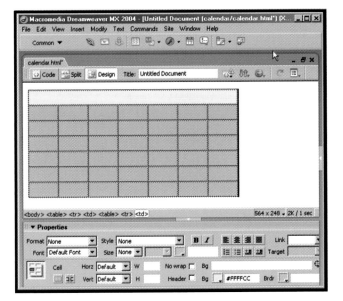

Tutorial
» Using Fixed Tables to Build the Home Page

You are designing this Web site to be viewed from a screen resolution of 800x600. If you are using a resolution higher than this, these Web pages may appear small to you. You want to design to the most common screen resolution—800x600—without making the users scroll to see the content on the home page.

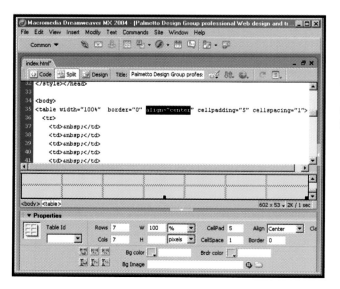

1. Open the `index.html` page, and click Show When File is Open option to deselect it.

2. Click OK to close the design note.

< N O T E >
I had you turn off the design note so it doesn't come up every time we open the index file. You can access it at any time by expanding the Files panel and double-clicking the Design Note icon.

3. Click the Insert Table icon from the Insert bar's Common category, accept whatever is in the Insert Table dialog box, and click OK.
   The Insert Table icon is also present in the Layout category of the Insert bar.

4. With the table still selected, choose the Center option in the Align field in the Property inspector.

5. Switch to Split view so you see the table and the code.
   The code for this table is highlighted in the code part of your document window. Notice where the code says `align= "center"`. This is deprecated (being phased out) code and does not render properly on all browsers. The better tag to use is `<div>`. You see how to use it in the next steps.

Looking at the Code

This is the complete code as seen when you center a table using Align in the Property inspector:

```
<table width="453" border="0"
align="center" cellpadding="0"
cellspacing="0">
```

This is the complete code as seen when you add the `<div>` tag to the `<body>` tag prior to inserting content:

```
<div align="center"></div>
```

This is how the code now looks after you inserted a table:

```
<div align="center">
<table width="601" border="0" cellspacing="0"
cellpadding="0" summary="Layout table">
 <tr>
 <td> </td>
 <td> </td>
 </tr>
</table>
</div>
```

6. **Delete your table.**

   I had you enter the table basically to show you how not to center it.

7. **Click the** `<body>` **tag in the Tag Selector.**

8. **Click the Align Center icon in the Property inspector.**

9. **Look in the code area and notice the code. It says**
   `<div align="center"></div>`.

   These are the opening and closing tags to center your table or content. The cursor placement is just before the closing `</div>` tag so that whatever you insert now has the `<div>` tag wrapped around it.

10. **Click the Insert Table icon from the Insert bar, and enter these values into the Insert Menu Table dialog box:**

    » Rows: **1**

    » Columns: **2**

    » Width: **601 pixels**

    » Border: **0**

    » Cell Padding: **0**

    » Cell Spacing: **0**

11. **Type** Layout Table **in the Summary area of the Accessibility dialog box.**

12. **Click OK.**

    Now look at the code. Notice that all the table tags are enclosed between the `<div></div>` tags.

13. **Click the word Assets next to the Files panel to activate it.**

    If you don't see a list of the assets for this site, click the top Image icon on the left.

14. **Select the tables single row by inserting your cursor into the table and selecting the** `<tr>` **tag from the Tag Selector.**

15. **In the Property inspector, click the arrow for the Vert field and select Top.**

    This positions anything you put into any row or column at the top.

16. **Click inside the left column of the table in your document.**

17. **In the Assets panel, find and select** logo.gif.

18. **Click the Insert button.**

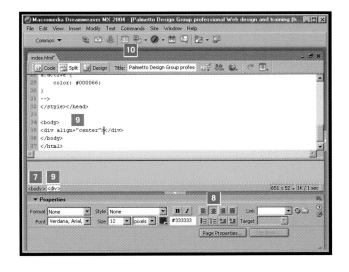

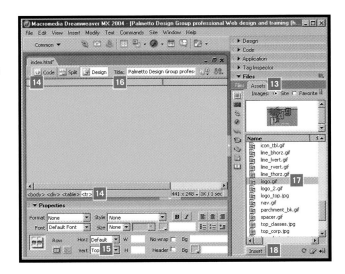

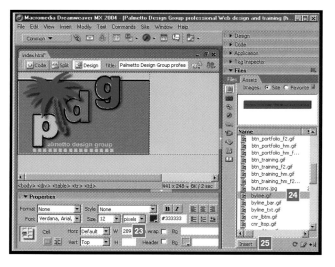

19. **Type** Palmetto Design Group Logo **in the Alternative Text field of the dialog box.**

20. **Click OK.**

 The image has been added to your table.

<NOTE>

The long description in the Alternative Text dialog box links to a text file that contains a longer description that is read by a screen reader.

21. **Look in the Property inspector, and note the width of the logo image.**

 It's 289 pixels wide.

22. **Press your keyboard's right-arrow key.**

 Your cursor is now in the cell. You could also click the <td> tag in the Tag Selector.

23. **Enter a Width of 289 in the Width (W) field in the Property inspector and then select Nowrap (you'll see a check mark when it's selected).**

<NOTE>

This collapses the column to the width of this image. If you didn't set the column width now and you added another image, it would collapse the column on the right because it has no content yet. Selecting a collapsed column is difficult, but not impossible. You only need to set the column width one time, so you don't need to do it again when you place images in the same column. By making the column the same width as the image, you can add more images that stack below the top one instead of side by side.

24. **With the logo cell still selected, select** byline.gif **in the Assets panel.**

25. **Click the Insert button.**

26. **Type** Professional Web Solutions and Training **for the Alternate text, and click OK.**

 The second image stacks right below the first image. It's because of this feature that you don't need additional rows to place your content into.

<NOTE>

Many of the applications that generate automatic tables for your images (Fireworks included) use separate rows for every image, making a table much more complex than necessary. The simpler the table, the faster it loads. Because this page is so graphic heavy (but still not bad at approximately 60KB), you want to keep the table as simple as possible.

27. **With the byline image still selected, select** `corporate.gif` **in the Assets panel.**

28. **Click the Insert button.**

29. **Type** Corporate Office Image **for the Alternative text, and click OK.**

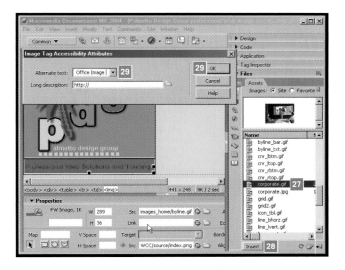

30. **If you can't see your entire table, then click on the word Properties (Property inspector title) to close it so you can view your Web page.**

31. **Click on it again to open the Property inspector again.**

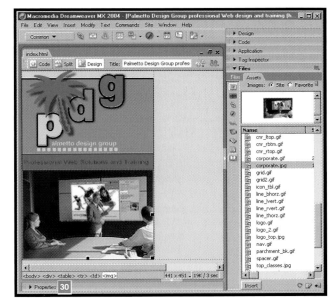

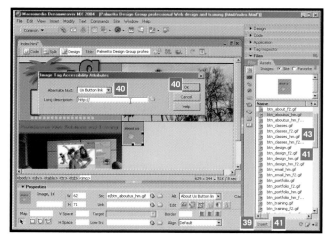

32. **Click in the right column.**
    Notice that your cursor is at the top. This is because you set the vertical alignment of the table to Top.

33. **Select** trees.gif **in the Assets panel.**

34. **Click the Insert button.**
    You can insert images in other ways, which you explore in Session 4. This method is my favorite.

35. **Type** Palm trees image **into the Alternative text dialog box, and click OK.**

36. **Look in the Property inspector, and note the width of the trees image.**
    The width is 312 pixels.

37. **Press your keyboard's right-arrow key to place your cursor in the right column.**

38. **In the Width (W) field in the Property inspector, type** 312.

39. **In the Assets panel, select** btn_aboutus_hm.gif **and click the Insert button.**

40. **Type** About Us Button link **in the Alternative text dialog box, and click OK.**

41. **In the Assets panel, select** btn_design_hm.gif **and click Insert.**

42. **Type** Design button link **in the Alternative text dialog box, and click OK.**

43. **In the Assets panel, select** btn_classes_hm.gif **and click Insert.**

44. **Type** Classes button link **in the Alternative text dialog box, and click OK.**

45. **In the Assets panel, select** btn_training_hm.gif **and click Insert.**

46. **Type** Training button link **in the Alternative text dialog box, and click OK.**

47. **In the Assets panel, select** btn_portfolio_hm.gif **and click Insert.**

48. **Type** Portfolio button link **in the Alternative text dialog box, and click OK.**

49. **In the Assets panel, select** btn_email_hm.gif **and click Insert.**

50. **Type** Email button link **in the Alternative text dialog box, and click OK.**

51. **In the Assets panel, select** books.gif **and click Insert.**

52. **Type** Books written by Palmetto Design Group **in the Alternative text dialog box, and click OK.**

<N O T E>
Knowing how the Assets panel alphabetizes helped me in naming the images. I preceded all the buttons with btn so they would appear together in the Assets panel.

<N O T E>
Be careful inserting the buttons, use the file name with hm at the end. Many of the names are similar and you'll be using them later. All the button images should have a gold button not green. If you see green you've accidently selected a file with f2 at the end.

53. **Preview in a browser by choosing one of these options:**

» Press Preview/Debug in Browser icon in the Document toolbar.

» Press F12 to access the primary browser.

» Press Ctrl+F12 (⌘+F12) for the secondary browser.

» Choose File➡Preview in Browser, and from the pop-up menu, select the browser in which you want to preview.

If you have a screen resolution of more than 800x600, change it so you can view your work the way someone using 800x600 would see it. This layout has no issues in Internet Explorer 6, Netscape 4.7, or Netscape 7.

54. **Save the file, and close it.**

You've made your first fixed-width Web page. That wasn't so painful, was it?

<NOTE>

You add the rollovers for the buttons in another session, and you add text links and copyright information below the table as well.

Tutorial
» Build the Interior Pages

Because you never know what size a user's browser is, you may want to build your Web site to accommodate any size browser window. Because you are designing to the lowest common denominator, it looks better for users who have higher resolutions to have the screen show more of your design by stretching to fill the extra browser window space. The tables you build for the interior page is the basis for autostretch (also known as fluid) tables for the site's interior pages. You'll actually make them autostretch in Session 4.

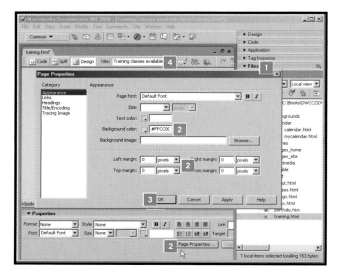

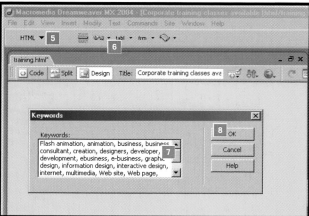

1. **Click on Files in the Files panel to activate it and double-click the** training.html **file.**

2. **Click the Page Properties button in the Property inspector, or press Ctrl+J (⌘+J), and enter these values:**

   » Appearance category—Background color: #FFCC00

   » Appearance category—All four Margin areas: 0

3. **Click OK.**
   Don't worry about the link colors. You actually change much of this information when you get to the session on Cascading Style Sheets.

4. **In the documents Title field, type:** Corporate training classes available.

5. **Select the HTML category in the Insert bar.**

6. **Click the arrow next to the Meta icon (or whatever you used last), and select Keywords.**

7. **In the Keywords dialog box, type these keywords:** Flash animation, animation, business, business consultant, creation, designers, developer, development, ebusiness, e-business, graphic design, information design, interactive design, internet, multimedia, Web site, Web page, corporate training, Dreamweaver, Fireworks, Flash, training, classes.

8. **Click OK.**

<NOTE>
You need to add the keywords again because this is a new page. For your other files, this is accomplished using a template, which you learn how to use later in this course.

9. **Click the arrow next to the keyword icon, and from the menu select Description.**

10. **Type this description into the dialog box:** Headquartered in Florida, Palmetto Design Group is a leading Web solution developer specializing in Ebusiness, Web Design, and corporate training.

11. **Click OK.**

12. **Click in the document window, and select the `<body>` tag in the Tag Selector.**

13. **Click the Align Center icon in the Property inspector.**

14. **Select the Common or Layout category of the Insert bar, click the Insert Table icon, and enter these values:**
    - » Rows: **1**
    - » Columns: **2**
    - » Width: **100 percent**
    - » Border: **0**
    - » Cell Padding: **0**
    - » Cell Spacing: **0**

15. **Type** Layout Table **in the Summary box, and click OK.**

16. **In the Property inspector, enter** #ACB7C5 **for the Bg color of the new table.**

17. **In the Table ID field of the Property inspector, type** logo.
    You see how useful this ID is when you start using CSS to style your table formatting.

18. **Place your cursor in the left column.**

19. **Click the Assets panel name to activate it. Click the Images icon if it isn't already.**

20. **Select** logo_top.jpg **from the Assets panel, and click the Insert button.**

21. **Type** Palmetto Design Group Logo **for the Alternative text, and click OK.**

22. **Check the width of the image in the Property inspector.**
    You see that it's 137 pixels.

23. **Click the image to return the focus to it; then press your keyboard's right-arrow key to place the cursor in the cell.**

24. **In the Property inspector, type** 137 **for the width (W) field.**

25. **Select the `<tr>` tag in the Tag Selector.**
    This selects the entire row, both columns.

26. **In the Property inspector, click the arrow for the Vert (vertical) field and select Top.**
    You add the rest of the images in Session 4.

27. **Save the file.**

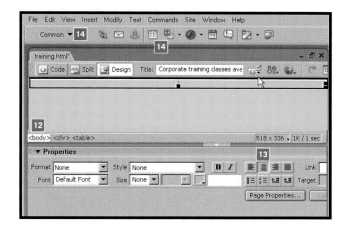

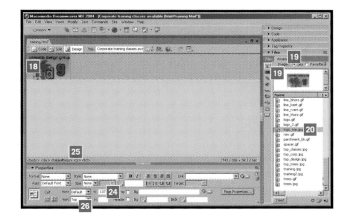

<NOTE>
I use multiple tables to keep a design modular; this makes it much easier to edit or alter. Each main area is contained in its own table.

Tutorial
» Adding the Navigation Table

In this tutorial, you add another table for the navigation. This site is considered to be a modular design because we are using individual tables. This method has great advantages, as you learn in this session.

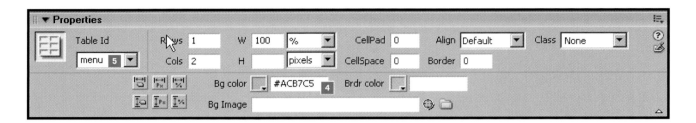

1. **With the** `training.html` **page open, in the Tag Selector, select table#logo.**
   The #logo is present in the table tag because of the ID name you gave it. This will help identify the table when you start using CSS styles.

2. **Select the Common or Layout category of the Insert bar, click the Insert Table icon, and enter these values:**

   » Rows: **1**

   » Columns: **2**

   » Width: **100 percent**

   » Border: **0**

   » Cell Padding: **0**

   » Cell Spacing: **0**

   Since these are the last values used, they will already be entered, unless you've used it between tutorials.

3. **Type** Layout Table **in the Summary box, and click OK.**
   You'll notice that even though the first table was selected, this table automatically stacked below it.

4. **In the Property inspector, enter** #ACB7C5 **for the Bg color of the new table.**

5. **In the Table ID field of the Property inspector, type** menu**.**

6. **Click inside the left column.**

7. **In the Property inspector set the vertical (Vert) to Top.**

8. **If you left the Table Widths on (green table ruler), choose View→Visual Aids→Table Widths and select to uncheck.**
   By clicking on Table Widths, you remove the check mark and deselect the option. The green table widths that you see in Dreamweaver are turned off. They interfere with our visual design using modular tables.

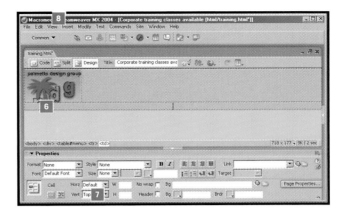

9. **In the Assets panel, select** logo2.gif **and click the Insert button.**
   Your cursor should still be in the left column.

10. **Type** Logo image **for the alternative text, and click OK.**
    The image aligns with the bottom of the image in the first table!

11. **In the Property inspector, check the width of the image.**
    It's 137.

12. **Select the logo image you just inserted to return the focus to it and press the keyboard's right-arrow key to place your cursor in the left column.**

13. **In the Property inspector, set the width (W) to 137.**
    You add the navigation buttons in Session 4.

14. **Save the file.**

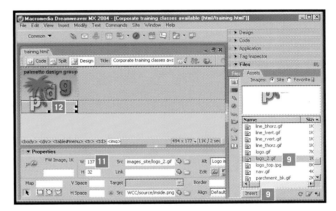

Tutorial
» Adding the Content Table

In this tutorial, you add the table that holds the content and the company byline.

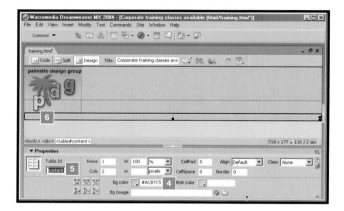

1. In the `training.html` page, click anywhere in the menu table. In the Tag Selector, select `<table#menu>`.

2. Select the Common or Layout category of the Insert bar, click the Insert Table icon, and enter these values:

   » Rows: **2**

   » Columns: **2**

   » Width: **100 percent**

   » Border: **0**

   » Cell Padding: **0**

   » Cell Spacing: **0**

3. **Type** Layout Table **in the Summary box, and click OK.**

4. **In the Property inspector, enter #ACB7C5 for the Bg color of the new table.**

5. **In the Table ID field of the Property inspector, type** content.

6. **Click inside the top-left cell.**

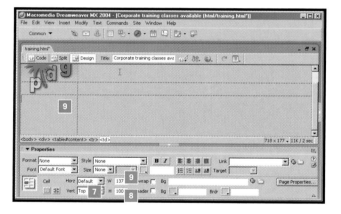

7. **In the Property inspector, set the vertical (Vert) to Top.**

8. **With your cursor still in the top-left cell, type** 100 **in the height (H) field in the Property inspector.**
   You can't specify a maximum height, but you can specify a minimum. This is just to open the cell for now. You add content in a later session.

9. **In the Property inspector, set the width (W) to** 137.
   This is the width of the images in the two tables above this one.

10. **Click to place your cursor in the left column of the second row.**

11. **In the Tag selector, select the** `<tr>` **tag to select the entire row.**

12. **In the Property inspector, set the height (H) to** 15.

13. **In the Property inspector, in the Bg (background color) field, type** #00659C.

14. **You can now save your page and close it.**

Tutorial

» Exploring the Layout View

If you have a very complex layout, the Layout view may be helpful. You can use a tracing image and draw your tables and cells visually. Don't confuse the Layout view with the Design view, Code view, or Split view. The Layout view is accessed from the Layout category of the Insert bar. This tutorial is not part of the book project; it's for learning only, so you may skip it if you want to. Personally, I never use this feature, but some people prefer it, so I want to at least introduce you to it.

1. **From the Start Page, click HTML in the "Create New" column.**
   If you have the Start Page preference turned off, choose File→New→Basic Page→HTML and click the Create button.

   <NOTE>
   You do not work on the Palmetto Design Group Web page for this tutorial. Because some of you may prefer to work this way, the main features of working in the Layout view are explained.

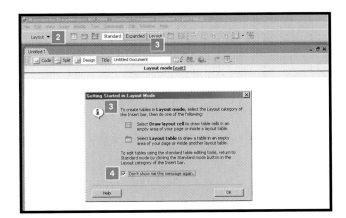

2. **Select the Layout category of the Insert bar.**

3. **Click the Layout button.**
   A Getting Started in Layout Mode dialog box opens with instructions. Note in the Insert bar that even though you selected Layout, the Standard button is still highlighted.

4. **Click Don't show me this message again option and click OK to close it.**
   The Layout button is now highlighted and a blue bar telling you the mode you are in and an Exit link are added visually to the document. This does not display in a browser.

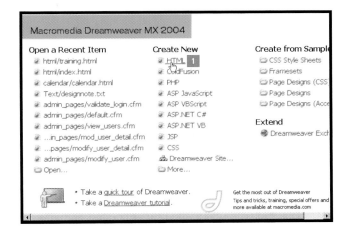

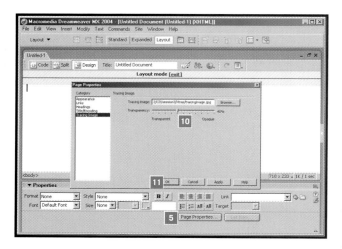

5. Choose Modify→Page Properties or click the Page Properties button in the Property inspector.

6. Click on the Tracing Image category.

7. Click the Browse button next to the Tracing Image field, and navigate to the Xtras folder inside the Session3 folder on the CD-ROM. Choose the `tracingimage.jpg` file, and click Open.

8. A warning about saving the page opens; click OK.

9. A dialog box opens asking if you want to save to your site; click NO. This dialog box opens because the Xtras folder is outside the DWCC defined root folder. Since this is practice only and not part of the site, you don't need to save the files here.

10. Move the Transparency slider to about 40 percent, and click OK. The image is now in your document.

11. Choose View→Tracing Image→Adjust Position. Use the keyboard's arrow keys to center the image. You can also enter specific coordinates to position the image. Click OK to close the dialog box.

12. Click the Layout Table icon, and place your cursor (now a crosshair) in the upper-left corner. Drag to cover the entire tracing image.

13. Check the Property inspector to see the available options. Notice that the properties are different in Layout view. You have the option of typing a value for a fixed width or selecting Autostretch, which automatically makes your table stretchy.

14. Notice the tab at the top indicating that it is a Layout Table.

15. If you click on the arrow by the number, you are given the option of making it Autostretch or adding a spacer image.

< N O T E >

Although both Standard Mode and Layout Mode insulate you from the underlying code, the two options are quite different. It's easy to switch between views and use them both on the same layout.

16. **Click the Draw Layout Cell icon in the Insert bar.**

17. **Drag from the left edge of the tracing image and around the horse banner and logo.**

18. **Notice that after you draw a cell, lines mark where other cells would be generated automatically. They are white lines and may be difficult to see.**

19. **Click the Draw Layout Cell icon, and drag around the puzzles picture, using the white line on the left side as a guide.**
    Notice that the white lines have automatically moved to generate new cell areas.

20. **Click the Layout Table icon, and drag a table in the cell around the horse banner.**
    Can't do it? Okay, it was a trick step. You can't draw a table inside a cell in Layout view. You can draw tables inside of tables but not tables inside of cells.

21. **Click the Layout Table icon again (it's not a trick), and drag a table in the area below the banner.**
    Another Layout Table tab is visible, so you can separate your tables from your cells. This design isn't really built for a stretchy table, but you can easily make any column autostretch by clicking the little arrow next to the fixed-width number and clicking Make Column Autostretch.

22. **You can close this file without saving.**

Using the Layout View

These tips will help you in using the Layout view.

» You can't overlap cells.

» You can add background and cell coloring from the Property inspector.

» To select a cell, move the cursor over the edge and, when you see the red line, click it.

» To move a cell, click and drag after you've selected it.

» Session Review

You covered lots of ground in this session, but it is important ground because table layout is the foundation for most Web sites today.

Answer the questions below to review the information in this session. The answer to each question can be found in the tutorial noted in parentheses.

1. What is the difference between cell padding and cell spacing? (See "Tutorial: Learning Table Basics.")

2. List two ways to select a table. (See "Tutorial: Selecting Table Elements.")

3. List two ways to select a row or column. (See "Tutorial: Selecting Table Elements.")

4. Can you add color to an individual table cell? (See "Tutorial: Changing Colors in a Table.")

5. What is the trick used to make a real 1-pixel table border? (See "Tutorial: Adding Custom Borders.")

6. What determines a fixed table? (See "Tutorial: Using Fixed Tables to Build the Home Page.")

7. Why don't we use the center="align" option? (See "Tutorial: Using Fixed Tables to Build the Home Page.")

8. Does each image need to have its own cell? (See "Tutorial: Using Fixed Tables to Build the Home Page.")

9. What makes a table autostretch, fluid, or stretchy? (See "Tutorial: Build the Interior Pages.")

10. How do you make a cell collapse to the same size as the content? (See "Tutorial: Build the Interior Pages.")

11. What setting forces content in a cell to align with the top of the cell? (See "Tutorial: Adding the Navigation Table.")

12. Can you specify a maximum cell height? (See "Tutorial: Adding the Content Table.")

13. List two advantages of using the Layout View. (See "Tutorial: Exploring the Layout View.")

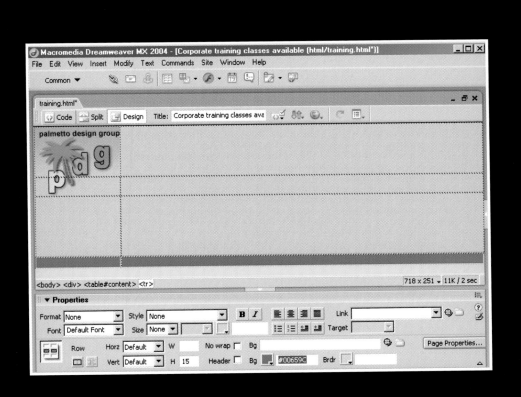

Working with Images

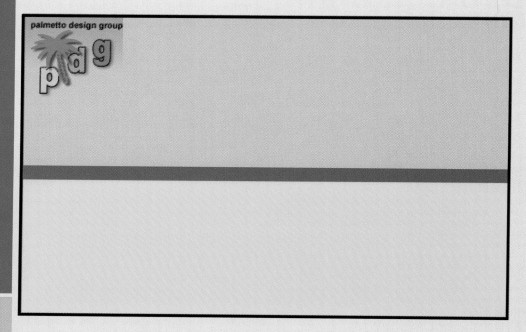

Tutorial: **Inserting the Masthead Images**

Tutorial: **Inserting the Navigation Images**

Tutorial: **Replacing Images**

Tutorial: **Making a Rounded Table Using Images**

Tutorial: **Using Background Images**

Session Introduction

Images are more than decoration. They can help locate content, navigate a site, evoke an emotional response, and provide a company identity. You should optimize and size your images in Fireworks or another image editor prior to laying them out in Dreamweaver, instead of relying on Dreamweaver to edit the bulk of your work. You should know something about the basic formats—GIF, JPEG, and SWF—that most browsers support.

GIF stands for Graphic Interchange Format, pronounced "jif." The GIF compression algorithm works best for line art and images with flat color, such as cartoons, logos, and type. GIF images are limited to 256 colors, but you can have a transparency in a GIF image, which is very important when you want to remove a background color. The GIF format is used for animation.

JPEG, pronounced "jay-peg," stands for Joint Photographic Experts Group. Because the JPEG compression algorithms excel at compressing millions of colors, photographs look best in JPEG format.

Although an exciting alternative created to combat patent holders who started charging for the GIF technology, PNG is only partially supported by Netscape and IE, which means it's not a viable option.

SWF, a vector format that Macromedia Flash uses, is viable because more than 96 percent of all users have the Flash player plug-in. Vector graphics are usually much smaller than GIF and JPEG graphics due to their method of generation. They are also scalable, which means that you can change their size without sacrificing image quality.

TOOLS YOU'LL USE
Property inspector, Assets panel, Insert bar, Document toolbar

MATERIALS NEEDED
session4_starterfiles if you didn't do the preceding sessions

TIME REQUIRED
90 minutes

Tutorial

» Inserting the Masthead Images

You can insert images into Dreamweaver in many ways. In this tutorial, you use each method at least once, and then in the instructions in the rest of this course I use the methods I have found to be most convenient through experience.

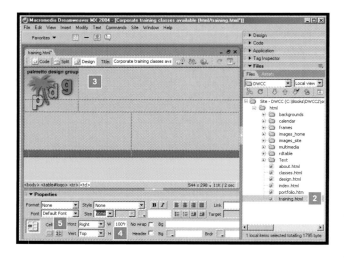

1. **Open the Files panel.**

2. **Double-click the** `training.htm` **page to open it.**

3. **Click in the right column of the first table.**
   Your cursor should be in the column to the right of the main part of the logo.

<NOTE>

If you find a cell or column difficult to select because it's collapsed, you can use the Expanded Table Mode. Choose View➜ Table Mode➜ Expanded View (F6). This adds visual space around the cells, but this extra space is not visible in a browser. Using Expanded Table Mode messes up how your visual layout appears in Dreamweaver, so I'd suggest using it when you need to and then turning it back off by clicking the icon again.

<NOTE>

You can also change your table view modes using the Layout category of the Insert bar.

4. **In the Property inspector, type** 100% **into the width (W) field.**
   Be sure to type the percent sign.

5. **Click the arrow for the horizontal (Horz) field, and select Right.**

6. **In the Insert bar's Common category, click the Insert Image icon.**

7. **Navigate to your DWCC/html/images_site folder and select** `top_trees.jpg`**. Be sure that Relative To: Document is selected, and click OK.**

<NOTE>

Relative to Document is the default linking method. The other linking method is Relative to Root Site. This method requires a server to test and is not the preferred method. All paths are mapped according to the root of the site.

8. **Type** Palm trees image **for the alternative text, and click OK.**

9. **Open the Assets panel, click and drag** top_classes.jpg **into the document to the right of the trees image.**

   I don't care for this method because you can easily drop an image in the wrong location.

10. **Type** Classroom image **for the alternative text, and click OK.**

11. **Click to the right of the classroom image and choose Insert→Image, navigate to your DWCC/html/images_site folder, select** top_design.jpg, **and click OK.**

<N O T E>

You don't really have to click to the right of the image if the previous image is still selected. If it's selected, the next image you insert will automatically go the right.

12. **Type** Web design image **for the alternative text, and click OK.**

    You used all the methods for inserting images. Now you can choose the one you prefer.

13. **Click to the right of the Web design image and in the Assets panel, select** top_corp.jpg **and click the Insert Button.**

14. **Type** Design meeting image **for the alternative text, and click OK.**

<N O T E>

If you are working on a laptop or a small screen, the last corporate image may appear below the other images in Dreamweaver.
But it isn't.

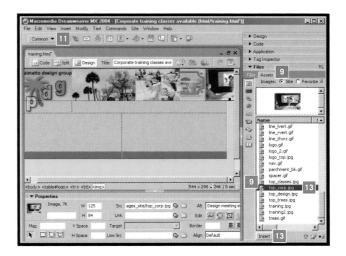

15. **Click on the Preview/Debug in Browser icon, and select Internet Explorer 6 (or whichever you prefer). Other preview options include:**

    » Pressing the keyboard shortcut F12 (or Ctrl/Cmd+F12 for secondary browser)

    » Choosing File→Preview in Browser→browser of your choice

16. **Adjust the size of your browser smaller and larger, and see how the stretchy column works.**
    Notice that when the window is larger, you can see blue between the logo and the trees image. The trees image needs to have the gradient that is behind the logo in this area.

17. **Click the tree image, and then press your keyboard's left-arrow key.**

    This places your cursor in the cell.

18. **In the Property inspector, click the yellow folder next to the bg field.**

19. **Navigate to the html/background folder, select** bk_top.jpg, **and click OK.**

20. **Save the file.**

21. **Press F12 to preview in your primary browser.**

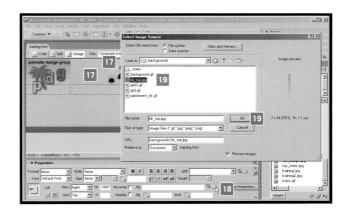

22. **Expand the browser to its full size, and notice your gradient.**

    You see the gradient now to the left of the tree image when the browser is expanded.

<N O T E>

The gradient image is actually only seven pixels wide. But when it's used as a background, it tiles in the browser. Table 4-1 lists the alignment attributes.

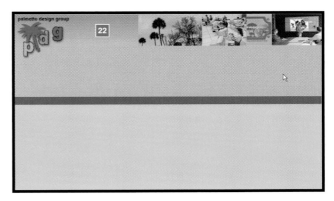

Table 4-1: Alignment Attributes

Property	Function
Default	The browser default; usually denotes bottom alignment.
Baseline	Bottom-aligns the images with the baseline of the first line of text.
Top	Top-aligns the top of the image.
Middle	Middle-aligns the middle of the image with the baseline of the first line of text.
Bottom	Bottom-aligns the bottom of the image with the baseline of the first line of text.
TextTop	Top-aligns the top of the image with the top of the first line of text.
Absolute Middle	Middle-aligns the middle of the image with the middle of the first line of text.
Absolute Bottom	Bottom-aligns the bottom of the image with the bottom of the first line of text.
Left	Aligns the image flush left on the page or in the cell; text is on the right.
Right	Aligns the image flush right on the page or in the cell; text is on the left.
Low Src	A URL for the image file that loads before the main image. It's usually a black-and-white version or a very low-resolution version of the final image.

Tutorial

» Inserting the Navigation Images

The images used for navigation go into the second table to the right of the lower half of the logo image on the `training.html` page. This tutorial teaches you how to place those images.

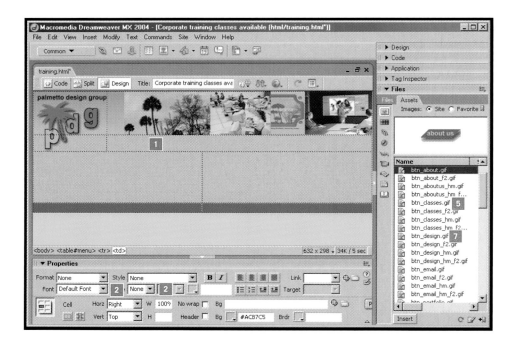

1. **Click in the right column of the second table to place your cursor.**
   This is the table below the masthead images.

2. **In the Property inspector, set the Horz field to Right. Type** 100% **into the width (W) field.**

3. **In the Assets panel, select** `btn_about.gif` **and click the Insert button.**

4. **Type** About us button link **for the alternative text, and click OK.**

5. **In the Assets panel, select** `btn_classes.gif` **and click the Insert button.**

6. **Type** Palmetto design group available classes button link **for the alternative text, and click OK.**

7. **In the Assets panel, select** `btn_design.gif` **and click the Insert button.**
   Notice that each button is being added to the right of the previous button automatically.

8. **Type** Design samples button link **for the alternative text, and click OK.**

9. **In the Assets panel, select** `btn_training.gif` **and click the Insert button.**

10. **Type** Corporte training button link **for the alternative text, and click OK.**

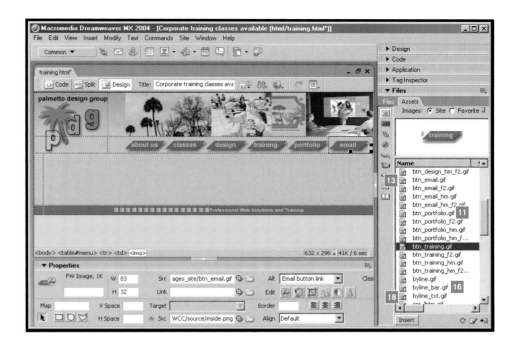

11. **In the Assets panel, select** `btn_portfolio.gif` **and click the Insert button.**

12. **Type** Portfolio button link **for the alternative text, and click OK.**

13. **In the Assets panel, select** `btn_email.gif` **and click the Insert button.**

14. **Type** Email button link **for the alternative text, and click OK.**

15. **Place the cursor in the right column of the bottom dark blue table, and set the Horz alignment to Center.**

16. **In the Assets panel, select** `byline_bar.gif` **and click the Insert button.**

17. **Press the spacebar for the alternative text, and click OK.**
    If you aren't using the automatic prompt for alternative text, you can also select `<empty>` from the Alt drop-down menu in the Property inspector.

18. **In the Assets panel, select** `byline_txt.gif` **and click the Insert button.**

19. **Type** Professional Web Design and Training **for the alternative text, and click OK.**

20. **Save and preview the file.**

<NOTE>
You may notice in Dreamweaver that the bottom table appears shorter than the navigation table. This is because you haven't yet set the right column to 100 percent.

<NOTE>
If your design requires that one image appear next to the other, except that the images appear in separate columns, you may need to set the cells to a horizontal setting of Left. In this design, the images in the second column are aligned to the right. But if they were left-aligned, there would probably be a space between the image in the right column and the one in the left column. Refer to the sidebar on V Space and H Space in Session 5 where you use these features.

Tutorial
» Replacing Images

You can replace images in several ways. None of the site images really needs to be replaced, so you replace the About Us button several times and then return the original image. This tutorial introduces you to quite a few additional tools; inevitably, you'll need to replace images in your own work.

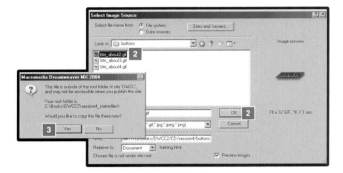

<NOTE>
Double-clicking the image name in the Assets panel does not produce the same result as in the document window. If you double-click the image in the Assets panel, your image editor opens.

1. **With the `training.html` file open, double-click the About Us button in the document window.**
   The Select Image Source dialog box opens.

<NOTE>
You navigate to the CD-ROM to get a few files in this tutorial. The images are accessed from outside your root folder intentionally. This shows you what to do if you need to use assets outside your currently defined site.

2. **Navigate to the session4/buttons folder on the CD. Open it, select `btn_about2.gif`, and click OK.**
   A dialog box opens that says:

   This file is outside of the root folder of site 'Complete_Course', and may not be accessible when you publish the site. Your root folder is: D:\DW_CC\Complete_Course\ (your path name would be here).

   Would you like to copy the file there now?

3. **Click Yes in the dialog box.**
   The Copy File As dialog box opens. Navigate to the images_site folder, and click Save. The new image file is now in the root folder.

4. **Look in the document window; the About Us button has been replaced.**
   Notice in the Assets panel that the new image is not listed in the list of image assets. The list needs to be re-created (as you do in Step 6) for the changes to show up.

5. **From the CD, copy the images inside the buttons folder from the Session4 folder. Paste them all into the images_site folder with the other icon images.**

6. **You can refresh the list of images in a number of ways in both the Files panel and the Assets panel. Use any of these options:**

   » With the Files panel selected, click the Options pop-up menu and select Site→Recreate Site Cache.
   This shows the new files in the Files panel only.

   » Click the Refresh icon on the bottom of the Assets panel.

   » With the Assets panel active, click the Options pop-up menu and select Recreate Site List or Refresh Site List. Now look in the Assets panel; the new button names are all in the list.

7. **Activate the Files panel by clicking its name.**

<NOTE>
Refresh Site List is used when you've added or removed assets from the site in Dreamweaver. If you add or remove from outside Dreamweaver using Windows Explorer or Finder, then you need to Recreate the Cache.

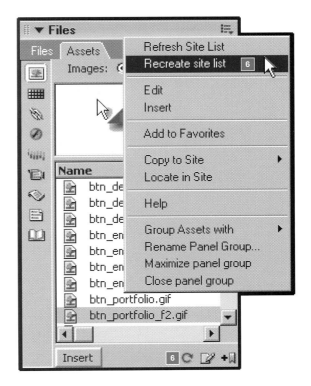

8. **Open the images_site folder by clicking the plus (+) sign next to it.**

9. **Select the About Us button in the document window.**

10. **In the Property inspector, click the Point-to-File icon to the right of the Src box. Drag from that icon to the** btn_about3.gif **image in the Files panel.**
    If necessary, fill in the Accessibility information again. The image is then automatically replaced with the new one.

<NOTE>
You don't really need to change the About Us button. These steps are to illustrate various methods of replacing images.

11. **Select the About Us button, and click the yellow folder to the right of the Src box in the Property inspector.**
    The Select Image dialog box opens.

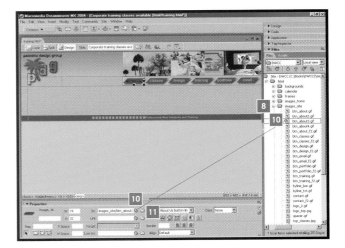

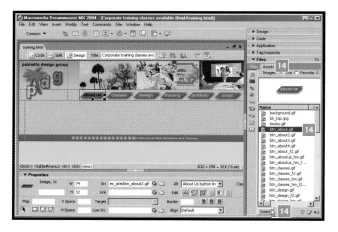

12. **Select the** `btn_about4.gif` **image from the images_site folder, and click OK.**

    Again, if necessary, fill in the Accessibility information. The About Us button is replaced.

13. **Select the About Us button and delete it.**

14. **Open the Assets panel, select** `btn_about.gif`, **and click the Insert button.**

15. **Type** About Us button link **for the alternative text, and click OK.**

    Your button returns to its original state. Because you are beginning to work with images, you may want to know the properties for the `<img>` tag. Table 4-2 lists the image attributes. You add or adjust all of these in this course.

16. **Save and preview in your browser(s).**

Table 4-2: Properties of the <img> Tag

Property	Function
Src	Specifies the URL of the location of the image file.
Align	Aligns the image to the specified margin.
Border	Shows the border around the image, measured in pixels.
Height	Indicates the height of the image measured in pixels. You should use the actual (rather than resized) height of the image, which Dreamweaver adds automatically.
Width	Indicates the width of the image measured in pixels. You should use the actual (rather than resized) width of the image, which Dreamweaver adds automatically.
Hspace	Indicates the horizontal whitespace around the image measured in pixels.
VSpace	Indicates the vertical whitespace around the image measured in pixels.
Alt	Displays text when images can't be displayed due to the Images Off option in browsers (or for accessibility readers).
Link	Inserts the URL for a hyperlink attached to the image.
Low Src	Loads a URL for the image file before the main image. It's usually a black-and-white version or a very low-resolution version of the final image.

Tutorial

» Making a Rounded Table Using Images

Tables with rounded corners are a popular table design. The rounded corners are achieved by using four corner images and background images for the outline. In this tutorial, you make a fluid rounded table. You should still have the `training.html` file open.

1. **Click in the right column of the third table (content table) to insert the cursor.**

2. **In the Property inspector, set the Horz value to Center and the width (W) to 100%.**
   Notice that the left cell has collapsed. That's okay.

3. **From the Common category of the Insert bar, click the Insert Table icon and use these values:**
   - » Rows: **3**
   - » Columns: **3**
   - » Width: **70%**
   - » Border: **0**
   - » Cell Padding: **0**
   - » Cell Spacing: **0**

4. **Type** Layout table **in the Summary field, and click OK.**
   The table is added to the center of the middle column. This is considered a "nested table."

5. **In the new table, click in the top-left cell of the first row.**

6. **In the Assets panel, select** `cnr_ltop.gif` **and click Insert.**

7. **Press the spacebar for the Alternate Text field of the Image Tag Accessibility Attributes dialog box, and click OK.**
   The spacebar adds empty double quotes that are used for the alternate text, because this image is decorative and offers no valuable information. You can also select ⟨empty⟩ from the Alt drop-down menu.

8. **Click the image in the top-left cell, and look in the Property inspector at the Width.**
   It's 14 pixels wide.

9. **Press the keyboard's right-arrow key once to place the cursor in the top-left cell.**

10. **In the Property inspector, add these values:**
    - » Horz: **Left**
    - » Vert: **Top**
    - » W: **14**
      Press Enter (Return). This collapses the entire column so that you don't have to add the width value to the bottom-left corner.

11. **Click in the top-right cell of the first row.**

12. **In the Assets panel, select** `cnr_rtop.gif` **and click Insert.**

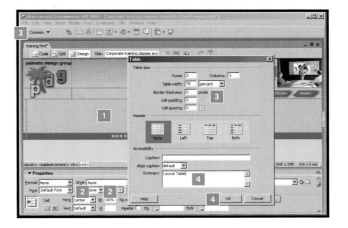

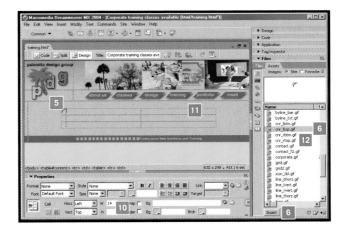

> **109**

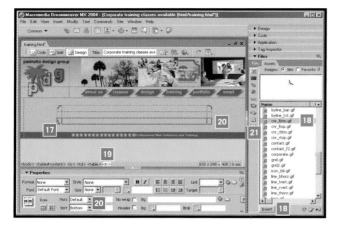

<NOTE>

With your cursor placed in the table, look in the code area and notice all the <td> </td> tags. These tags indicate that this cell has a non-breaking space ( ) in it. Dreamweaver automatically adds this code so that content appears in each cell. When you add "real" content, such as an image or text, the non-breaking space is removed. In Netscape, this space does not render properly unless real content is included.

13. **Press your spacebar in the Alternate Text field of the Image Tag Accessibility Attributes dialog box, and click OK.**
Pressing the spacebar or using double quotes produces an empty Alt field that won't come up as a missing field if you run a search for missing Alt tags.

14. **Look in the Property inspector at the Width.**
It's 14 pixels wide, the same as the left corner.

15. **Select the image, and press the right-arrow key once to place the cursor in the top-left cell.**

16. **In the Property inspector, add these values:**
    » Horz: **Right**
    » Vert: **Top**
    » W: **14**
    Press Enter (Return).

17. **Click in the bottom-left corner cell.**

18. **Insert the** cnr_lbtm.gif **from the Assets panel using the spacebar for the Alternative description.**

19. **Look in the Tag Selector and click the** <tr> **tag.**

20. **Set the Vert to Bottom.**
This sets the vertical for the entire row instead of just the one cell as you did for the top row.

21. **Now select the** <td> **tag (cell only) by selecting the left corner image, press the right-arrow key and select** <td> **using the Tag Selector, and set these properties:**
    » Horz: **Left**
    » Width: **14**
    Press Enter (Return).

22. **Click in the bottom-right corner cell.**

23. **Insert the** cnr_rbtm.gif **image from the Assets panel using the spacebar for the Alternative description.**

24. **Place your cursor in the cell or select the** <td> **tag, and set these properties:**
    » Horz: **Right**
    » Width: **14**
    Press Enter (Return). Notice that the Vert is already set to Bottom. All the corners are added to the table. Now add the vertical and horizontal lines to the table. The lines are used as background images.

25. **Select the center cell of the top row.**

26. **Set the W to 100%. Be sure to manually type the percent sign.**
    The center column now fills up 100 percent of the available space. The table itself uses 70 percent of the available space of the column it's in, and this cell uses 100 percent of the available space of this table.

27. **Set the Vert to Top.**

28. **Select** `spacer.gif` **from the Assets panel, and click the Insert button (press the spacebar for Alt text).**
    You can use the default of 1px by 1px. You add a spacer because it is considered real content. Later, you add a background image to this cell. Without the spacer, the image wouldn't render in Netscape.

29. **Open the Files panel.**

30. **Open the rdtable_images folder.**

31. **Place your cursor in the top row's center cell in the Property inspector, click and drag the Point-to-File icon for the Bg to the** `line_thorz.gif` **image in the rdtables folder, and release the mouse.**
    Notice the line from the Point-to-File icon to the selected image, which is indicated by the rectangular outline. When you release the mouse button, this image is inserted where the cursor is positioned. Alternatively, you can click the folder icon to the right of the Bg box in the Property inspector and select the image from the Select Image Source dialog box.

32. **Place your cursor in the bottom row's center cell, and repeat Steps 24 through 29 using the** `line_bhorz.gif` **image. The Vert alignment is already set to Bottom so don't change that as in Step 24.**
    You now have horizontal lines that connect the top and the bottom corners.

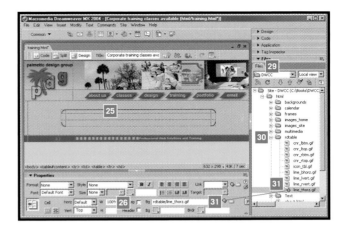

< N O T E >
If you recall, when you started this tutorial, the table was set at 70 percent. The right and left columns are now both fixed-width columns set at 14px each. You make the center column fluid so that it stretches depending on the browser size.

< N O T E >
This is actually a very small image; it's 2 pixels wide by 26 pixels high. By placing it in the background of the cell, it tiles to fill up the available space. The height was determined by the top corner images, which are 26 pixels high.

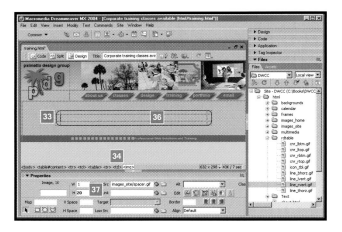

33. **Click in the center row of the left column (below the curved corner), and insert a spacer image.**

34. **Click in the cell off the spacer image (or select the `<td>` tag). Set the Bg image using the Point-To-File method or by clicking the yellow folder and selecting the `line_lvert.gif` image.**

35. **Repeat Steps 33 and 34 for the right side using the `line_rvert.gif` image.**

36. **Insert the cursor in the center cell of the center row.**

37. **Insert a spacer image. Press the spacebar for the alternative text, and click OK. In the Property inspector, highlight the 1 and type 20 in both the width (W) and height (H) fields.**
    A spacer image is added to the center cell to prevent the cell from collapsing until some real content is added.

<**N O T E**>
Notice the Property inspector width (W) and height (H) fields after you change the size of the spacer image. It is bolded, indicating that it is not the original size. A curved arrow is also present. If you ever want to convert back to the image's original size, just click the curved arrow. This comes in handy when you accidently change an image's size.

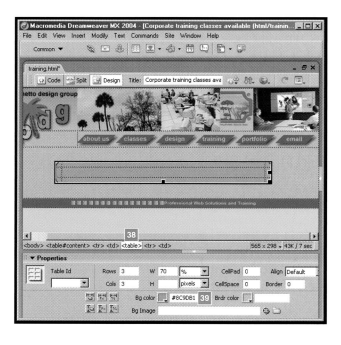

38. **Click anywhere in the rounded cornered table, and click the `<table>` selector tag.**

39. **In the Property inspector, set the Bg color to `#8C9DB1`.**

40. **Preview in all your test browsers.**
    Your table and background color should render properly in Internet Explorer 6 and Netscape 7. In Netscape 4.79, the cells are colored, but the background lines won't show.

<**N O T E**>
If you preview before saving, Dreamweaver asks if you want to save. Just click OK and preview.

<**N O T E**>
If you have cells with no background color, you missed a spacer image. Add it, and the cells show the background color.

Tutorial

» Using Background Images

Earlier in this session, you used background images in cells for the horizontal and vertical lines of the rounded cornered table. Now you learn how to use background images for an entire page or table.

1. **With the** `training.html` **page still open, click the Page Properties button in the Property inspector (Modify→ Page Properties).**

NOTE

The Page Properties button in the Property inspector will only be visible if nothing else is selected. You can click on the `<body>` tag to get the proper Property inspector.

2. **In the Page Properties dialog box, click on the Appearance category.**

3. **Click the Browse button next to the Background Image box. Navigate to the backgrounds folder, and click the** `background.gif` **image and click OK.**

4. **Click OK to close the Page Properties dialog box.**

5. **Preview your work in the browser.**
   This image is only 130 pixels by 130 pixels. Because it's applied as a background image, it tiles to fit the available browser space. Later in this course, you learn how to use a background image that does not tile, but that requires CSS styles.

6. **Click Edit→Undo Set Page Properties to remove the background.**

7. **Choose Modify→Page Properties.**

8. **Still in the Appearance category, navigate to the background folder and choose** `parchment_bk.gif.`
   Notice how much nicer and less distracting a texture looks?

9. **Click OK.**

10. **Close the page without saving.**

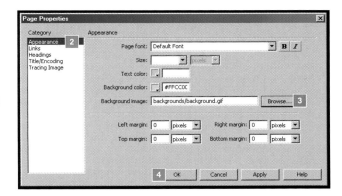

<NOTE>

Background images can be GIF, JPEG, or PNG. If you want to use background images, be sure that they do not distract from the content of your pages. Very pale backgrounds work best. Whatever you do, don't put text on top of a colorful or busy background. This is the mark of an amateur designer. Pale pastels or textures work best as backgrounds.

» Session Review

It's time to test out those newly acquired skills. If you don't know the answers to certain sections, you might want to rework that tutorial to expedite your learning curve.

Answer the questions below to review the information in this session. The answer to each question can be found in the tutorial noted in parentheses.

1. Name three ways to insert an image. (See "Tutorial: Inserting the Masthead Images.")

2. When selecting an image from the Select Image Source dialog box, there is an option to make the path Relative to the Site Root or Document. Which method is used most often? (See "Tutorial: Inserting the Masthead Images.")

3. How do you set the alignment of a cell or column? (See "Tutorial: Inserting the Navigation Images.")

4. What is H space and V space? (See "Tutorial: Inserting the Navigation Images.")

5. If an image is selected and you insert another from the Assets panel, is the original image replaced? (See "Tutorial: Replacing Images.")

6. How do you collapse a column to fit the image size? (See "Tutorial: Making a Rounded Table Using Images.")

7. What type of image was used for the horizontal and vertical lines of the rounded corner table? (See "Tutorial: Making a Rounded Table Using Images.")

8. Why did you add a spacer image to a cell that contained only a background image? (See "Tutorial: Making a Rounded Table Using Images.")

9. You used a background image of 130 pixels by 130 pixels. How can such a small image fill the entire canvas? (See "Tutorial: Using Background Images.")

palmetto design group

pd g

about us   classes   design   training   portfolio   email

Professional Web Solutions and Training

Session 5

Adding Text

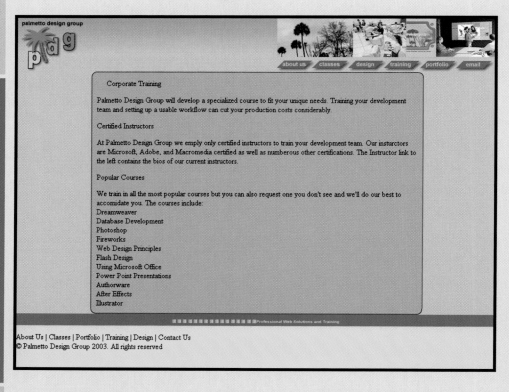

Tutorial: **Adding Text**

Tutorial: **Importing Text**

Tutorial: **Adding Structural Formatting**

Tutorial: **Wrapping Text around an Image**

Tutorial: **Making a List**

Tutorial: **Adding Flash Text**

Session Introduction

Dreamweaver provides a few methods for formatting your text. The bulk of text formatting is done using Cascading Style Sheets. But you add the structural formatting such as headings (H1, etc.) and lists using the Property inspector. Dreamweaver versions prior to Dreamweaver MX 2004 applied font tags to text when you used the Property inspector.

Font tags are deprecated (on their way out) items of code that bloat your page's code. Also, font information is presentational code so it belongs in a style sheet. By separating presentation from content, you make your site more accessible and portable. It is compliant with more devices, such as PDAs and cell phones. But you need to add a few HTML tags to the content. When you add structural tags such as ⟨h1⟩ for a level-1 heading and ⟨li⟩ for a list, your page's content can be correctly interpreted by a screen reader. Also, these tags can be referenced in a style sheet and formatting added there. Then when you need to make presentational changes, you simply change the style sheet and the change affects your entire site—what a timesaver!

TOOLS YOU'LL USE
Property inspector, Assets panel, Insert bar, Flash Text, Spell Checker

MATERIALS NEEDED
session5_starterfiles if needed

TIME REQUIRED
60 minutes

Tutorial

» Adding Text

This tutorial shows you how to insert text into your Web pages and how to format the text. Knowing a bit of HTML when editing text is helpful so that you know how the code should look. We look at code as we work with text in this session.

Refer to the O'Reilly reference guide for HTML help. You can click the Reference icon (<?>) on the toolbar; you can also find O'Reilly HTML Reference in the Reference panel, which is part of the Code panel group. But you can no longer apply code such as `<font>` tags via the Property inspector. Macromedia has come a long way in this version of Dreamweaver helping you use Web standards by using CSS Styles instead of HTML. The reference guide contains not only definitions and descriptions of HTML tags, but many other topics as well, including reference material for CSS and CFML.

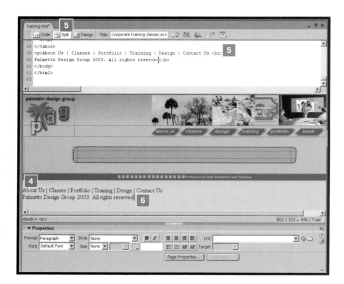

1. **Open the** `training.html` **file from the HTML subfolder of the DWCC root folder in the Files panel.**

2. **Place your cursor outside the bottom table containing the byline.**
   If you are having a problem getting your cursor in the right place, click anywhere in the table and select it's `<table>` tag and press the keyboard right-arrow key.

3. **Press Enter (Return) to add a paragraph space.**
   Click on Split view, and look in the code part of your document window; you notice that `<p> </p>` is added after `</table>` (the closing table tag). In this new tag, the `<p>` is the opening paragraph tag, ` ` is a non-breaking space, and the `</p>` is the closing paragraph tag. The non-breaking spacer is removed when you add content in the paragraph.

4. **With your cursor below the last table, type the following text for what will become text links:**
   About Us | Classes | Portfolio | Training | Design | Contact Us

5. **Press Shift+Enter (Shift+Return) to add a single line break.**
   Click the Split view icon and look at the code. A `<br>` tag is added after Contact Us. Click the Design view icon to continue.

6. **Type the following copyright notice:**
   Palmetto Design Group 2003. All rights reserved.

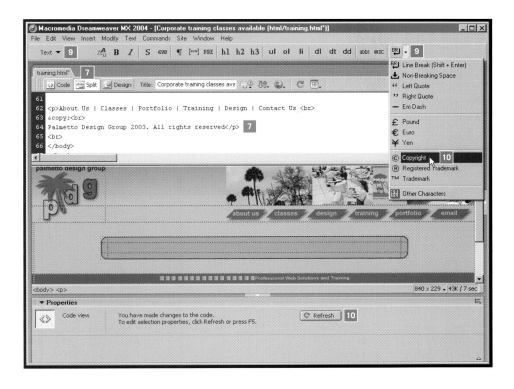

7. **Now look at the code that was added. Click on Split view.**
   Both lines of text are enclosed inside the paragraph tags.

8. **Place the cursor in front of the word Palmetto in the copyright notice.**

9. **Select the Text category in the Insert bar, and click the Characters icon (last icon in the row) arrow to open the menu.**

10. **Click the copyright symbol. Click the Refresh button in the Property inspector.**
    The copyright symbol is added in front of the copyright statement. This is all the formatting we do in this area for now. This site is formatted using CSS styles in Session 7.

<N O T E>

Whenever you make changes in the code directly, you'll see a Refresh button in the Property inspector. You can click it if you'd like. But if you click anywhere in the document, the page will be refreshed with the new code.

Tutorial

» Importing Text

This tutorial shows you how to import text from a text file and from a Microsoft Word document. This text has no formatting, but you see that the Word file has all kinds of markups, which must be removed.

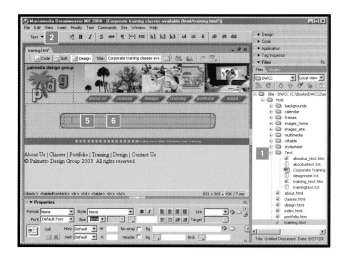

1. **In the Files panel, open the Text folder (inside the html folder) and double-click the `trainingtext.txt` file to open it.**

2. **Click Edit→Select All, or press Ctrl+A (Option+A).**

3. **Copy the text by choosing Edit→Copy or pressing Ctrl+C (Option+C).**

4. **Close the text file.**

5. **Click in the center cell of the rounded table to place the cursor.**
   Your cursor should be in the main content area of the table. Don't select the spacer image; place the cursor in the cell itself.

6. **Paste the text into the center cell by clicking Edit→Paste or pressing Ctrl+V (Option+V).**
   You may want to memorize the copy and paste keyboard short-cuts; they save lots of time.

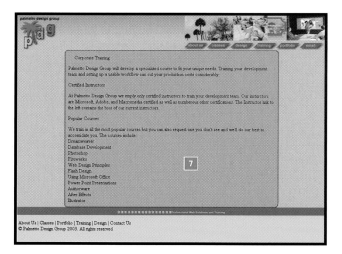

7. **Preview your work in all the target browsers.**

8. **Return to Dreamweaver, and highlight and delete all the text in the center cell of the rounded table.**

9. **Place the cursor in the center cell of the table below the spacer image.**

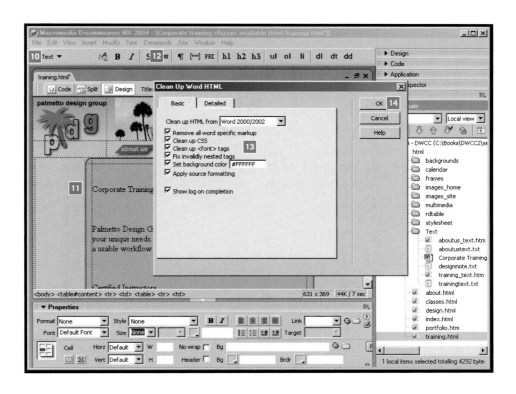

10. **Choose File→Import→Word Document.**

11. **Navigate to the Text folder, click the** `Corporate Training.doc` **file, and then click Open.**
    You'll notice there are extra paragraph spaces. Now you'll clean up the code for this text.

12. **Choose Commands→Cleanup Word HTML.**
    The Clean Up Word HTML dialog box opens.

13. **Leave everything checked in the Basic and Detailed tabs of the Clean Up Word HTML dialog box.**

14. **Click OK.**

15. **Click OK on the Results dialog box that opens.**
    Five extra paragraph spaces were removed.

Tutorial

» Adding Structural Formatting

Structural tags such as headings and lists are applied to add structure to your page. The tags can then be referenced in an external style sheet for the formatting of the appearance of the text. This logical structure also helps screen readers correctly interpret the hierarchy of the site.

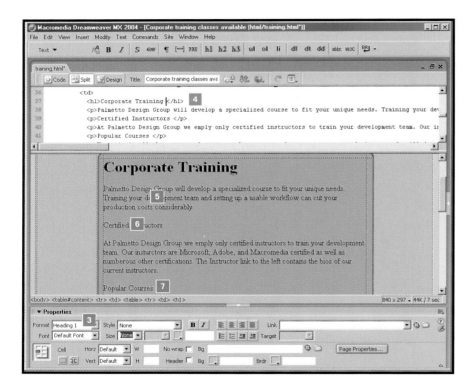

1. **Click in the top-left corner of the area containing the text.**
   You should be able to select the spacer.gif image. Delete it.

2. **Place the cursor in the words Corporate Training.**
   You don't have to highlight the text; just place the cursor within the text that you want to change.

   <NOTE>
   If no paragraph spacing appeared below the Corporate Training text, the entire section including the paragraph text would be changed.

3. **In the Property inspector, click the Format arrow and click Heading 1.**

4. **Look at the code that you just added.**
   Notice the `<h1>` heading tag and the closing `</h1>` tag surrounding the words Corporate Training.

5. **Place the cursor in the paragraph text.**
   Notice that it is already set for Paragraph; don't change it just yet.

6. **Place the cursor in the Certified Instructors text, and set the Format to Heading 2.**

7. **Place the cursor in the Popular Courses text, and set the Format to Heading 2.**

8. **Place the cursor in the first paragraph of text.**

Table 5-1: Font Groups in Dreamweaver

Font	Type
Default Font	Usually Times New Roman or Arial
Arial, Helvetica, sans-serif	Proportional sans-serif font
Times New Roman, Times, serif	Proportional serif font
Courier New, Courier, mono	Mono-spaced serif font
Georgia, Times New Roman, Times, serif	Proportional serif font
Verdana, Arial, Helvetica, sans-serif	Proportional sans-serif font
Geneva, Arial, Helvetica, sans-serif	Proportional sans-serif font
Edit Font List	Add fonts

9. **Click the <p> tag selector, which selects the entire paragraph.**

10. **Click the down arrow in the Font box area, and choose Verdana, Arial, Helvetica, sans-serif.**
    You should choose multiple fonts because you don't know what fonts a user may have. If a user doesn't have Verdana, Arial is displayed. If the user doesn't have Arial, Helvetica or the default sans-serif font is used. Refer to Table 5-1 for a list of the font groups in Dreamweaver and an explanation of the types of fonts. A sans-serif font is easier to read on the screen than a serif font (one that has little "feet"). A serif type font is best used for large text, perhaps a heading or title.

11. **Click the down arrow in the Size box, and click 12.**

12. **Click in the color box to the right of the Size box, and select a red color.**
    You are not going to keep this color. I just want you to see how to use the tool and look at the code.

13. **Click and drag over the color number in the Property inspector, and delete the color.**
    Black is the default text color, so we don't need to add the code to make it black.

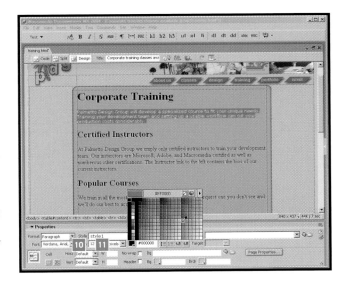

< N O T E >
You can also click Edit Fonts and specify your own. If you specify a custom font, one that may not be available on all computers, you should always specify a standard font as another choice. For example, suppose that you really want to use Akzidenz Grotesk for a heading. If the viewing (or client) computer doesn't have that font installed, you could use Swiss721 . . . or as a last choice, Arial. You'd then set up your font list as Akzidenz Grotesk, Swiss721, Arial.

```
        <h1>Corporate Training </h1> 14
15  [   <p class="style1">Palmetto Design Group will develop a spe
        <h2>Certified Instructors </h2> 14
        <p>At Palmetto Design Group we emply only certified instru
        <h2>Popular Courses </h2>
        <p>We train in all the most popular courses but you can al
        <p>Dreamweaver </p>
        <p>Database Development </p>
        <p>Photoshop </p>
```

```
1  <html>
2  <head>
3  <title>Corporate training classes available</title>
4  <meta http-equiv="Content-Type" content="text/html; charset=iso-8859-1">
5  <style type="text/css">
6  <!--
7  body {background-color: #FFCC00;}
8  .style1 {                    16
9     font-family: Verdana, Arial, Helvetica, sans-serif;
10    font-size: 12px;
11    color: #FF0000;
12  }
13  -->
14  </style>
15  <meta name="description" content="Headquartered in Florida, Palmetto Des
16  </head>
```

< N O T E >

The style is still in the head of the document—you'll remove it later. But the code added to the paragraph itself telling the browser to use style1 for its formatting—has been removed.

14. **Click inside your first paragraph to place the cursor, and switch to Code view.**

    Take a quick look at the horrible code that you just added to the page. Although it's CSS styles, it's still not the best way to mark up your text. The head tags are fine, but not the classes added to each paragraph.

15. **Notice the tags around the text. The <p> tag is fine, but also notice that a class was added (style1).**

    Classes are explained in Session 7, when all this will make sense to you. For now, I want to demonstrate that using the Property inspector to format paragraph text is NOT the way to go.

16. **Scroll up to the head of the document where you see <style> tags added with a new style named style1.**

    This is the embedded style sheet. You'll see one added for the background that you added in Page Properties and then style1 which you just added.

< N O T E >

To keep it short for now, the problem with adding formatting to each paragraph is that a class is added to each one (a span). Using CSS styles, you can define one style that is automatically applied to all paragraph tags—eliminating the redundant use of a class tag in every paragraph.

17. **Select the first paragraph text again.**

18. **In the Property inspector, select None from the Style drop-down menu.**

    This removes all the code that was added to your paragraph. You deal with the rest in Session 7.

19. **Save the file.**

Tutorial

» Wrapping Text around an Image

You can position text around images in many ways, and you do that in this tutorial using the text alignment options as well as with vertical and horizontal spacing.

1. **Place the cursor in front of the first word of the first paragraph (Palmetto).**

2. **In the Assets panel, click the** `training.jpg` **image and click the Insert button.**

3. **In the Alternative text box (or Alt field), type** Training image **and click OK.**
   Notice that the text is aligned with the bottom of the image. It doesn't look very attractive. Dreamweaver has nine alignment options; refer to Table 4.1.

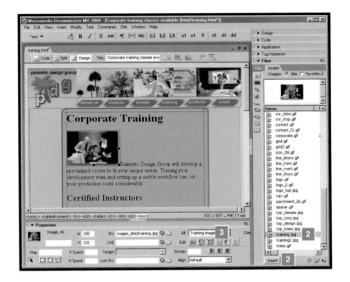

4. **Click the image.**

5. **Click the down arrow in the Align box in the Property inspector.**

6. **Click Left.**
   Notice that the text wraps around the image on the right.

7. **With the image still selected, type** 5 **where you see H Space in the Property inspector.**
   H Space adds the desired amount of pixels around the right and left sides of the image. V Space adds space to the top and bottom of the image (which we don't need).

<N O T E>
Left alignment is just one of nine alignment choices. The best way to understand these choices is to try each one and see the effect. When you are finished, continue with Step 8.

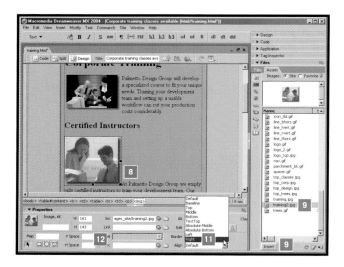

8. **Place the cursor in front of the word At in the second paragraph.**

9. **Click the** `training2.jpg` **image in the Assets panel, and click the Insert button.**

10. **Add the Alternative text** Instructor image.

11. **Click the arrow for the Align drop-down menu in the Property inspector and select Right.**

12. **Set the H Space to 5.**

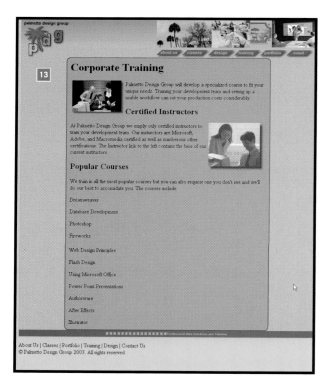

13. **Preview your work in a browser, and make the browser window large.**
    Notice that the text and images change position according to the size of the browser. This is because the middle cell, which contains the content, is a fluid column. The images are also considered floating images and move with the text as it moves.

14. **Go back to Dreamweaver, and click Text→Check Spelling.**

    » The word employ is displayed in the Change To box; click Change.

    » Click Change for instructors.

    » Click Change for numerous.

    » Click Change for accommodate.

    » Click Add to Personal for Macromedia, Dreamweaver, Photoshop, Authorware.

    » Click OK for spelling check completed.

    » Don't forget to run the spell checker whenever you have text in a document. Misspelling a word is very easy. Of course, these mistakes were made on purpose (smile).

15. **Save your file.**

Tutorial
» Making a List

Dreamweaver uses several kinds of lists. We add one to our training page in this tutorial; you can try out the others on your own.

1. **Place the cursor in front of the word Dreamweaver in the list below the Popular Courses paragraph, and drag to highlight the remaining text (all the way to the bottom of the page).**

2. **Click the Unordered List icon in the Property inspector.**
   Notice that Dreamweaver automatically adds the bullets.

3. **Now click the Ordered List icon.**
   Notice that the list is now numbered.

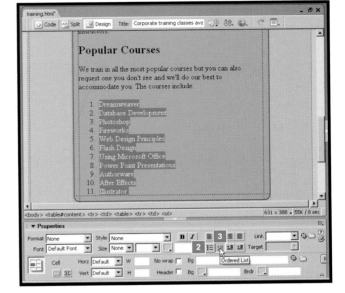

4. **Click the Unordered List icon again.**
   This is the type of list we want for this document.

5. **Look at the code, and notice the `<ul>` tag before the list and the `</ul>` at the end. Also notice that each list item has a `<li>` list tag.**
   This is good formatting.

6. **Save your file.**

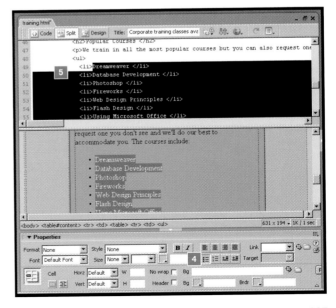

Tutorial
» Adding Flash Text

Macromedia Flash has quickly become the number one software program for generating vector-based animations. Because vectors are based on mathematical formulas, the file sizes are normally smaller and they load faster. We add some simple Flash text in this tutorial.

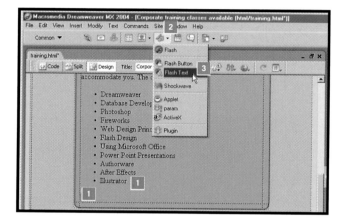

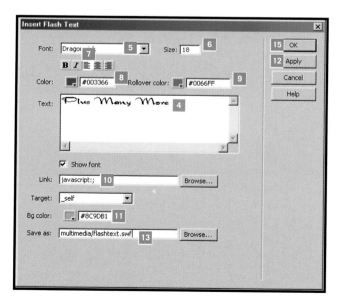

1. **In Design view, click to place your cursor behind the word Illustrator (bottom of the page) and press Enter (Return) twice.**

2. **In the Insert bar's Common category, click the arrow next to the Media icon to access the menu.**

3. **Click the Flash Text icon.**
   The Insert Flash Text dialog box opens.

4. **Type the text** Plus Many More **in the Text box.**

5. **Click the down arrow in the Font box, and choose a decorative font.**
   I have Dragonwick, so it's what I chose. One advantage of Flash text is that the users don't have to have the font installed—just you.

6. **Type a size.**
   I used 18, but the size depends on the font you use.

7. **Click the Left align icon.**

8. **Type #003366 for the Color field.**

9. **Type #0066FF for the Rollover color.**

10. **Type** javascript:; **in the link field for a null link.**

11. **Click in the Bg Color box, and use the eyedropper to sample the blue background of the content table color.**

12. **Click the Apply button to see if the text looks like what you want.**
    Is it the correct size? If not make changes until you are satisfied.

13. **Click the Browse button for the Save As field, and name the file** flashtext.swf.

14. **Navigate to the Multimedia folder, and select it.**

15. **Click OK, and type** Plus many more classes available **in the accessibility box.**
    The text may look jaggy in Dreamweaver, but when you preview it in a browser, you see that the edges look great.

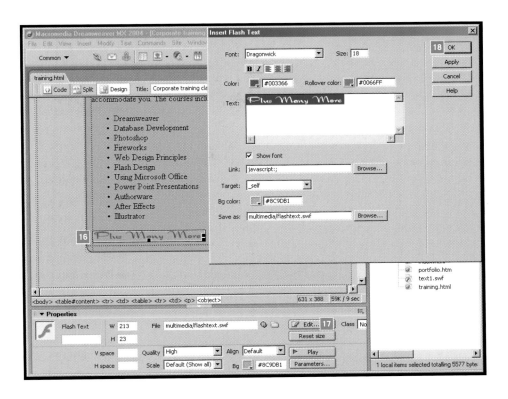

16. **Click the Flash text to select it.**

17. **In the Property inspector, click the Edit button.**
    The Insert Flash Text dialog box opens.

18. **Make changes if you'd like (I'm not); then click OK to close the dialog box.**

19. **Save and preview your work in the browsers.**

20. **You can close the file.**

» Session Review

You probably found this session on the easy side. Adding and formatting text isn't difficult in Dreamweaver.

Answer the questions below to review the information in this session. The answer to each question can be found in the tutorial noted in parentheses.

1. What is the difference between a paragraph space and a break? (See "Tutorial: Adding Text.")

2. What are the tags for paragraph and for break? (See "Tutorial: Adding Text.")

3. Where do you find the copyright symbol? (See "Tutorial: Adding Text.")

4. How do you clean up the text imported from Microsoft Word? (See "Tutorial: Importing Text.")

5. Where does the style go in the code when you add text formatting from the Property inspector? (See "Tutorial: Adding Structural Formatting.")

6. What does <h1> stand for? (See "Tutorial: Adding Structural Formatting.")

7. How do you wrap text around an image? (See "Tutorial: Wrapping Text around an Image.")

8. What are the two kinds of lists with which you practiced in this session? (See "Tutorial: Making a List.")

9. When you add Flash text, must the user have the font on his machine to view it properly? (See "Tutorial: Adding Flash Text.")

10. Once you add Flash text, can you then edit it? (See "Tutorial: Adding Flash Text.")

palmetto design group

about us   classes   design   training   portfolio   email

Corporate Training

Palmetto Design Group will develop a specialized course to fit your unique needs. Training your development team and setting up a usable workflow can cut your production costs considerably.

Certified Instructors

At Palmetto Design Group we employ only certified instructors to train your development team. Our instructors are Microsoft, Adobe, and Macromedia certified as well as numerous other certifications. The Instructor link to the left contains the bios of our current instructors.

Popular Courses

We train in all the most popular courses but you can also request one you don't see and we'll do our best to accommodate you. The courses include:

- Dreamweaver
- Database Development
- Photoshop
- Fireworks
- Web Design Principles
- Flash Design
- Using Microsoft Office
- Power Point Presentations
- Authorware
- After Effects
- Illustrator

Plus Many More

Professional Web Solutions and Training

About Us | Classes | Portfolio | Training | Design | Contact Us

Adding Navigational Links

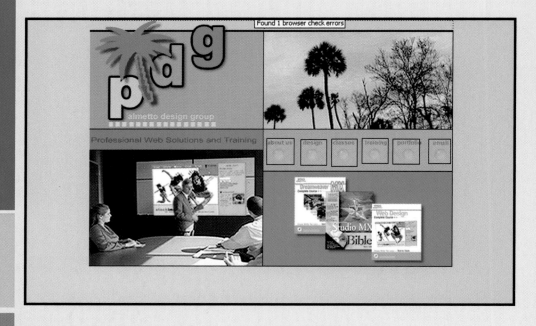

Found 1 browser check errors

Tutorial: **Adding Links**

Tutorial: **Adding Rollovers**

Tutorial: **Making an Image Map**

Tutorial: **Adding a Flash Button**

Session Introduction

This session looks at some of the more common types of navigational links. So far, your Web site is a simple and clean format that can be viewed in older browsers. The type of linking you do in this session fits with this simple design. You make a rollover, in which one image is swapped for another, and an image map, which is one image with multiple links attached to it. You also add an e-mail link and a Flash button.

Some of the more sophisticated navigation schemes require layers or frames, so they are discussed later in the book. But because of the layers and frames, these pages are compatible with version 4 browsers and later.

TOOLS YOU'LL USE
Property inspector, Insert bar, Flash button, Hotspot tools

MATERIALS NEEDED
session6_starterfiles if you need them or your working DWCC root folder; the Index2.html file in the session6_starterfiles folder

TIME REQUIRED
75 minutes

Tutorial
» Adding Links

Adding links in Dreamweaver is quite easy. A link is a behavior that tells the browser, "When a user clicks here, open this page." You add some of the links in this tutorial and more in other tutorials in this session.

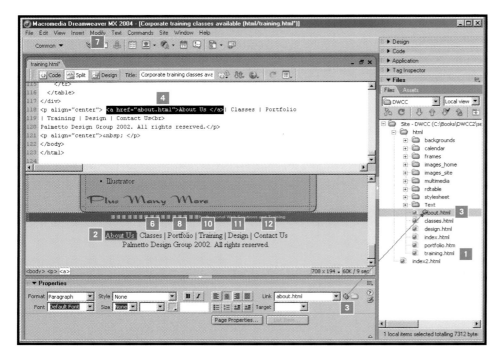

1. **Double-click the** `training.html` **file in the Files panel to open it.**

2. **Place your cursor in front of the About Us text at the bottom of the page below the tables, and drag to highlight About Us.**
   Don't highlight the pipe symbol, just the text.

3. **Add a link in the Property inspector. The easiest way is to drag the Point-to-File icon (right of the Link field) to the** `about.htm` **file in the Files panel.**

4. **Click Split view or Code view (if you're in Design view), and look at the code.**
   You see this:

   ```
   <p><a href="about.htm">About Us</a> | Classes |
   Portfolio | Training | Design | Contact Us<br>
   ```

   Notice the anchor tag (`<a>`) that was added before and after the About Us text.

5. **Click in the document to deselect the text.**
   Notice that the link is now blue and underlined.

6. **Highlight the word Classes.**

7. **Click Modify→Make Link, navigate to the DWCC/html folder, select the** `classes.html` **file, and click OK.**
   This is another way to add a link.

8. **Highlight the Portfolio text.**

9. **In the Property inspector, click the yellow folder, navigate to the** `portfolio.html` **file, select it, and click OK.**

10. **Highlight the word Training, and link to** `design.html` **using your favorite method.**

11. **Highlight the word Design, and link to** `training.html` **using your favorite method.**

12. **Highlight the Contact Us text.**
    This time, you make an e-mail link, which is a bit different than regular links. With an e-mail link, the user's default e-mail client opens.

13. **In the Email Link box of the Property inspector, type the words** mailto:info@palmettodesigngroup.com **to quickly add a link.** You simply type **mailto:** and add any e-mail address to it to create a link. Don't put a space between the mailto: and the e-mail address.

14. **Look at the code. Notice that the e-mail link still uses the <a> tag.** The only difference between an e-mail link and a regular link is that the mailto: is added before the e-mail address.

15. **Place the cursor to the right of the copyright line and add a line break by pressing Shift+Enter (Shift+Return).**

16. **Click Insert→Email Link.**

17. **Type the e-mail address (**info@palmettodesigngroup.com**) for both the Text and the E-Mail fields.** You don't need to type in the **mailto:** for the e-mail address. You typed the e-mail address instead of a link name so that users who don't have an e-mail client for their Web browser can see the address and type it manually.

18. **Click OK.**

<NOTE>

To automatically include a subject line, use this text: mailto:info@palmettodesigngroup.com?Subject=Yoursubjectline.

19. **Preview your work in a browser.**

20. **Pass your cursor over your new links.** The cursor changes into a hand to indicate that these are links. The blue text and underline also indicate that these are links. When you pass your mouse over a link, it shows up in the status bar.

21. **Save your file.**

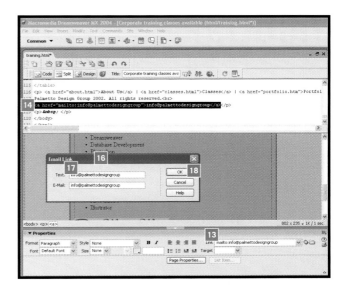

<TIP>

After you've used a link in your site, you can access it from the Link drop-down menu instead of typing it again. It is also available in the Link category of the Assets panel.

<NOTE>

Open the Assets panel and click the URL icon. You see two links that you've used so far in this site. The first one you didn't actually add; it was added with the Flash text. It's a link to the Flash player. But notice that the e-mail link is now in the Assets panel. You can use this just like any other asset. Also click the Colors icon to see the colors used in your site. It's a great way to keep a specific color palette for a site.

Tutorial

» Adding Rollovers

A rollover is a behavior that causes one image to swap with another one when the mouse cursor passes over it. Users normally recognize that an image that changes is a link to another page or section. In this tutorial, you add rollover images and links to the navigational icons in the `training.htm` page.

1. **Double-click the** `training.html` **page to open it if you closed it.**

2. **Select the About Us button at the top of the page.**
   The illustration here has the Table Width view on; that's why you see the faint green bar over the buttons.

3. **Type** aboutus **in the Image box of the Property inspector.**
   You need a name for the image when you attach different behaviors to it. This is a good habit to get into. If you look at the status bar, you see that the `<img>` tag now has `#aboutus` added to it.

4. **Click the Tag Inspector name in the panel group area to expand the group.**

5. **Click Behaviors to open the Behaviors panel.**

6. **Click the plus (+) sign.**

7. **Click Swap Image.**
   The Swap Image dialog box opens. The selected image is highlighted. You have lots of unnamed images in the document, but you remedy that shortly.

8. **Be sure that the image called "aboutus" is in fact highlighted.**

9. **Click the Browse button, navigate to the images_site folder, select** `btn_about_f2.gif`, **and click OK.**

10. **Click OK to close the Swap Image dialog box.**

11. **Preview your work in a browser.**

12. **Pass your mouse over the About Us button.**
    You should see the text change from gold to green.

13. **Check the code.**
    Just in front of the `<img>` tag, you see the JavaScript behavior:
    ```
    onMouseOver="MM_swapImage('aboutus','','images_site/
    btn_about_f2.gif',1)"
    onMouseOut="MM_swapImgRestore()">
    ```

    This says that when the mouse passes over the image called aboutus, the program swaps it with `btn_about_f2.gif`. When the mouse moves off the icon, the program restores the icon to the original state.

14. **Click the Classes icon, and delete it.**
    You delete it so you can learn another way of inserting both the original and the swap image at the same time.

15. **Click the Rollover Image icon (in the images menu) from the Common category of the Insert bar.**

    The Insert Rollover Image dialog box opens.

16. **Type** Classes **in the Image Name box.**

17. **Click Browse next to the Original Image box, and navigate to the images_site folder. Select** btn_classes.gif, **and click OK.**

18. **Click Browse to the right of the Rollover Image box, and navigate to the Icons folder. Select the** btn_classes_f2.gif **image, and click OK.**

19. **Type** Classes PDG Offers **for the alternate text.**

20. **Click Browse to the right of the When Clicked, Go To URL: box, navigate to the** classes.htm **file, select it, and click OK.**

21. **Click OK to close the Insert Rollover Image dialog box.**

    In the Property inspector, you see that the name field has been filled in with classes, but the <img> tag in the status bar does not have the image name attached to it.

22. **Preview in a browser, and mouse over both the About Us and Classes buttons.**

23. **Repeat the method that you prefer on the remaining buttons in the top navigation area.**

    Because the buttons are in place, using the Behavior panel is the easiest method. Also remember to name each button in the Property inspector before you add the Swap Image behavior.

24. **Open the Files panel.**

25. **Click each of the buttons, and use the Point-to-File method of adding links by dragging the Point-to-File link icon to each .html file for the respective icons:**

    » About Us to about.html
    » Classes to classes.html
    » Portfolio to portfolio.html
    » Training to training.html
    » Design to design.html

26. **Select the email button.**

27. **Open the Assets panel, and click the Link icon.**

28. **Click the e-mail address, and click the Apply button at the bottom of the Assets panel.**

    Notice in the Property inspector that the link has been added.

29. **Save your file, and close** training.html **for now.**

30. **Open** index.html, **and repeat this tutorial for its buttons. The images are in the images_home folder.**

    Remember that you select and name the button, and then add the Swap Image behavior and link the button to the appropriate file. The button names for the home page have hm in the file name. The rollover version of the button has f2 at the end of the file name.

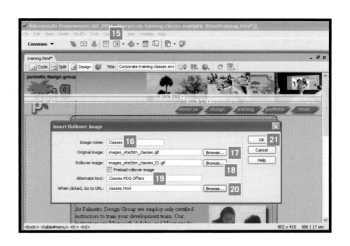

Tutorial
» Making an Image Map

An image with many links is an image map. Links are attached to different areas of the same image by using hotspots. Clicking the hotspot takes you to the respective link. We don't use an image map in this site because having individual buttons for the navigation is a better method. But you may find that you need to use this feature in later sites you design. So for your learning experience, I've provided a sample file for you to use in the session6_starterfiles folder.

<TIP>
If you have Dreamweaver open already, you may not see the file after it's added in the Files panel. In the Files Options pop-up menu, select Site➔Recreate Site Cache. Your file can now be seen in Dreamweaver.

<NOTE>
You can edit a shape by clicking to deselect the drawing tool, then select the hotspot and drag any one of its control points (small rectangles). You can move a shape by simply dragging it. You also can copy and paste shapes to place them in new locations.

1. **Copy** index2.html **into your DWCC root directory.**

2. **Open Dreamweaver, and double-click** index2.html **to open it.**

3. **Click the area that contains the navigation icons.**
   Notice that the icons are all one image.

4. **Click the expander arrow in the Property inspector to see the image map properties.**
   The expander arrow in the lower-right corner reveals additional properties. Personally, I always leave this panel expanded.

5. **Select the Rectangular Hotspot tool. Click OK to close the warning message.**
   In the bottom-left corner, you see three blue shapes. These are the Rectangular Hotspot tool, the Oval Hotspot tool, and the Polygon Hotspot tool. You use the Rectangular Hotspot tool for this tutorial.

6. **In the Map field, type** mainnav.
   It's especially important to name your image maps with unique names when you have more than one image map on a page. Notice that I said a unique name; this does not give you the option to skip this step. If you don't enter a map name of some sort, you are unable to use the Hotspot tools.

Hotspot Tool Tips

You use the Rectangular and Oval Hotspot tools by clicking and dragging out the shape. The Polygon Hotspot tool differs in that you click around an irregularly shaped area. As you click, the points are connected. You continue to click until the area is defined and finish by clicking the Arrow tool to close the shape.

7. **Place the cursor at the top-left corner of the About Us button, and drag toward the bottom right of the button covering the text and button to define the shape.**

   After a hotspot is defined, you see the hotspot properties in the Property inspector.

8. **Click and drag the Point-to-File icon for the Link field to the** about.html **file in the Files panel.**

9. **Type the Alt text** About Palmetto Design Group.

10. **Repeat Steps 7 through 9 for the rest of the buttons, replacing the alt text with the following:**

    » Design: design.html Alt: **PDG Design Concepts**
    » Classes: classes.html Alt: **Online Classes Available**
    » Training: training.html Alt: **Corporate Training Available**
    » Portfolio: portfolio.html Alt: **Portfolio**
    » Email: mailto:palmettodesigngroup.com Alt: **Contact Us**

    You can copy and paste the first hotspot area for all the rest because the icon sizes are all pretty close. Just move the pasted shape over another icon.

11. **With Email selected, select the e-mail link from the Assets panel and click the Apply button.**

12. **Look at the code, and notice that the map information is located at the bottom of the .html file, just before the closing body tag.**
    This code shows the map name and the specific coordinates (yours may vary) of the hotspots, with the Alt text included.

```
<map name="mainnav">
  <area shape="rect" coords="5,14,51,60" href=
"about.html" alt="About Palmetto Design Group">
  <area shape="rect" coords="61,17,105,62" href=
"design.html" alt="PDG Design Concepts">
  <area shape="rect" coords="112,16,155,64" href=
"classes.html" alt="Online Classes Available">
  <area shape="rect" coords="162,15,206,59" href=
"training.html" alt="Corporate Training Available">
  <area shape="rect" coords="214,15,259,59" href=
"portfolio.htm" alt="Portfolio">
  <area shape="rect" coords="272,16,309,59" href="#">
</map>
```

13. **Save the file, and then preview and close it.**

Tutorial
» Adding a Flash Button

In this tutorial, you learn how to add a Flash button to your page, which adds personality to your site. Don't overdo it with Flash, though, because you can make it harder for search engines to recognize your site.

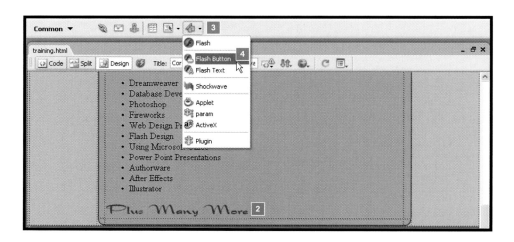

1. **Double-click the** training.html **page in the Files panel to open it (or the** training.html **tab at the top of the document if you still have it open).**

2. **Click to the right of the Plus Many More Flash text at the bottom of the rounded table.**

3. **Click the Media category icon in the Common category in the Insert bar.**

4. **Click the Flash Button icon.**
   The Insert Flash Button dialog box opens.

<NOTE>
The Macromedia Exchange has additional styles that you can download—usually for free. Third party developers frequently provide free and low cost extensions for Dreamweaver. The Get More Styles button takes you to the Macromedia Exchange site to download more styles.

5. **In the Style area, select the Navigation-Next (Green) style.**
   If you click the style in the preview window, you can see what the button looks like in a browser.

6. **Leave the Button Text area blank because you are using an arrow instead of a text button.**
   If you click the style sample in the preview window, it does not reflect the text change. The changes appear in Design view after you insert the button.

7. **Click the Apply button to insert the button in the document immediately.**

8. **If you use a button that needs text, you can choose any font style.**
   It doesn't matter which font you use because it is embedded in the Flash movie. The user doesn't need to have that font on his system. I used Splash because I used it for the Flash text.

9. **If you are using a button, select a size of text that fits on the button.**

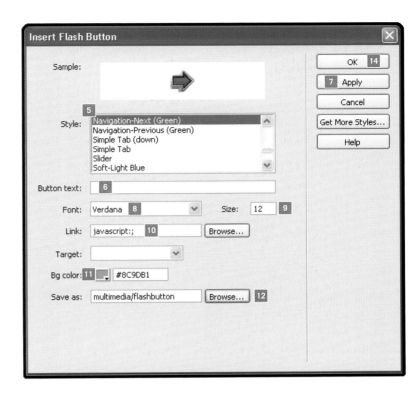

10. **Type a null link of** javascript:;.

11. **Click in the Bg Color box, and use the eyedropper to sample the blue of the table background. Click Apply again to see the results in the document.**
    The background color is the color that shows through transparent areas of the Flash button.

12. **In the Save As field, click the Browse button and save in the Multimedia folder. Name the image** flashbutton.swf.

13. **Click the Apply button to see the updated button in the document.**
    The advantage of clicking Apply first is that the dialog box stays open, so you can make alterations if needed.

14. **Click OK to close the dialog box. Type** More Classes **in the accessibilty dialog box and click OK.**

15. **Notice that the Property inspector has changed.**
    No loop and autoplay options are available. Now you see an Edit button, which opens the Insert Flash Button dialog box.

16. **Preview in your browsers.**
    Notice that the button lines up with the Flash text even though it appeared lower in Dreamweaver. But the arrow is too close to the text.

17. **Place your cursor in front of the arrow.**

18. **In the Assets panel, click the images icon and then click** spacer.gif **and the Insert button.**

19. **Change the Width of the spacer to** 15, **and press Enter (Return).**

20. **Save and preview your work again.**

< N O T E >

Site root relative links are not recognized with Flash movies, so use an absolute URL, which in this case is www.palmettodesigngroup.com/ media/buttonname.swf. You can also save the .swf file in the same folder as the .html file. To save the .swf in the root folder with the .html file, click the Browse button to the right of the Save As field. Navigate to your root folder, and save the file there.

< N O T E >

If you notice that the background color shifts or doesn't look accurate, be sure that you have Snap to Web Safe color option turned off. To do this, click the color box in the Property inspector and click the right-pointing arrow; if you see a check mark next to Snap to Web Safe, click it to uncheck it and turn it off.

» Session Review

Well, it's that time again—time to see how much of this information has stuck in your head. Roll up your sleeves, and let's get started.

Answer these questions to review the information in the session. The answer to each question is in the tutorial noted in parentheses.

1. What kind of tag is used for links? (See "Tutorial: Adding Links.")

2. How do you add an e-mail link? (See "Tutorial: Adding Links.")

3. Where can you look for additional help with .html code? (See "Tutorial: Adding Links.")

4. What is a rollover? (See "Tutorial: Adding Rollovers.")

5. Where do you find the Swap Image behavior? (See "Tutorial: Adding Links.")

6. How is an image map different from other images or links? (See "Tutorial: Making an Image Map.")

7. Do you have to name the image map, or can you skip this step? (See "Tutorial: Making an Image Map.")

8. Where do you find the code for the image map? (See "Tutorial: Making an Image Map.")

9. What type of URL do you have to use for a Flash button? (See "Tutorial: Adding a Flash Button.")

10. How can you preview a Flash button? (See "Tutorial: Adding a Flash Button.")

Certified Instructors

At Palmetto Design Group we employ only certified instructors to train your development team. Our instructors are Microsoft, Adobe, and Macromedia certified as well as numerous other certifications. The Instructor link to the left contains the bios of our current instructors.

Popular Courses

We train in all the most popular courses but you can also request one you don't see and we'll do our best to accommodate you. The courses include:

* Dreamweaver
* Database
* Development
* Photoshop
* Fireworks
* Web Design Principles
* Flash Design
* Using Microsoft Office
* Power Point Presentations
* Authorware
* After Effects
* Illustrator

Plus Many More

Professional Web Solutions and Training

About Us | Classes | Portfolio| Training | Design | Contact Us
Palmetto Design Group 2002. All rights reserved.
info@palmettodesigngroup

Part III:
Automating the Design Process

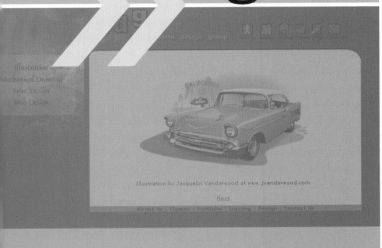

Session 7 **Using Cascading Style Sheets (CSS)**

Session 8 **Using Templates and Libraries**

Session 9 **Adding Forms and Behaviors**

Session 7

Using Cascading Style Sheets (CSS)

Tutorial: **Removing Embedded Styles**

Tutorial: **Attaching a Style Sheet**

Tutorial: **Editing the BODY Tag**

Tutorial: **Grouping Selector Tags**

Tutorial: **Applying Custom Classes**

Tutorial: **Using Pseudo-Class Selectors**

Tutorial: **Assigning a Class Name to the Footer Area**

Tutorial: **Using a Contextual Selector to Add a Style**

Tutorial: **Adding Space Using CSS**

Session Introduction

The use of cascading style sheets (CSS) is on the rise. Dreamweaver MX 2004 includes lots of new and improved CSS features that are compatible with the World Wide Web Consortium (W3C) standards.

Style sheets are formatting rules that control the appearance of content in a Web page. Style sheets are a collection of formatting rules—known as styles—that control the appearance of content in a Web page. These style rules are governed by a cascading hierarchy that uses the principles of inheritance, specificity, and importance to determine which rule applies when a conflicting rule exists. CSS styles can be implemented in three ways. One is inline, which is placed directly in the code of your Web page. This is similar to embedded, which embeds the entire style sheet into the `<head>` of an individual document. Neither of these methods is recommended, however. They increase the download time because of all the extra code written to the file. They also defeat the ease of updating your styles site-wide.

External style sheets are the way to go for the most part. With this method, you actually link your HTML page or template to the CSS, and it becomes accessible to the entire site. Making modifications is as easy as changing one file. Some of the benefits include maintaining a consistent look across all pages that link to the style sheet, easily updating the look of all pages by changing the values in one file, and making your pages much smaller and quicker to download, because all the style information is in one file.

TOOLS YOU'LL USE
CSS Styles panel, Tag Selector, Quick Tag Editor, Property inspector

MATERIALS NEEDED
session7_starterfiles if needed

Optional but important: Any browser that your target audience might be using. I've tested with Netscape 4.79, Netscape 7, and Internet Explorer 6 for this book. Netscape 4X causes the most problems.

TIME REQUIRED
90 minutes

Tutorial

» Removing Embedded Styles

Remember that embedded styles can be problematic; therefore, styles are better implemented by writing your own. The first step is to remove the embedded styles to an external style sheet.

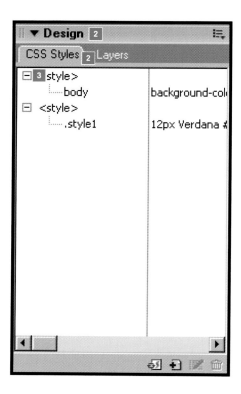

1. **Open the Files panel, and double-click** `training.html` **to open it.**

2. **Open the Design panel and click on CSS Styles to activate it.**
   You'll see two styles, one for the body and one named .style1.

3. **Select the style that says body.**

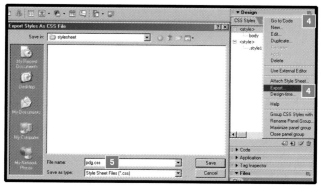

4. **Open the CSS Styles Options pop-up menu and select Export.**

5. **Navigate to the stylesheet folder and open it. Name the file** `pdg.css.`

6. **Click OK.**

7. To see the style sheet in the Files panel, open the Options pop-up menu and select View→Refresh.

8. Open the stylesheet folder and double-click on pdg.css to open it.

9. Notice that both the background and the style1 style are now in an external style sheet.

10. Close the style sheet.

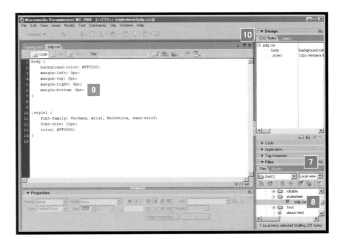

11. In the CSS Styles panel, select the top `<style>` and click on the trash can icon to delete it. Repeat for the remaining style.

12. Switch to Code view to see if the styles have been removed from the head of the document.

13. Scroll to the top to check. I have a stray `<style>` tag left. If you do as well, delete it.

    I highlighted it in yellow so you could identify where the stray code was. It won't be yellow.

14. Save your file, and switch to Design view.

Tutorial
» Attaching a Style Sheet

Previously, you defined the background properties using the Modify→Page Properties dialog box, which you removed and placed into an external style sheet. In this tutorial, you attach the style sheet to your document. For your own site, if you don't have a style sheet already saved to start with, then skip this tutorial. Normally, I wouldn't have any embedded styles to delete or put into a style sheet. The only reason you do in this instance is that I wanted to demonstrate how to use the Property inspector for text and the Page Properties dialog box.

1. **Open the Files panel, and double-click** `training.html` **if you closed it.**

2. **Click on the Design panel group name, and then select CSS Styles.**

3. **Click the Attach Style Sheet icon on the bottom of the panel.**

4. **Navigate to the stylesheet folder in your DWCC root.**

5. **Select** `pdg.css`.
   Notice the URL and the fact that it is Relative to the Document. Leave these default settings.

6. **Link is selected by default; leave it this way and click OK.**

<NOTE>

In the Attach External Stylesheet dialog box is a Preview button. You can click it and see how the document will look with the styles attached. You won't see much since there are only two styles so far.

7. **Notice the CSS Styles panel and the Relevant CSS panel.**

   You can see the style for the <body> tag and style1 added. If you recall, your style sheet contains only the background color and margins for the body properties and the style1 that was added when you were practicing with the Property inspector. Style1 got transferred to the style sheet when you exported, but you don't need it now.

8. **Select style1 in the CSS Styles panel and click the trash can icon.**

9. **Close and save the** pdg.css **file.**

Tutorial
» Editing the BODY Tag

So far, the `<body>` tag only has a style added for the background color and the margins. In this tutorial, you define the font, size, and color of any body text.

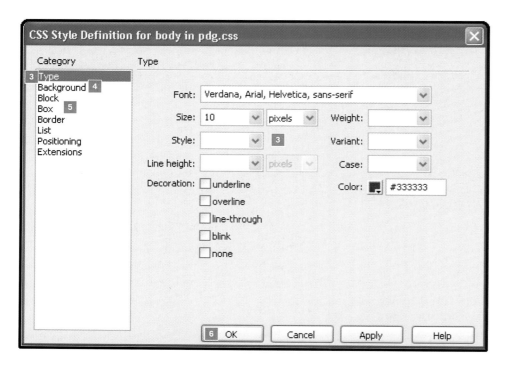

1. **Click the CSS Styles panel tab to make it the active panel, if it isn't already.**

2. **Select body, and then click the Edit Styles icon (pencil).**
   The CSS Style Definition for body in pdg.css dialog box opens.

3. **Select the Type category, and set the following properties:**
   » Font: **Verdana, Arial, Helvetica, sans-serif**
   » Size: **10 pixels**
   » Color: **#333333**
   Leave the default settings for everything else.

4. **Click the Background category.**
   Don't make any changes; just notice that the color is already entered.

5. **Click the Box category, and notice that all the margins are set to 0 (zero).**
   All margins are set to zero by setting the Top to zero and selecting the Same for all checkbox.

6. **Click OK to close the dialog box.**

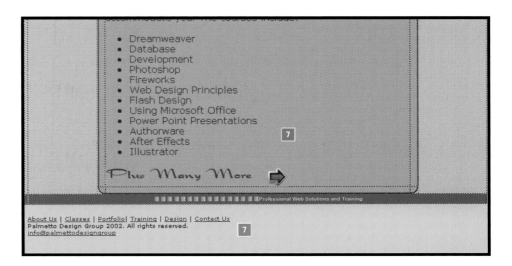

7. **Look at your document.**

Notice that all the body text is now in Verdana. You did not have to do anything to apply this style. It was applied automatically because of the selector that you redefined, in this case, the `<body>` tag.

<NOTE>

Did you notice that the font size of the text in the table in Step 7 still didn't change? The `<body>` tag style did, in fact, set the Font attribute, but it isn't controlling the paragraph, heading, or table tags. That's why the font size didn't change. Look at the link text at the bottom of the document; this text is inside the body, so its size is changed. But the text inside the table is Verdana and 12-point type. You defined the `<body>` tag, not the `<p>` or `<td>` tags (more on this later).

8. **Test your page in your target browsers.**

It renders as expected in Netscape 4.79, Netscape 7, and Internet Explorer 6. The text in the body (copyright and e-mail address) has been changed to 12-point Verdana type.

9. **Choose File→Save All. This saves the `training.html` page and the `pdg.css` page.**

<NOTE>

When you edit the style sheet, it opens. You are usually not even aware of it because it opens quietly in the background. If you close out documents and it's ever open, be sure to save it.

CSS Rules

Each rule has two parts: a selector and the declaration. The selector is often an HTML element such as `<H1>`, `<body>`, `<p>`, and so on. The declaration is a combination of properties and values. A declaration is always formatted as a property followed by a colon, a value, and a semicolon. Each style sheet is made up of a series of rules. You don't need to know how to actually write the rules (although understanding how they work is a good idea), because Dreamweaver has a great interface that lets you choose the properties and values you want. Dreamweaver writes all the code for you.

Tutorial

» Grouping Selector Tags

In this tutorial, you add the same style to the paragraph tag (`<p>`) and the table cell tag (`<td>`) in order to define the text that is contained inside the table. You also re-declare the text properties.

1. **Open** `training.html` **if you've closed it.**

2. **In the CSS Styles panel, click the New CSS Style icon.**

3. **Click the Advanced (IDs, contextual selectors, etc) option in the Selector Type category.**

4. **In the Selector field, type** p, td **(that's p comma space td).**
   You could also use the Tag option (which redefines the look of a specific tag), but it allows you to define only one tag at a time.

5. **Click the radio button for Define In, and select** pdg.css **if it isn't already selected.**
   If you have more than one style sheet and the proper one isn't listed by default, you select the one you want from the drop-down menu.

6. **Click OK.**

7. **Set the following properties for the Type category:**
   - » Font: **Verdana, Arial, Helvetica, sans-serif**
   - » Size: **12px**
   - » Color: **#333333**
     Leave the default settings for everything else.

8. **Click OK.**

9. **Place your cursor in front of Certified Instructors, and press Enter (Return).**
   This adds a paragraph space and puts the title below the image.

10. **Save your page, and then preview it in your test browsers.**

Tutorial
» Applying Custom Classes

In this tutorial, you define some custom classes and then apply them to different selectors.

1. **Open** `training.html` **if it's closed.**

2. **Open the CSS Styles panel.**

3. **Click the plus sign (+) to add a new style.**
   The paragraph tag was previously defined for font, size, and color. Now you add a class that is applied to the content paragraphs to add space around them.

<NOTE>
If you were to define the space for the paragraph tag itself, it would be applied to all paragraphs, including ones that weren't content—such as the footer area.

4. **Click the "Class (can apply to any tag)" radio button in the Selector Type category.**

5. **Click the Define In radio button.**
   Because we have only one style sheet, the `pdg.css` is shown by default.

6. **Type** .para **in the Name field.**
   Be sure to type a period before the word para.

7. **Click OK.**

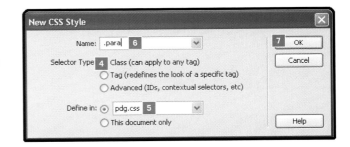

<NOTE>
Notice that the name begins with a period. Custom classes always begin with a period. They can't start with a number, nor can they include spaces or special characters.

8. **Click the Box category to make it active.**

9. **In the Margin values area, uncheck the Same for All check box by clicking it.**

10. **Set the following values:**
    - » Top: **0 pixels**
    - » Right: **10 pixels**
    - » Bottom: **blank**
    - » Left: **10 pixels**

11. **Click OK.**

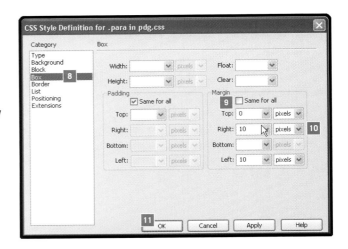

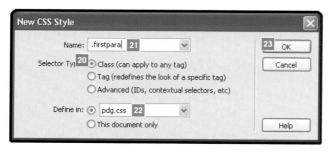

12. **Place your cursor inside the first paragraph, and click anywhere.**
Now you apply the new Custom Class of .para to the paragraph.

13. **In the Property inspector, select Para from the Style drop-down list.**

14. **Notice that the Tag Selector now says `<p.para>` instead of just `<p>`.**
This indicates that it's a paragraph with the class of para added to it.

15. **Repeat Steps 12 and 13 for the remaining paragraphs, but not the bulleted list.**

< N O T E >

Notice that extra space is added around the paragraph. If you look closely, though, you notice that no 10-pixel margin (which you defined in the box values of the .para style) appears around the pictures. That's because the picture is part of the paragraph and the 10 pixels are added to the left side of the top image and to the right side of the second image.

16. **Select the first image that is left aligned.**

17. **In the Property inspector, change the H Space to 10.**
This moves the text away from the edge of the picture a bit more.

18. **Select the second image, and change the H Space to 10 as well.**

19. **In the CSS Styles panel, click the Add New Style button.**
This time, you define a custom class that adds some space between the lines of text for the first paragraph only.

20. **Click the Class radio button.**

21. **Type .firstpara in the name field.**

22. **Set Define In to pdg.css.**

23. **Click OK.**

24. In the Type category, type 150 in the Line Height field and choose percent (%) from the drop-down menu.

25. Click OK to close the dialog box.

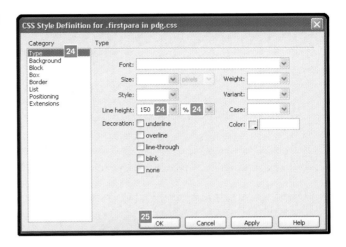

< N O T E >

Now the style is defined. You can't, however, just apply it to the paragraph because the paragraph already has a style applied to it. You need to add a `<span>` tag that wraps around the specific text that you have selected. Then the new style is applied to that. This same method is how you add bold or change the format of one or several words in a sentence.

26. Select the entire first paragraph.

27. Press Ctrl+T (⌘+T) to access the Quick Tag Editor. You see Wrap Tag <>. If you don't, press Ctrl+T (⌘+T) until you do.

28. Place your cursor between the <>, type the word span (or select it from the menu), and press Enter (Return) to close the Quick Tag Editor. You may need to press Enter (Return) twice.

< N O T E >

Span tags are inline tags which surround the text or image it is being applied to. A span tag can be useful if you need to change the properties on a few words. A DIV tag is a block tag. For example, a table is a block element, so is a paragraph. If you want to check the code, you see that the opening and closing span tags are now added in front of and behind the selected text.

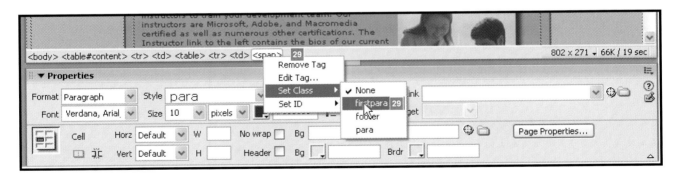

29. Right-click (Ctrl+click) the `<span>` tag in the Tag Selector, and select Set Class to .firstpara.

The first paragraph now has more space between the lines, and it lines up nicely with the image.

30. Save your page, and preview it in your target browsers.

Tutorial
» Using Pseudo-Class Selectors

Pseudo-class selectors change the appearance of all hyperlinks using the <a> tag. In the CSS1 specification, the only pseudo-class selectors include :visited, :link, and :active. Notice that pseudo-classes begin with a colon. What makes pseudo-class selectors different is that they are dynamic. They can be used to add rollover effects without images in browsers that support them. You can use text as links and using CSS change the text color on rollover. When defining more than one of the pseudo-class selectors, you need to do it in this order: a:link, a:visited, a:hover, a:active. Be sure to test your styles in all your target browsers. To test unvisited links, you need to clear your link history and then refresh the browser page. (To clear your link history in Internet Explorer, choose Tools→Internet Options→General→Clear History. In Netscape Navigator 4, choose Edit→Preferences→Navigator→Clear History.)

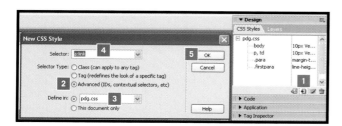

1. **In the CSS Styles panel, click the Add button (+) to make a new style.**

2. **Click Advanced (IDs, contextual selectors, etc) in the Selector Type category.**

3. **Click the Define In radio button.**

4. **In the Selector field, type a:link (or choose it from the drop-down menu).**

5. **Click OK.**

6. **In the Type category, set the color to** #000099.
   Because the font size is already 12 points and the font style of Verdana is set (and I like both), nothing else needs to be done. Inheritance takes care of the rest. But if you like your links to be a different size, font, and so on, you can change them.

7. **Click OK.**
   This style is applied to all links, regardless of their location. Sometimes, you may have links on a page that need to be different colors to be visible. That can be accomplished by using contextual styles, which you do later in this tutorial.

8. **In the CSS Styles panel, select the a:link style that you just made.**

9. **Click the CSS Styles panel option pop-up menu, and click Duplicate.**
   Alternatively, you can right-click (Ctrl+click) the name, and the same menu is available.

10. **In the Duplicate CSS Style dialog box, type or select** a:visited.

11. **Make sure that the Define In box lists** pdg.css **as the style sheet.**

12. **Click OK.**

13. **Double-click a:visited to edit it.**

    This opens the actual style sheet. If you are more comfortable not working directly with the code, then you can click the Edit Syles icon as you've done before.

14. **Locate the a:visited style, and change the color number to**
    #0066FF.

    If you use the Edit icon, you need to change the color to #0066FF in the Type category.

15. **Choose All.**

16. **Make a duplicate of a:visited (refer to Step 13).**

17. **In the Duplicate CSS Style dialog box, type or select** a:hover.

18. **Click OK.**

    You now discover yet another way to edit a styles property.

19. **In the CSS panel, click in the area to the right of hover that shows**
    the color number.

20. **Look at the Tag Inspector panel.**

    The name has changed to Rule "a:hover". You see the Font Color property listed.

21. **Click in the Color box, and pass the eyedropper over the green**
    part of the palm tree in the logo.

    If you want to check the style sheet to see the changed color, just double-click the style in the CSS Styles panel. Be sure to close the style sheet again.

22. **Save your work, and test in your target browsers.**

    The hover effect does not work in older browsers.

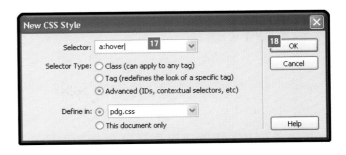

Tutorial

» Assigning a Class Name to the Footer Area

In this tutorial, you set up a class that is used to designate a specific region to accept a style. This is beneficial if you want certain tags to have one style while the rest have another.

1. **In the CSS Styles panel, click the New CSS Style icon.**

2. **Click the Advanced (IDs, contextual selectors, etc) radio button.**

3. **Enter .footer in the Selector field.**

4. **Make sure that the** pdg.css **style sheet is selected.**

5. **Click OK.**

6. **In the Type category, type** 150 **into the Line Height field and select the percent sign from the drop-down list.**

7. **Click OK.**

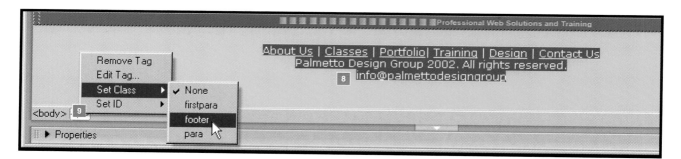

8. **Click in the copyright and e-mail area.**

9. **In the Property inspector, select footer from the Styles drop-down list.**

10. **In Code view, notice that the code,** class="footer", **is added to the** <p> **tag of the link area.**

    You just designated the footer area (where your links are) as a class. What you really did was give this paragraph a class name, which is like giving a table an ID name.

11. **Save the file.**

Tutorial
» Using a Contextual Selector to Add a Style

Contextual selectors use rules that apply whenever the specific selector occurs within a container using a class style. For example, the <p> tag or the <a> tag can have only one style applied, but by adding a contextual style, you can format each paragraph or link differently.

As it happens, we have only text links in the footer area. But if you had links in other areas of the text or design, they all would have the same formatting. This technique can be used for every link area you may have on your site to change the look. For example, if our footer links were in the table with a blue background, you would probably want the link colors to be different than links on a gold background.

1. **In the CSS Styles panel, click the New CSS Style icon.**

2. **Click the Advanced (IDs, contextual selectors, etc) radio button.**

3. **Type** .footer a:link **into the Selector field.**
   Don't forget to start the name with a period.

4. **Be sure that Define In is set to the** pdg.css **style sheet.**

5. **Click OK.**

<NOTE>

This concept works extremely well for IDs that you may have added. You may recall that we added ID names to each table in Session 3. You see in the next tutorial how to use an ID to assign a style. An ID is also considered a contextual selector.

6. **In the Type category, click Decoration none.**
   This removes the underline from the e-mail address.

7. **In the Color field, type** #000099 **to set the color to a dark blue.**

8. **Set the Weight to bold.**

9. **Click OK.**
   This setting won't affect the copyright line even though it is part of the footer because this contextual selector only affects the <a> tag.

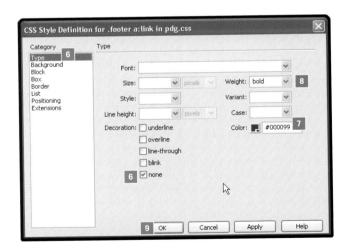

10. In the CSS Styles panel, select the **.footer a:link** style and open the Options Pop-up menu. Select Duplicate.

11. Type .footer a:visited **into the Selector field.**

12. **Click OK.**

13. **Click the .footer a:visited style, and then click the Edit Styles icon.**

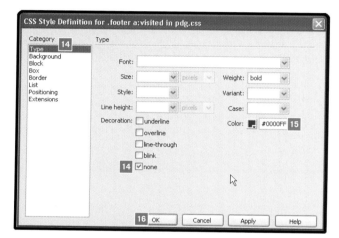

14. **In the Type category, leave the Decoration set to none.**

15. **In the Color field, type** #0000FF **to set the color to a lighter shade of blue.**

16. **Click OK.**

17. **Duplicate .footer a:visited.**

    This time, you edit in the Rule panel (the Tag Selector automatically changed to the Rule Inspector). You see the CSS Properties panel, the Font category, and the color and weight defined.

18. **Type** .footer a:hover **into the Selector field.**

19. **Click OK.**

20. **Click in the color area of the Font color, and change the color to** #000099.

21. **Down a few lines, click in the Text decoration. From the drop-down menu, select Underline.**

    As you've seen, you can edit and apply styles in several ways. It's your choice to use whichever works best for you.

22. **Click the** pdg.css **file tab, and choose File→Save.**

    Even if you don't specifically open the style sheet, it opens when you are editing and adding styles. Be sure to always save this file if it is open.

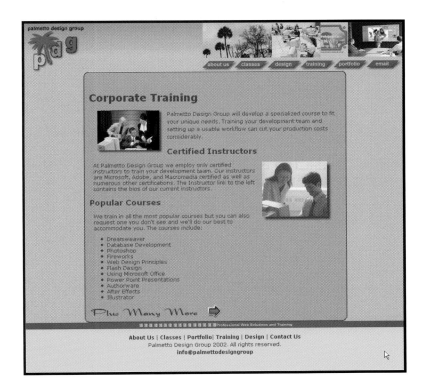

<NOTE>
When you preview, take note that the images and buttons at the top are against the right edge. The buttons are also too close to the rounded table, and the rounded table is too close to the byline. You fix this in the next tutorial.

23. **Save the file, and do a browser check.**

The hover does not work in Netscape 4X, but it does in Internet Explorer 6 and Netscape 6 and 7.

Tutorial

» Adding Space Using CSS

In this tutorial you see that the positioning problem you saw when you previewed the training page can all be handled with CSS. When you set up the table structure, I had you give each table a unique ID name just in case you needed it. This is a time when you can use it. The ID name allows you to add a style to each specific table independent of the others.

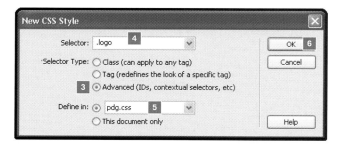

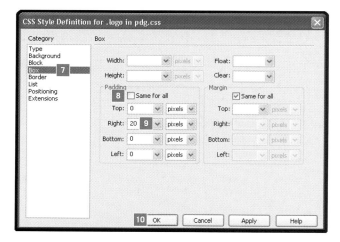

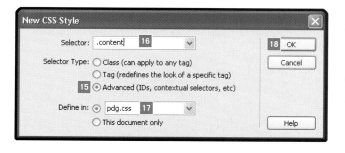

1. **Open** `training.html` **if you closed it.**

2. **In the CSS Styles panel, add a new style.**

3. **Click the Advanced (IDs, contextual selectors, etc) radio button.**

4. **Type** .logo **in the Selector field.**
   This is the ID name of the table with the logo and the images.

5. **Be sure that Define In is set to the** `pdg.css` **style sheet.**

6. **Click OK.**

7. **Select the Box category.**

8. **In the Padding category, click Same for All to deselect it.**

9. **Enter** 0 **for all fields except for Right. Enter** 20 **there.**

10. **Click OK.**

11. **Click anywhere in the logo table. In the status bar, right+click (Ctrl+click) on the** `<table#logo>` **tag and select Set Class→logo.**

12. **Preview in your browsers.**
    A 20-pixel space is added to the right side of the images.

13. **Repeat Steps 2 through 11 for the button table, but substitute** .menu **for** .logo **as the Selector name.**

14. **In the CSS Styles panel, add a new style.**

15. **Click the Advanced (IDs, contextual selectors, etc) radio button.**

16. **Type** .content **in the Selector field.**
    This is the ID name of the table with the rounded table inside. You add space above and below.

17. **Be sure that Define In is set to the** `pdg.css` **style sheet.**

18. **Click OK.**

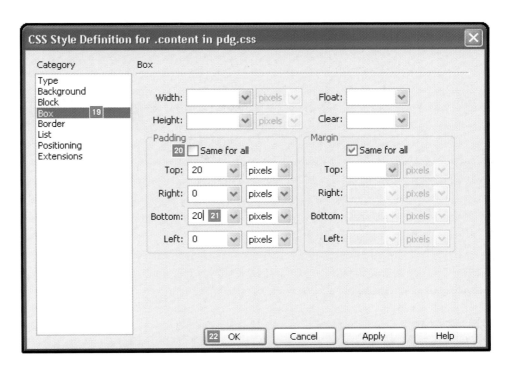

19. **Select the Box category.**

20. **Click in Same for All in the Padding category to deselect it.**

21. **Enter 0 for Right and Left, and enter 20 for Top and Bottom.**

22. **Click OK.**

23. **In the status bar, right+click (Ctrl+click) on the** `<table#content>` **tag and select Set Class→content.**

24. **Preview in your browsers.**
    A 20-pixel space is added to the top and bottom of the rounded table.

25. **You may notice some gold showing on the right side of the menu table. This table needs a background color. Select the .menu style in the CSS panel and click the Edit icon.**

26. **In the Background category, click in the color box for background color and select the color from the menu table in your document.**

27. **Click OK and test.**

28. **Save (File→Save All) and close the files** (`training.html` and `pdg.css`).

» Session Review

If you've never used CSS styles before, your mind is probably boggled at this point. You may want to repeat this session a time or two until you get the hang of it.

Answer the questions below to review the information in this session. The answer to each question can be found in the tutorial noted in parentheses.

1. How do you get embedded styles into an external style sheet? (See "Tutorial: Removing Embedded Styles.")

2. How do you attach a pre-existing style sheet to your document? (See "Tutorial: Attaching a Style Sheet.")

3. When you edit the `<body>` tag, can you change all the font attributes for the entire page? (See "Tutorial: Editing the BODY Tag.")

4. How do you apply a body style? (See "Tutorial: Editing the BODY Tag.")

5. Name two ways to edit a style. (See "Tutorial: Editing the BODY Tag," "Tutorial: Applying Custom Classes," and/or "Tutorial: Using a Contexual Selector to Add a Style.")

6. How do you define the text within a table? (See "Tutorial: Grouping Selector Tags.")

7. Can you add a style to just one word in a paragraph that already has a style applied? (See "Tutorial: Applying Custom Classes.")

8. Name the three pseudo-class selectors. (See "Tutorial: Using Pseudo-Class Selectors.")

9. Can you have links in different locations of the document with different styles applied to them? (See "Tutorial: Using a Contexual Selector to Add a Style.")

10. Which browser doesn't recognize hover? (See "Tutorial: Using a Contexual Selector to Add a Style.")

11. How did you add space to specific tables? (See "Tutorial: Adding Space Using CSS.")

about us | classes | design | training | portfolio | email

Corporate Training

Palmetto Design Group will develop a specialized course to fit your unique needs. Training your development team and setting up a usable workflow can cut your production costs considerably.

Certified Instructors

At Palmetto Design Group we employ only certified instructors to train your development team. Our instructors are Microsoft, Adobe, and Macromedia certified as well as numerous other certifications. The Instructor link to the left contains the bios of our current instructors.

Popular Courses

We train in all the most popular courses but you can also request one you don't see and we'll do our best to accommodate you. The courses include:

- Dreamweaver
- Database Development
- Photoshop
- Fireworks
- Web Design Principles
- Flash Design
- Using Microsoft Office
- Power Point Presentations
- Authorware
- After Effects
- Illustrator

Using Templates and Libraries

Tutorial: **Using an Existing Document as a Template**

Tutorial: **Applying a Template**

Tutorial: **Editing a Template**

Tutorial: **Detaching a Template**

Tutorial: **Making a Library Item**

Tutorial: **Inserting Library Items**

Tutorial: **Editing Library Items**

Session Introduction

Using templates in your site saves lots of time and aggravation. By using a template, you can determine which elements should appear on each page and which elements can be edited. This assures the designer/developer that others adding content can't alter the design.

Another benefit of templates is that changes can be made directly to the template. After it is saved, you can automatically update all the pages attached to the template. This is particularly important when a site swells to hundreds of pages.

Be sure to test any design in multiple browsers prior to making it into a template to assure that it is performing as you expect.

TOOLS YOU'LL USE
Assets panel, Library category, Templates category, CSS Styles panel

MATERIALS NEEDED
session8_starterfiles if you didn't complete the previous tutorial

TIME REQUIRED
60 minutes

Tutorial
» Using an Existing Document as a Template

You use the `training.html` file as a template for the rest of the site. The navigation, header, and footer are all in place. Now is the perfect time to make it into a template.

1. **Open the Files panel, and double-click** `training.html` **to open it.**

2. **Click the Templates icon in the Common category of the Insert bar.**

3. **Click the Make Template icon.**

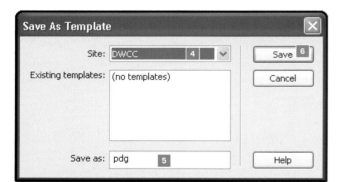

4. **Select DWCC for the Site, if it isn't already selected.**

5. **Type** pdg **in the Save as: field.**

6. **Click Save.**

7. **Click Yes to update links.**
   All regions of the document are locked by default except for the title. In order to use this template, we need to set a region that is editable.

8. **Click in the cell with the rounded table in it.**

9. **Select the `<table.content#content>` tag in the Tag Selector.**

10. **Click the Editable Region icon in the Template menu in the Insert bar.**

11. **Type** content **into the Name: field of the New Editable Region dialog box.**

12. **Click OK.**
    Notice an overlay over the table that is editable as well as a label that says content (to the top left of the table). This is the only part of this document that can be edited when the template is applied to documents in the site.

13. **Click anywhere in the Corporate Training table and then click the `<td>` tag in the Tag Selector.**
    This selects the entire table.

14. **Press the Delete key to delete this content.**
    It's not needed in the template because this area will contain content appropriate to the different pages.

15. **Open the Assets panel.**

16. **Click the Templates icon.**
    You see a preview of the template in the preview pane.

17. **Save the template file (File→Save). You can close this file.**
    If you get a message to update all files using the template, just click No because there are none yet.

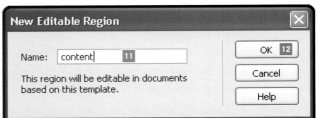

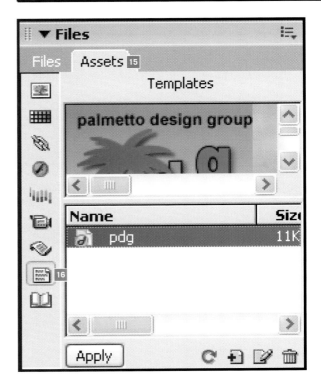

Tutorial
» Applying a Template

In this tutorial, you apply the PDG template to the `training.html` page and the rest of the site's pages as well.

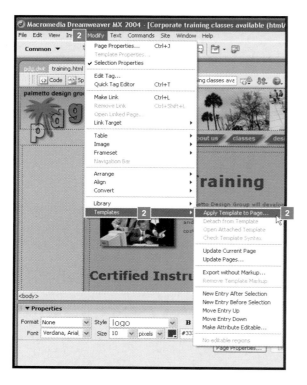

1. **Click the Files panel to open it, and double-click on `training.html` again.**
   Your other open file was converted into the template file (`pdg.dwt`).

2. **Choose Modify→Templates→Apply Template to Page.**

3. **Click pdg.**
   The Update page when template changes option is checked by default. Leave it that way.

4. **Click Select.**
   The Inconsistent Region Names dialog box opens. This happens when a document has never had a template applied before or if it has another template applied with different regions. In this case, your document has content that it doesn't know what to do with.

5. **Click Document body.**

6. **Click Nowhere in the Move Content to New Region drop-down menu.**

   You choose Nowhere because the body content is already in the template that you are applying. If you put it anywhere else, the page would contain two copies of the document body.

7. **Click Document head.**

8. **Click Nowhere in the Move Content to New Region drop-down menu.**

<TIP>

You can also select the Use for All button in the Inconsistent Regions dialog box after you select what to do with the content.

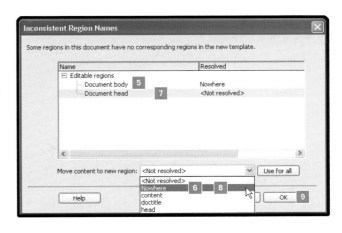

9. **Click OK.**

10. **Notice the top-right corner of the document window.**

    A template marker is added to the entire document. Yellow indicates that it is not editable. When you move your cursor over the icons, you get the "no" symbol.

11. **Notice the blue marker titled content.**

    This one is editable. If you place your cursor in the content area, you can change the content. The extra gold that you see on top of the content table will not appear in a browser. The content template tag added the space visually.

12. **Look in the status bar.**

    When your cursor is in the content area, the Tag Selector also denotes that it is editable.

13. **Save the file.**

14. **In the Files panel, double-click** about.html.

<NOTE>
You use a different technique for the design page.

<NOTE>
Getting some of your main keywords into your title is a good idea.
Some search engines use the title text to help index your content.

15. **In the Assets panel, click the Template icon.**

16. **Select the pdg template.**

17. **Click Apply.**
No dialog box opens this time because you have no content to deal with. But notice that your entire design is now in the about.html file.

18. **Type the following as the page title:** About Palmetto Design Group.
The title area is the only area other than the content area that is not locked. Adding a title right away is a good habit to get into. It's very easy to forget to do this, and seeing Untitled Document in the Browser title bar and in the Favorites list can be very annoying.

19. **Save and close all open files.**

20. **Repeat Steps 14 through 20 for the classes and portfolio pages using these titles:**

    » classes.html: Online graphic design classes

    » portfolio.html: Professional Web site design portfolio

    » design.html: Brochures, illustration, magazines, and print designs

21. **Close and save all files.**
Next you see how to create a new page based on a template.

22. **Choose File→New. Click on the Templates tab, select the DWCC site name then select** pdg.dwt. **Click the Create button.**

23. **Choose File→Save As and save it as** design.html **overwriting the copy in the sites html folder. You can close this file.**

Tutorial
» Editing a Template

In this tutorial you change the name of the about.html page to aboutus.html. After you're finished, you can see how the change is applied automatically to the entire page to which the template is applied.

1. **In the Assets panel, double-click the pdg template to open it.**

2. **Select the About Us button.**

3. **In the Property inspector change the link name to** aboutus.html.

4. **In the Files panel select the** about.html **file name.**

5. **From the Options pop-up menu select File→Rename and rename it** aboutus.html.

6. **Click the Update button.**

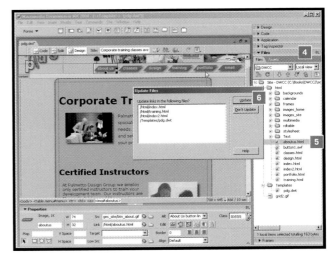

7. **In the template page scroll down to the footer text. Change the copyright year from 2002 to** 2003.

8. **Save the template (File→Save).**
The Update Template Files dialog box opens with a listing of all the documents that are using the PDG template.

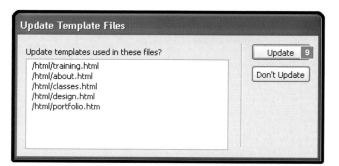

9. **Click Update to apply the changes to all the pages.**
The Update Pages dialog box opens and reports which files were updated, including how many were examined and how many were updated. If for any reason files can't be updated, you are told so in this dialog box.

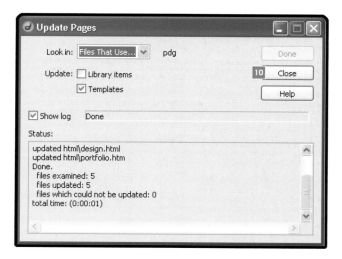

10. **Click the Close button to close the Update Pages dialog box.**

Tutorial

» Detaching a Template

You want to edit pages in a site separately from the rest of the site. For example, you may want to make changes to one page that doesn't conform to the template. To do this, you need to detach the template from the page. In this tutorial, you detach the template because you make a few Library elements from some of the content in the next tutorial. You then attach the template again.

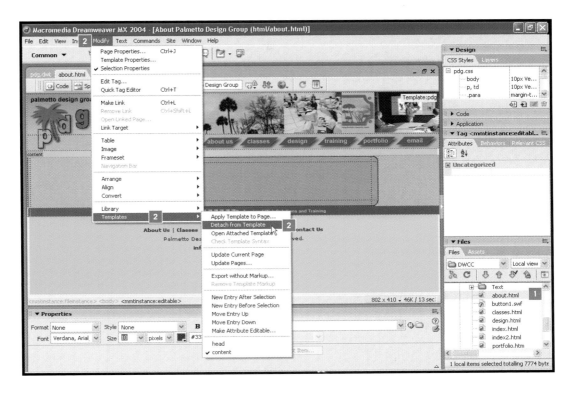

1. **Double-click the** about.html **file in the Files panel to open it.**

2. **Click Modify→Templates→Detach from Template.**
   That's all there is to it. If you want your page to remain without the template, you should save it now. (But you don't want to do that, so don't save the page.) If you close and save this page before completing the next tutorial, you need to apply the template again.

<NOTE>
When you detach the template from a page, it no longer updates when a change is made to any of the un-editable areas of the document. You can even make design changes and make a new template if you want to. Many sites have more than one template.

Tutorial
» Making a Library Item

This tutorial shows you how to make a Library item. Library items can be added to individual pages and updated just as easily as templates. Library items contain the necessary code with them, so you can insert, for example, a table with specific formatting with the click of your mouse.

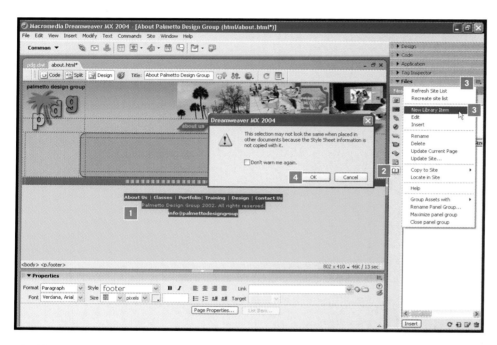

1. **With the** `training.html` **page open, click inside the text navigation (footer area). Select the** `<p class="footer">` **tag from the Tag Selector.**

After you select the footer text in the document, check the code. Be sure that the opening `<p class="footer">` and closing `</p>` tags are included in the selection.

2. **Click the Library icon in the Assets panel.**

3. **Click the Options pop-up menu, and then click New Library Item.**
   A warning dialog box opens stating that "This selection may not look the same when placed in other documents because the Style Sheet information is not copied with it." That's okay; you can edit it later. The links remain with the Library item.

4. **Click OK.**
   In the Assets panel, you see a preview of the new Library item. Also notice that the name untitled is highlighted and ready to change.

5. **Type** footer **for the name of the item, and press Enter (Return).**
   The new Library item is now available for use.

6. **Close the** about.html **file without saving it.**
   This way, the template is still attached.

7. **In the Files panel, click Site→Recreate Site Cache from the Options pop-up menu to see the Library items and template folder added to the Files panel.**

<NOTE>
Notice that two new folders were added that you didn't make. One is templates, and the other is Library. These folders are automatically generated by Dreamweaver. You don't upload these to your server; they are strictly internal folders for Dreamweaver's use.

Tutorial
» Inserting Library Items

This tutorial shows you how to add the text navigation and the copyright Library items to the index page of the site.

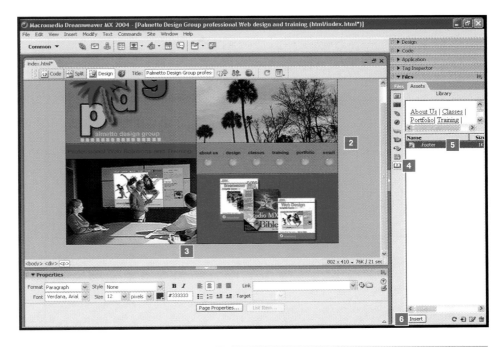

1. **Double-click the** `index.html` **file in the Files panel to open it.**

2. **Click on the right side of the document in the gold area to place your cursor.**

3. **Press Enter (Return) to add a paragraph space.**
   The cursor is now below the site design.

4. **Click the Library icon in the Assets panel.**

5. **Click footer.**

6. **Click the Insert button.**

7. **Save the file.**

<NOTE>

That's all there is to inserting Library items in a document. The items are highlighted with yellow to indicate that they are Library items. Also notice the code—it is highlighted as well. You can't edit the Library item in an individual document unless you detach it first. Detaching it does not allow the items to be updated if the original Library item is updated or changed.

Library Item Facts

You can also copy a Library item to another site. Select the Library item in the Assets panel, and click the Options pop-up menu. Click Copy to Site, and choose the site to which you want to copy it. This works great for Library items such as the ones you made, because they are text-only. But if you make a Library item that contains images, the images don't move with the Library. You need to copy the images or the folder with the images and paste them into the new site. Be sure that you keep the same structure so the links work. A Library item is actually linking to the images in your site. If you want to copy a Library item to another site, you can do that and then separately place the images in a folder into the new site. Be sure, though, that the folder has the same name as the original so the links work properly.

Tutorial

» Editing Library Items

You can edit any Library item by double-clicking it in the Assets panel. After you are finished, you are prompted to save the file and update any uses of the item. In this tutorial, you make a separate style sheet for each of the Library items you added to the home page.

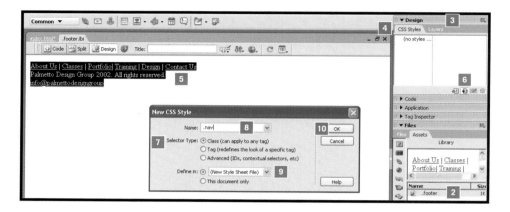

1. Open the `index.html` page if you've closed it.

2. Double-click the footer Library item in the Assets panel.

3. Click on Design to open the Design panel group.

4. Make the CSS Styles panel active by selecting it.

5. Select the footer text.

6. Add a new style in the CSS Styles panel.

7. In the New CSS Style dialog box, click Class (can apply to any tag).

8. Name the style `.nav`.

9. Click Define In (New Style Sheet File).

10. Click OK.

11. **Name the style sheet** homepage, **navigate to the Stylesheet folder, and save it.**

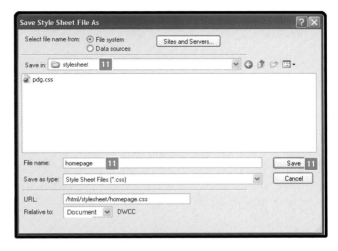

12. **In the Type category, select the font Verdana, Arial, Helvetica, sans-serif.**

13. **Choose a size of 10.**

14. **Click OK.**

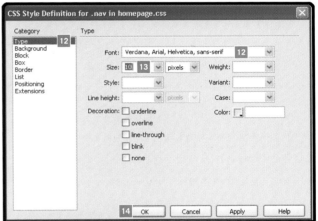

15. **Click in the footer area.**

16. **In the Property inspector, select nav from the Styles drop-down list.**

17. **Save the Library item.**

18. **If prompted to update, click the Update button.**

19. **Save the file, and preview your work in a browser.**

20. **Close any open documents.**

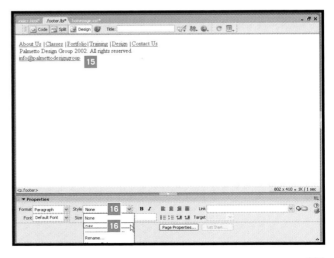

» Session Review

This session should have been pretty easy for you. Answer these questions to review the information in the session. The answer to each question is in the tutorial noted in parentheses.

1. What is editable in a new template by default? (See "Tutorial: Using an Existing Document as a Template.")

2. Must a document have content in it to have a template applied to it? (See "Tutorial: Applying a Template.")

3. How do you edit a document that has a template attached to it? (See "Tutorial: Editing a Template.")

4. Why would you want to detach a template from a document? (See "Tutorial: Detaching a Template.")

5. Where are Library items stored? (See "Tutorial: Making a Library Item.")

6. Why are Library items useful? (See "Tutorial: Making a Library Item.")

7. How do you get a Library item into a document? (See "Tutorial: Inserting Library Items.")

8. After you insert a Library item, how do you edit it? (See "Tutorial: Editing Library Items.")

pdg
palmetto design group

Professional Web Solutions and Training

about us   design   classes   training   portfolio   email

About Us | Classes | Portfolio | Training | Design | Contact Us
Palmetto Design Group 2002. All rights reserved.
info@palmettodesigngroup

Session 9

Adding Forms and Behaviors

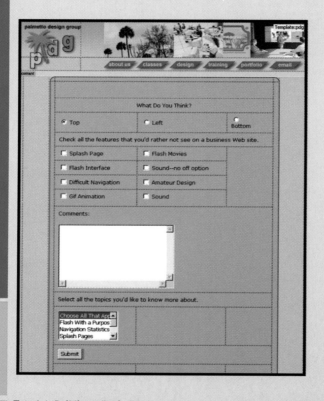

Tutorial: **Building a Basic Form**

Tutorial: **Adding Submit and Clear Buttons**

Tutorial: **Inserting Radio Buttons**

Tutorial: **Inserting Check Boxes**

Tutorial: **Inserting a Text Area and a List**

Tutorial: **Using Jump Menus**

Session Introduction

HTML forms are used to collect data from users. That data is then sent to the server. Three form attributes allow the form to interact with a program on your server: the Form Name, the Actions, and the Methods. The Form Name can be referenced by scripts to perform different actions. Actions are taken when the Submit button is clicked. Two Methods, GET and POST, are used to submit the form's data. GET is limited to ASCII data, which is no larger than 8KB, and it is a bit insecure. POST is the preferred method. It sends the data to the processing agent that the Action attribute specifies; it can handle encrypted files.

In this session, you learn how to insert and label form objects. You make several forms on blank pages so that you can insert them into any document. Forms need to be linked to a CGI script to actually work, so I walk you through the steps you need to take to set up a script. But you need to have a server that supports CGI, and you need a CGI script (you can get one of the free scripts by entering CGI e-mail scripts into a search engine) in order to make your forms fully functional.

TOOLS YOU'LL USE
Form insertion icons, Property inspector, Behaviors panel

MATERIALS NEEDED
session9_starter files if needed. Copy send.gif from the session9_starterfiles folder into your html/images_site folder.

Access to a CGI script designed to process forms on a server

TIME REQUIRED
60 minutes

Tutorial
» Building a Basic Form

In this tutorial, you add a form field, a form element, and a Submit button. You build the form on a blank page so you can copy and paste it into other documents or make a library item of it.

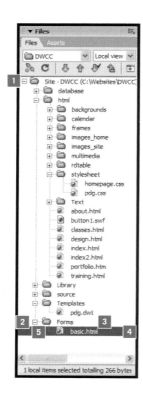

1. **In the Files panel, right-click (Ctrl+click) the root folder name, and click New Folder.**

2. **Name the folder** Forms.

3. **Right-click (Ctrl+click) the Forms folder, and click New File.**

4. **Name the file** basic.html.

5. **Double-click** basic.html **to open it.**

6. **Click the Forms category on the Insert bar.**
   Pass your mouse cursor over each icon to familiarize yourself with what is available. You use many of these options in this session.

7. **Click in the page, and then click the Form icon.**
   You see a red dotted line box; this is the empty form. If you can't see the red box, click View→Visual Aids→Invisible Elements.

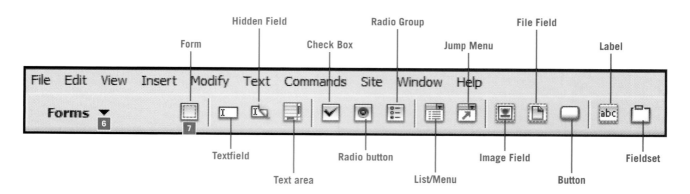

8. **Click the Split View (Show Code and Design Views) to see the code.**
   Notice the code added after the <body> tag. It says <form name="form1" method="post" action=""> </form>. Your form is between these opening and closing form tags.

9. **Switch back to Design view. At the top of the document in the Title text field, highlight Untitled and type in** Sample forms.
   This is a good habit to get into—titling every page.

10. **In the Property inspector, change the Form Name to** contact.
    If you look at the code now, the form name has changed to name="contact".

11. **Click your cursor inside the red lines that define the form area.**
    In the next steps, you insert a table inside the form area to make the form objects look nicer. You don't have to use tables to organize form objects.

12. **Switch to the Common category of the Insert bar, and click the Insert Table icon.**

13. **Type these values in the Insert Table dialog box:**

    » Rows: **13**

    » Border: **0**

    » Columns: **2**

    » Cell Padding: **0**

    » Width: 340 **Pixels**

    » Cell Spacing: **0**

14. **Type** layout table **in the Summary box, and click OK.**

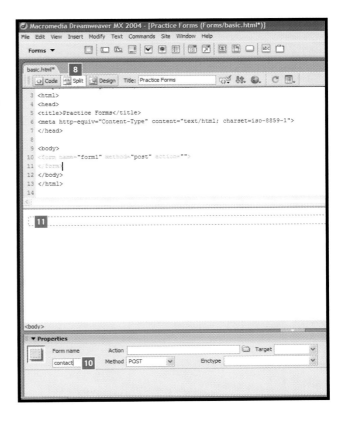

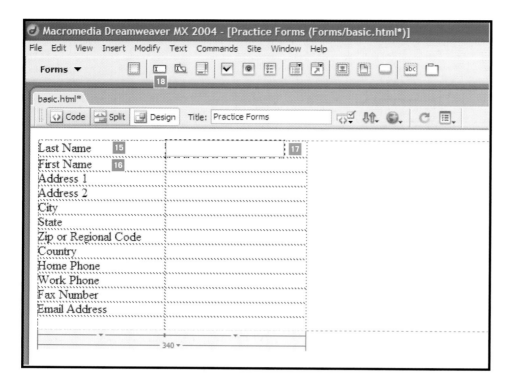

15. **Place your cursor in the first cell of the first row (top-left corner), and type** Last Name.

    You can use the Tab key to move between cells.

16. **Place your cursor in each of the remaining rows on the left side of the column, and type these entries:**

    » **First Name**

    » **Address 1**

    » **Address 2**

    » **City**

    » **State**

    » **Zip or Regional Code**

    » **Country**

    » **Home Phone**

    » **Work Phone**

    » **Fax Number**

    » **Email Address**

17. **Place your cursor in the first cell of the right column, and click to place the cursor.**

18. **Click the Text Field icon in the Forms category of the Insert bar.**

    Notice that a text field is now visible in your document. If you have left the Accessibility options on, use No Label and type a letter for the Access key. This letter, when used with the Ctrl key, tabs through the form fields.

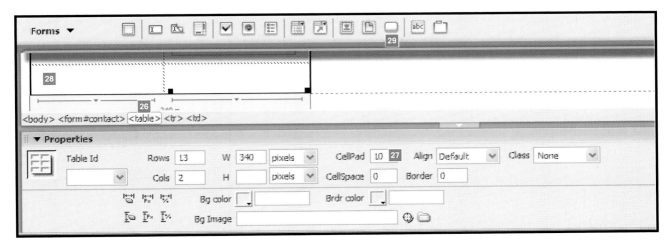

19. **In the Property inspector, leave Max Chars (Maximum Characters) blank.**
    By leaving Max Chars blank, you eliminate the possibility of cutting letters off the end of a long last name.

20. **In the Char Width field, enter a value of** 25.
    If you click in the document or press Enter (Return) to activate the changes, you notice that the text field box got a little larger after you changed the width. By specifically changing the character width, you can control the appearance of all the text fields.

21. **Click the Single Line radio button to select it, if it isn't selected already.**
    It's selected if you see a black dot in the radio button.

22. **Type a text field name of lastname.**
    Avoiding spaces in field names is best.

23. **Repeat Steps 17 through 22 for the rest of the entries, replacing the text field name with an appropriate name for the entry.**

<NOTE>
A quick way to add numerous text fields with the same values is to select the first field and copy it. Then paste it into each of the desired rows. When you paste, the names will be lastname 2, lastname 3, etc. Select each field, and change the name to match the label.

24. **Look at the code, and notice that each text field has an input name.**
    You can see the properties of each such as the type, size, and ID.

    ```
    <td><input name="email" type="text" id="email"
    size="25"></td>
    ```

<NOTE>
The input name helps you identify the entered information when you receive the form. You set up a database application in Part V of this course. You also set up a form that actually inserts the form's data into the provided database.

25. **Click the Design View icon.**

26. **Select the table tag in the Tag Selector.**
    The table content is much too crowded, so you add some padding to the cells.

27. **In the Property inspector, type** 10 **in the CellPad field. Press Enter (Return).**
    The form looks much better now. You can add more or less padding depending on your taste.

28. **Click in the left column of the last row.**

29. **Click the Button icon in the Forms category of the Insert bar. In the next tutorial you code the button to send the form information.**

Tutorial
» Adding Submit and Clear Buttons

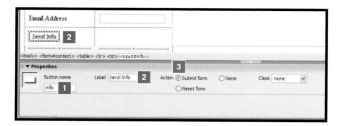

1. **In the Property inspector, change the Button name from Submit to info.**

2. **Change the Label field to** Send Info.

3. **Leave the Action set to Submit form. Press Enter (Return).**
   Notice that the button expands to fit your text.

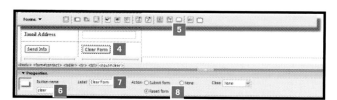

4. **Place your cursor in the right column of the last row.**

5. **In the Insert bar (Forms category), click the Button icon.**

6. **Change the Button name field to** clear.

7. **Change the Label field to** Clear Form.

8. **Change the Action to Reset form, and press Enter (Return).**

9. **Click in the Last Name cell, and drag down to select all the text in the first column.**
   You see a solid black line around the entire left column indicating that it is selected.

10. **In the Property inspector, change the Horizontal alignment to Right.**
    This makes the text go to the right of the column. The form looks much better, but it needs some text formatting. When you use this form on a Web page, use CSS styles to format the text.

11. **Save the file.**

12. **Preview your work in the appropriate browsers. Close the file.**

< N O T E >

When you test the form, you can enter text at this point, but it won't work because it needs to have a CGI-BIN set up with a CGI script with your ISP. I show you how to link a form to a CGI script in the "Inserting a Text Area and a List" tutorial. This particular form connects to a database in Part V.

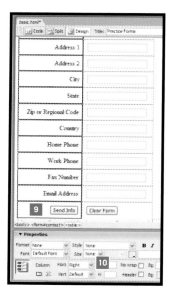

Tutorial
» Inserting Radio Buttons

In this tutorial, you insert three radio buttons with different options. The user can choose just one of the options.

1. **Right-click (Ctrl+click) the Forms folder in the Files panel, and click New File.**

2. **Name the file** survey.html, **and double-click the file to open it.**

3. **Click the Form icon to insert the form field.**

4. **In the Property inspector, change the Form Name to** Survey.

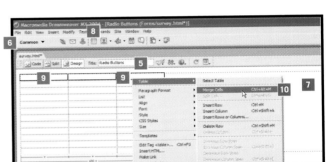

5. **In the Document Title field, type** Radio Buttons Form.

6. **Change the Insert bar category to Common.**

7. **Click inside the red form lines to place your cursor.**

8. **Click the Table icon, and enter these values:**

   » Rows: **12**

   » Border: **0**

   » Columns: **3**

   » Cell Padding: **0**

   » Width: **500**

   » Cell Spacing: **0**

   Type **layout table** in the Summary field, and click OK.

9. **Click into the first left cell, and drag horizontally to select the entire first row.**

10. **Right-click (Ctrl+click), and click Table→Merge Cells.**

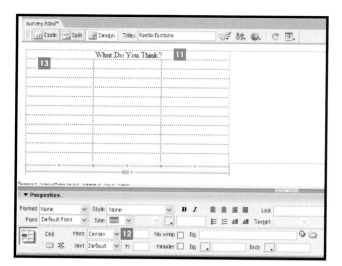

11. **Type** What Do You Think? **into the merged row.**

12. **With your cursor still in the merged row, go to the Property inspector and set Horz to Center.**

13. **Place your cursor in the first cell (on the left) of the second row.**

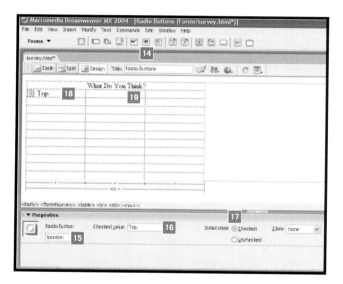

14. **In the Forms category of the Insert bar, click the Radio button icon.**

15. **In the Property inspector, type** location **in the Radio Button field.**

16. **In the Checked Value field, type** Top.

17. **Click the Initial State of Checked.**

18. **In the document, to the right of the radio button, type** Top.

19. **Place your cursor in the center cell of the second row.**

20. **Click the Radio Button icon to insert the radio button.**

21. **In the Radio Button field, name it** location **again.**

    The buttons have the same names because you want readers to be able to select only one button. If each radio button had a different name, the users could select all the options.

22. **In the Checked Value field, enter** left.

23. **For the Initial State, click Unchecked.**

24. **In the document, to the right of the center radio button, type** Left.

25. **Place your cursor in the right cell of the second row.**

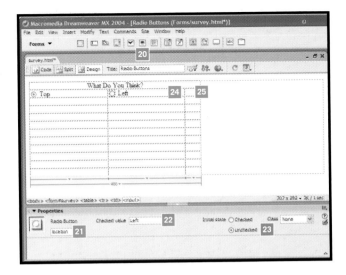

26. **Click the Radio Button icon to insert the radio button.**

27. **Name it** location **again.**

28. **In the Checked Value field, enter** left.

29. **For the Initial State, click Unchecked.**

30. **In the document, to the right of the right radio button, type** Bottom.

31. **Click on the Split View icon, and look at the code.**

    Notice the input type is radio, the name is location, the value is left, and so on.

32. **Save the document, and leave it open.**

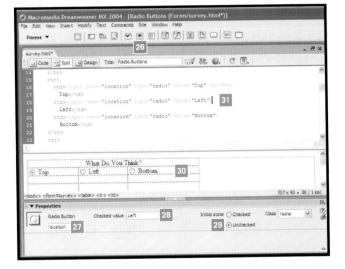

Tutorial

» Inserting Check Boxes

When you want to allow multiple selections, you need to use check boxes instead of radio buttons. In this tutorial, you add a series of check boxes.

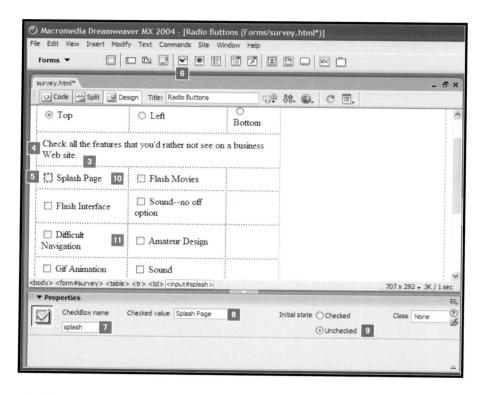

1. Select the table tag in the Tag Selector, and enter 10 for the CellPad.

2. Merge the third row by selecting the row, right-clicking (Ctrl+clicking), and clicking Table→Merge Cells.

3. With the cursor in the third row, set the Horz to Left in the Property inspector.

4. Type Check all the features that you'd rather not see on a business Web site.

5. Place your cursor inside the first cell of the fourth row.

6. Click the Check Box icon in the Forms bar.

7. In the Property inspector, change the CheckBox name to splash.

8. Type Splash Page for the Checked Value.

9. Click Unchecked for the Initial State.

10. In the document, to the right of the check box, type Splash Page.

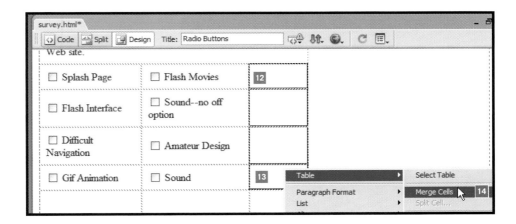

11. **Add radio buttons and text for the following, and enter a new name for the CheckBox name and the Checked Value name for each. For the initial state, leave them all unchecked:**

   » Flash Movies: Type **flashmovies** into both the CheckBox name and Checked Value fields.

   » Flash Interface: Type **flashinterface** into both the CheckBox name and Checked Value fields.

   » Sound-no Off Option: Type **noff** into both the CheckBox name and Checked Value fields.

   » Difficult Navigation: Type **difnav** into both the CheckBox name and Checked Value fields.

   » Amateur Design: Type **amateur** into both the CheckBox name and Checked Value fields.

   » GIF Animation: Type **gifanim** into both the CheckBox name and Checked Value fields.

   » Sound: Type **sound** into both the CheckBox name and Checked Value fields.

   The location of each check box entry is not important.

12. **Click in the third column (far right) of the first check box.**

13. **Click and drag down to the last row of the check boxes.**

14. **Right-click (Ctrl+click), and select Table→Merge Cells.**

15. **Save the file, and leave it open.**

Tutorial
» Inserting a Text Area and a List

In this tutorial, you add a text area that can be used for comments and a list from which users can select multiple options.

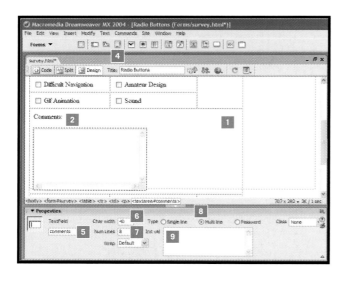

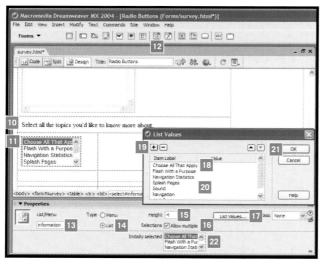

1. **Merge row 9 (under the last check boxes).**

2. **Type** Comments:.

3. **Press Enter (Return).**

4. **Click the Text Area icon in the Forms category of the Insert bar.**

5. **In the Property inspector, in the TextField field, type** comments **for the name.**

6. **Set the Char Width to** 40.

7. **Set the Num Lines to** 8.

8. **Leave Multi Line option checked.**

9. **Leave the Init Val field empty.**
   The Initial Value field is where you can explain how the text area is being used.

10. **Merge the next row, and type** Select all the topics you'd like to know more about.

11. **Place your cursor in the first cell of the next row.**

12. **Click the List/Menu icon in the Forms category of the Insert bar.**

13. **Change the List/Menu name to** information.

14. **Click List for the Type.**

15. **Set the Height to** 4.

16. **Click Allow multiple selections.**

17. **Click the List Values button.**

18. **Type** Choose All That Apply.

19. **Click the plus sign (+).**

20. **Repeat Steps 18 and 19 for the following values:**

    » Flash with a purpose

    » Navigation statistics

    » Splash pages

    » Sound

    » Navigation

    » Web design

21. **Click OK.**

22. **In the Initially Selected field, click Choose All That Apply.**

23. **Merge the next row.**

24. **Insert your cursor in the merged row.**

25. **Click the Image Field icon in the Forms category of the Insert bar.**

    The Image Field allows you to use a graphical button for the Submit and Reset buttons.

<NOTE>

You won't use the File field, but it adds a Browse button to enable the user to send a file to you.

26. **Navigate to the html/images_site folder, and click** send.gif. **Click OK.**

    If you don't see this file, you need to copy the send.gif file from the session9_starterfiles folder on the CD-ROM into your html/images_site folder.

27. **In the Property inspector, name the Imagefield Send.**

28. **Set the Alt tag to** Send.

29. **Click inside the form but outside the table.**

30. **In the Tag Selector, click** form#survey.

31. **In the Property inspector, choose a Method of POST.**

32. **The Action field is where you enter the path to a CGI-BIN folder with a CGI script in it.**

    Refer to the CGI Scripts sidebar.

33. **Save the file, and leave it open.**

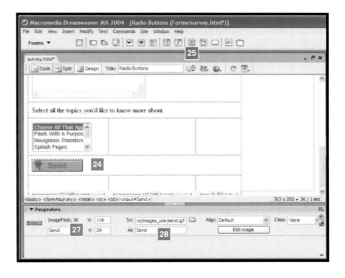

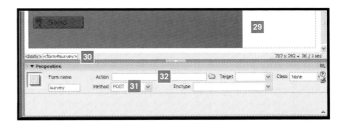

CGI Scripts

The path to a script can be obtained from your hosting service if it allows CGI and if it provides the script. You can also find free scripts on the Internet. Just be sure that you get them from a reputable source. I have provided a couple of links on the CD-ROM.

Tutorial
» Using Jump Menus

In this tutorial, you make a jump menu (whereby you click an item from a list and go somewhere else). You discover how similar jump menus are to list menus. In fact, you make the list menu that you made earlier into a jump menu.

1. **Select the list form object, and copy it.**
   Click in the list that says Choose All That Apply to select it. Press Ctrl+C (⌘+C) to copy it.

2. **Close the** survey.html **page.**

3. **In the Files panel, right-click (Ctrl+click) the Forms folder, and click New File.**

4. **Name the new file** jump.html.

5. **Double-click** jump.html **to open it.**

6. **Click the Form icon in the Forms category of the Insert bar.**

7. **Insert your cursor inside the form box.**

8. **Click Edit→Paste, or press Ctrl+V (⌘+V).**

9. **Select the list form.**

10. **In the Property inspector, click List for the Type.**
    Notice that the list box has changed to a single line.

11. **Click the List Values button.**

12. **Click the Choose All That Applies text, and type** Information.

13. **Click Flash With a Purpose, and press the Tab key.**
    This puts you into the Value field. This is where you enter the URL that activates when the user clicks on the Flash With a Purpose text.

14. **For now, enter a null link of** javascript:;.

15. **Copy the javascript:; text.**

16. **Press the Tab key twice, and paste the text.**
    This puts the focus into the value field of Navigation statistics.

17. **Press the Tab key twice again, and paste for the remaining text items.**

18. **Click OK.**

19. **In the Property inspector, click Information for the Initially Selected item.**

20. **This menu has no behavior attached to it yet, so click the Tag Inspector in the Panels group to open it.**

21. **Click Behaviors to activate the Behaviors panel.**

22. **Click the plus sign (+).**

23. **Click Jump Menu.**

24. **When the Jump Menu dialog box opens, click one of the entries.**
    Notice that the null links are already entered. If you don't do this from the Property inspector, you can also add the link fields here in the When Selected, Go To URL: field.

25. **Click Select First Item after URL Change, if you'd like the Information entry to show after the page loads again.**

26. **Click OK.**

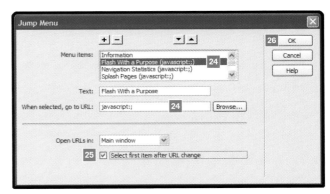

27. **Look at the behavior added to the Behaviors panel.**
    The Event should read onChange. You can always change the event that triggers the behavior by selecting the Jump Menu behavior and clicking the little arrow to choose a new event.

28. **Save the file, and preview your work in the appropriate browsers.**

Jump Menu Form Object

I chose to show you how to convert a list object into a jump menu by adding the links and a behavior. If you want to, you can accomplish the same thing by clicking the Jump Menu icon in the Forms bar. The dialog box that opens is almost identical to the one with the Jump Menu behavior. You have the additional option of adding a Go button. You don't have to add a behavior manually when you use the Jump Menu form object because it is added automatically.

» Session Review

In this session, you learned how to add a variety of forms from a simple text field to a jump menu. You made these forms on separate pages so that you can add them to any document where you can customize the backgrounds and the text.

Now that you know how to add various forms, you can give yourself this quick test to evaluate how much you can recall. The answer to each question can be found in the tutorial noted in parentheses.

1. Where do you find the form objects? (See "Tutorial: Building a Basic Form.")

2. What tags are required for every form object? (See "Tutorial: Building a Basic Form.")

3. What technique do you use to line up your form objects? (See "Tutorial: Building a Basic Form.")

4. Can you customize the names on a form button? (See "Tutorial: Adding Submit and Clear Buttons.")

5. Can you select more than one object in a set of radio buttons? (See "Tutorial: Inserting Radio Buttons.")

6. What makes check boxes different from radio buttons? (See "Tutorial: Inserting Check Boxes.")

7. Name a few values that you can specify for a text area. (See "Tutorial: Inserting a Text Area and a List.")

8. How does a list work? (See "Tutorial: Inserting a Text Area and a List.")

9. Can you change the event that triggers a behavior? (See "Tutorial: Using Jump Menus.")

10. What is the difference between a list and a jump menu? (See "Tutorial: Using Jump Menus.")

11. Do you need to add a behavior when you add a jump menu form using the Jump Menu icon in the Forms bar? (See "Tutorial: Using Jump Menus.")

» Other Projects

If you want to practice making a jump menu, you can add one to the `default.asp` page of the DataBase intranet site. Session 14 has you repeat Step 1 if you choose not to use it.

1. Copy the DataBase folder from the CD-ROM to your hard drive (not in the DWCC folder). Define the site in Dreamweaver, and name it **PDGdynamic**.

2. Open the `default.asp` page. You notice that the jump menu is already there, but plenty of space appears below it on which to practice.

3. Add the form field.

4. Add the jump menu.

5. Add the following List Values (you can add the links now or in the Jump Menu behavior):
   » Intranet Home: Link of: `../Library/default.asp`
   » Contacts List: Link of: `contacts_list.asp`
   » View Contacts: Link of: `../Library/view_contacts.asp`
   » Add Contact: Link of: `../Library/add_contact.asp`
   » Modify Contact: Link of: `../Library/mod_contact.asp`
   » Delete Contact: Link of: `../Library/delete_contact.asp`

6. Add the Jump Menu behavior. Don't choose the Select First Item after URL Change option.

7. In the Behaviors panel, be sure that the Event of the behavior is onChange.

8. Close the document, and don't save the changes.

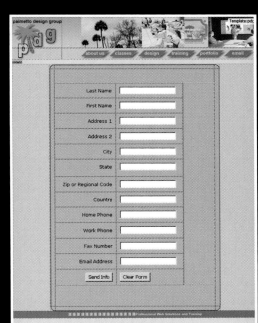

palmetto design group

Template:pdg

about us | classes | design | training | portfolio | email

Last Name	
First Name	
Address 1	
Address 2	
City	
State	
Zip or Regional Code	
Country	
Home Phone	
Work Phone	
Fax Number	
Email Address	

Send Info   Clear Form

Professional Web Solutions and Training

About Us | Classes | Portfolio| Training | Design | Contact Us
Palmetto Design Group 2003. All rights reserved.
info@palmettodesigngroup

Part IV:
Publishing the Site

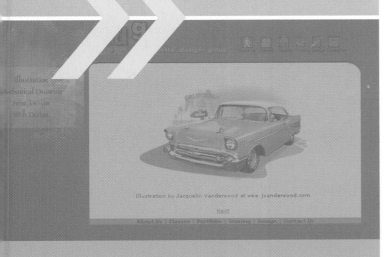

Session 10 **Editing Images with or without an Image Editor**

Session 11 **Performing Site Checks**

Session 12 **Getting Your Web Site Online**

Session 10

Editing Images with or without an Image Editor

Corporate Training

Palmetto Design Group will develop a specialized course to fit your unique needs. Training your development team and setting up a usable workflow can cut your production costs considerably.

Certified Instructors

At Palmetto Design Group we employ only certified instructors to train your development team. Our instructors are Microsoft, Adobe, and Macromedia certified as well as numerous other certifications. The Instructor link to the left contains the bios of our current instructors.

Popular Courses

We train in all the most popular courses, but you can also request one you don't see and we'll do our best to accommodate you. A few of the courses include:

- Dreamweaver
- Photoshop
- Fireworks
- Flash Design
- InDesign
- GoLive
- Authorware
- After Effects
- Illustrator

About Us | Classes | Portfolio | Training | Design | Contact Us

Tutorial: **Cropping Images in Dreamweaver**

Tutorial: **Resampling an Image**

Tutorial: **Adding Brightness, Contrast, and Sharpening in Dreamweaver**

Tutorial: **Using External Image Editors**

Tutorial: **Optimizing Images in Fireworks**

Tutorial: **Editing a Source Image in Fireworks from Dreamweaver**

Session Introduction

In this session, you learn to edit images from within Dreamweaver. You can perform simple functions such as cropping, resampling, adding brightness and contrast, and sharpening without even owning an image editor. But for more robust editing, you learn how to use Macromedia Fireworks for more precise optimization, editing source files, and so on. You also see how to change the preferences in Dreamweaver to use Adobe Photoshop or another image editor. When you have Fireworks installed, Dreamweaver makes it possible to edit in Fireworks and, with a click of the button, allows you to automatically apply changes to your Dreamweaver layout.

You also discover how to insert a fully functional and linked navigational graphic from Fireworks into Dreamweaver.

You need to install Fireworks to take full advantage of the second portion of this session. If you don't have it already, a trial version is available on the CD-ROM.

TOOLS YOU'LL USE
Fireworks MX 2004, Preferences panel, Property inspector,
Fireworks edit, Optimize in Fireworks, Crop, Resample,
Brightness/Contrast, Sharpen

MATERIALS NEEDED
The session10_starterfiles. Copy the Editing folder to your
hard drive but not into the DWCC root folder.

TIME REQUIRED
90 minutes

Tutorial
» Cropping Images in Dreamweaver

Being able to do simple edits directly in Dreamweaver without an external editor can be a tremendous advantage for someone working on a Web site without a graphics editor. You may need to crop an image when you want to bring more focus into the main subject and eliminate portions that detract from the focus.

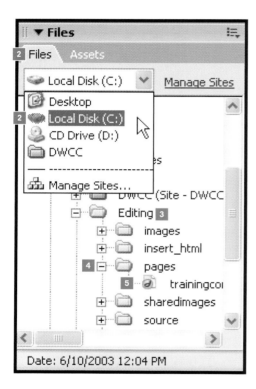

<NOTE>

To complete the first three tutorials in this session (Cropping Images in Dreamweaver; Resampling an Image; and Adding Brightness, Contrast, and Sharpening in Dreamweaver), you *do not* need to have Fireworks or any other image editor installed. Also, these features in Dreamweaver work *only* for JPEG and GIF image file formats.

1. **Copy the Editing folder from the CD-ROM onto your hard drive. Do not put it into your DWCC root folder.**
   This session stands on its own and is not part of the main site design. You use a practice page, so you can experiment with editing images without destroying any of the ones needed for your design.

2. **Open the Files panel, and select Local Disk from the drop-down menu.**

3. **Navigate to where you saved the Editing folder.**
   This is a new feature in Dreamweaver MX 2004. You no longer are required to define a site to be able to work in a different folder. Because this is not part of the DWCC site, this feature comes in handy.

4. **Click the plus sign (+) next to the pages folder to expand it.**

5. **Double-click on** `trainingcontent.html` **to open it.**
   This is a modified page from Chapter 16 that you can practice editing on.

6. **Select the image on the right.**

7. **In the Property inspector, click the Crop tool icon.**

8. **Click OK, and you see a message that says "**The action you are about to perform will permanently alter the selected image. You can undo any changes you make by selecting Edit→Undo."

<NOTE>

This message in Step 8 tells you that your original file is going to be overwritten. For this reason, you should always have backup copies of your site before doing any editing.

9. **Click and drag the center-right square to the left. Move the line to the left of the ear. Move the bottom up just a bit to remove the shadowed edge.**
   You can drag any of the squares to redefine the part of the image that you want to see. Whatever is inside the "box" remains after the crop.

10. **Double-click inside the crop area to accept the change.**
   By using the crop tool, you not only made the image's physical size smaller, but you decreased the file size as well. If you compare the original training2.jpg file on the CD (images folder) to the one now in your Editing→images folder, you see that it's a couple of kilobytes smaller in file size.

The only way to undo the crop is to use the Edit menu (Edit→Undo).

> 207

Tutorial

» Resampling an Image

Resampling an image either adds pixels to or substracts pixels from a JPEG or GIF image (the only formats that you can resample in Dreamweaver). After you change the dimensions of an image, you can resample it. For example, if you make the image larger, pixels are added; if you make it smaller, pixels are removed.

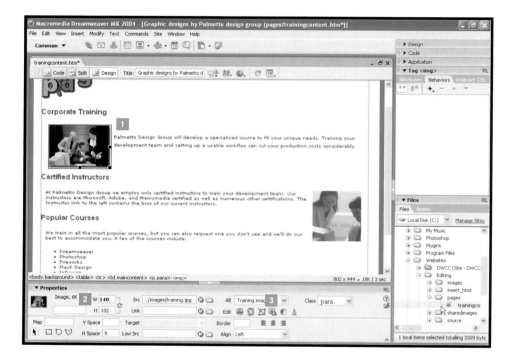

1. **Select the top-left image.**

2. **In the Property inspector, highlight the width (W), type** 140, **and press Enter (Return) to make the image smaller. Or you can also drag one of the little black boxes surrounding the image to resize visually.**
   Notice that the Resampling icon is now available in the Property inspector. Prior to making a dimension change, it was grayed out.

   <NOTE>
   Note the little curved arrow between the height and width. If you click this, the dimension change reverts to the original.

3. **Select the Resample icon.**

4. **Click OK to make the warning go away.**
   The Resample is done automatically with no user interaction.

   <NOTE>
   After the resample is done, the only way to revert to the original is to choose Edit→Undo. The reverse symbol (little cured arrow) for the dimension is no longer available.

Tutorial

» Adding Brightness, Contrast, and Sharpening in Dreamweaver

You can use the Brightness/Contrast feature of Dreamweaver to adjust the highlights, shadows, and midtones of an image, making them darker or lighter. You can sharpen an image by contrasting the edges within an image. This technique is used for images that appear a bit too "soft." Sharpening makes an image appear sharper.

1. **Select the left image.**
   This image is a bit dark, so you lighten it in the next steps.

2. **In the Property inspector, click the Brightness/Contrast icon.**

3. **Click OK in the Warning dialog box.**

4. **Drag the Brightness slider to the right, or type a value.**
   I used 10.

5. **Drag the Contrast slider to the right, or type a value.**
   I used 5.

6. **Click OK when you are satisfied.**
   If you leave the Preview option selected, you see the changes to the image before clicking OK.

< N O T E >

If you type a value, press the Tab key to move away from the text box—or to see the change. Don't press Enter (Return); this accepts the change and closes the dialog box.

7. **Select the right image.**

8. **Click the Sharpen icon.**

9. **Click OK to close the Warning dialog box.**

10. **Move the slider until the image looks good to you.**
    I used 4.

11. **Experiment with the slider. Move it all the way over, and notice how bad the image looks.**

12. **Click OK to close the Sharpen dialog box when you get it the way you want it.**

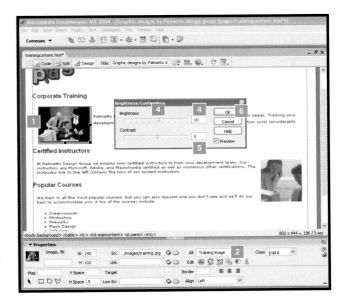

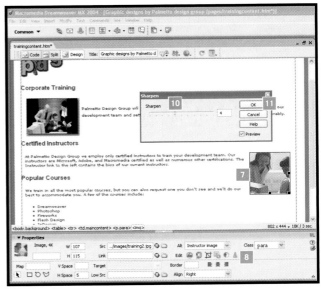

Tutorial
» Using External Image Editors

In this tutorial, you set up the graphics editor of your choice (Fireworks MX 2004 best integrates with Dreamweaver) to open and edit images from within Dreamweaver. The tutorials in this session assume that you installed Fireworks MX 2004 (a trial version is on the CD-ROM). If you installed the Macromedia Studio MX 2004, the steps in this tutorial are done in the installation process, so you can skip to the next tutorial.

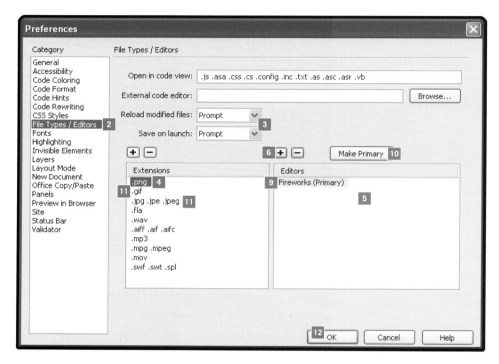

1. **Click Edit→Preferences.**

2. **Click the File Types/Editors category.**
   The bottom portion, where you see the extensions, is the part you're interested in right now.

3. **Reset the Reload Modified Files if you want to.**
   I prefer to be prompted, so I leave the default of Prompt. Do the same for Save on Launch.

4. **Click the** `.PNG` **extension in the Extension area.**

5. **If any editors are specified for this file type, they appear in the Editors section.**
   If Fireworks is already there, you can skip to Step 12.

6. **Click the plus sign (+) if no editor is present or if you want to add one.**
   For example, you can add Photoshop as an editor. But in order for it to open from Dreamweaver, you need to make it the Primary editor for a specific file type.

7. **Navigate to the application folder for Fireworks MX 2004 (or the editor of your choice), and select the executable file.**

8. **Click Open.**

9. **Select Fireworks MX 2004 in the Editors section.**

10. **Click the Make Primary button.**
    If only one editor is listed, it is Primary by default.

11. **Repeat these steps for the** `.GIF` **and** `.JPG` **extensions.**

12. **Click OK to close the Preferences dialog box.**

Tutorial

» Optimizing Images in Fireworks

If you want to optimize an image, you can access the Fireworks Optimize dialog box from Dreamweaver. You have lots of options available to reduce the size of your image. You can reduce the colors, change the file format, and crop and/or scale the image. An animation tab is available for editing frames.

1. **Open the** `trainingcontent.html` **file if you closed it.**

2. **Select the top-left image.**

3. **In the Property inspector, click the Optimize in Fireworks icon.**

4. **Click Use This File.**

   Usually, if you have the Fireworks\source file used for the image, you would click Use a PNG. But often, you may not have the source file, especially if it was created with another program.

Avoid editing a JPEG if you can. It recompresses each time, loosing quality with each compression.

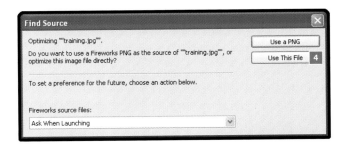

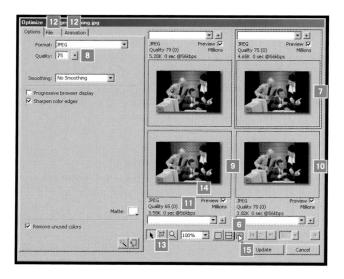

5. **Take a moment to check out all the options available in the Optimize dialog box.**

6. **Click the 4 Preview Windows icon.**
   This displays four previews in which you can set different optimization settings for comparison.

7. **Select the top-right image.**

8. **On the left side, leave the format as JPEG, but change the quality to** 60.
   You can change the format if you want to see how a GIF compares to a JPEG.

9. **Select the bottom-left image, and change the quality to** 65.

10. **Select the bottom-right image, and change the quality to** 70.

11. **Notice each of the preview windows. You see the quality setting and the file size, along with the preview. Decide which one is acceptable, and select it.**
    I selected the bottom-left one, with the quality at 65.

12. **Click on the Files tab, and look at what's available. Look at the Animation tab as well.**

13. **Select the Crop icon.**
    You'll see dotted lines around the image.

14. **Drag the right and bottom lines to remove the shadow.**
    The shadow was added on a blue background and doesn't look good on the white one.

15. **Click the Update button.**

16. **Click on the image and notice that the image has been altered automatically in Dreamweaver.**
    Your file in the images folder has also been altered.

Tutorial

» Editing a Source Image in Fireworks from Dreamweaver

In this tutorial, you see how you can edit the Fireworks PNG file that you used to create an image. Using this method is the most powerful because you can make changes to the original. This is especially important when editing JPEGs because each time you edit a JPEG directly, as we did in the preceding tutorial, it gets compressed again. If you do that too many times, the quality really goes down. But if your original is a vector such as the one used for the logo, you can easily alter color or even the text. It's important to always keep your source files handy.

1. **Select the logo in the** `trainingcontent.html` **page.**

2. **Click the Edit icon.**
   If you set up another image editor, it opens instead of Fireworks.

3. **Click the Use a PNG option.**
   If you haven't moved files around since you exported an image, clicking this option automatically opens to the correct source files. This is the information stored in the notes folders that you see added by Dreamweaver. Because this sample folder has been moved, you need to locate the source image.

4. **Navigate to** `Editing/source/framelogo.png`, **select the file, and open it.**

5. **Notice that it says Editing from Dreamweaver.**

6. **Also notice that all the layers are intact.**

7. **Also note the Optimize panel displaying all the current settings.**

8. **Click in the Matte box, and select white.**

9. **Click the Preview tab to see the changes.**
   White pixels are added around the letters instead of the blue pixels that were there.

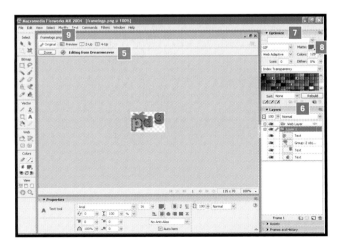

> **213**

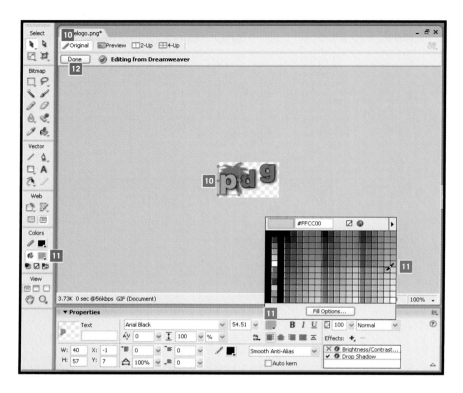

10. **Click the Original tab again, and select the P.**

11. **Click the color box for the fill (in the Property inspector or Tools panel), and select gold.**

12. **Click Done.**
When you click Done, the file is automatically exported using your new changes, and the GIF or JPEG image is replaced in Dreamweaver. The PNG file is also saved.

<NOTE>
A really cool feature is that if you change the format of an image—for example, a JPEG to a GIF—you are prompted to update all references in your site of that image. When you click OK to the prompt, all instances of the image are updated.

13. **In Dreamweaver, you see that the logo color for the P has been changed and the blue fringe is gone.**

14. **Select the left image, and click the Edit icon (the yellow icon with the Fireworks logo) in the Property inspector.**

15. **Select Use this file.**

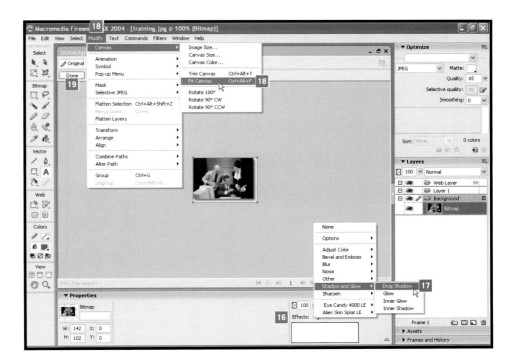

16. **In Fireworks, click the plus sign (+) for Effects in the Property inspector.**

17. **Select Shadow and Glow→Drop Shadow, and accept the default. Press Enter (Return).**
    You won't see any change in the document because the shadow falls outside the current image size.

18. **Choose Modify→Canvas→Fit Canvas.**
    This type of modification actually increases the size of the canvas to fit the additional shadow you added.

19. **Click Done.**

20. **Repeat Steps 13 through 19 for the remaining photo.**

21. **In Dreamweaver, notice that the shadows have been added to both images.**

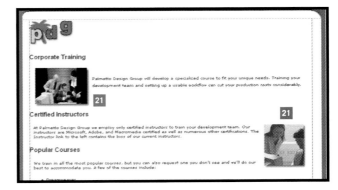

» Session Review

Answer the questions below to review the information in this session. The answer to each question can be found in the tutorial noted in parentheses.

1. Must you have Fireworks installed to crop an image from Dreamweaver? (See "Tutorial: Cropping Images in Dreamweaver.")

2. Must you define a new site to use the supplied Editing folder for this session? (See "Tutorial: Cropping Images in Dreamweaver.")

3. Why should you keep backup copies of your images? (See "Tutorial: Cropping Images in Dreamweaver.")

4. What do you need to do before the Resample icon becomes available for use? (See "Tutorial: Resampling an Image.")

5. What does Resample do? (See "Tutorial: Resampling an Image.")

6. What do you need to do to preview a change if you've typed in the value for Brightness/Contrast instead of using the slider? (See "Tutorial: Adding Brightness, Contrast, and Sharpening in Dreamweaver.")

7. What does Sharpen do? (See "Tutorial: Adding Brightness, Contrast, and Sharpening in Dreamweaver.")

8. How do you set up Dreamweaver to use various image editors? (See "Tutorial: Using External Image Editors.")

9. Do you need Fireworks installed to use the Optimize Images in Fireworks feature? (See "Tutorial: Optimizing Images in Fireworks.")

10. Do you have to re-export an image after you've made changes to it? (See "Tutorial: Editing a Source Image in Fireworks from Dreamweaver.")

Corporate Training

Palmetto Design Group will develop a specialized course to fit your unique needs. Training your development team and setting up a usable workflow can cut your production costs considerably.

Certified Instructors

At Palmetto Design Group we employ only certified instructors to train your development team. Our instructors are Microsoft, Adobe, and Macromedia certified as well as numerous other certifications. The Instructor link to the left contains the bios of our current instructors.

Popular Courses

We train in all the most popular courses, but you can also request one you don't see and we'll do our best to accommodate you. A few of the courses include:

- Dreamweaver
- Photoshop
- Fireworks
- Flash Design
- InDesign
- GoLive
- Authorware
- After Effects
- Illustrator

Performing Site Checks

Tutorial: **Running a Site Report for Links**

Tutorial: **Checking Site Reports**

Tutorial: **Using Find and Replace**

Tutorial: **Doing Browser Checks**

Session Introduction

You don't really need to replace anything in the site that you are developing for this course, but the Find and Replace function is a powerful tool that you'll find is indispensable when you have to edit a site. It's inevitable—a client changes his or her mind. You may need to change the name of something, or you may discover a word that was misspelled—or worse, someone's name is incorrect. These things are extremely easy to fix, whether the error occurs on one page or throughout an entire site. But you can also search for tags or for text inside tags; you can use wildcards and develop some pretty complex searches. In this session, you learn how to add a style sheet link to an entire site that currently has no style sheets.

In this session, you also discover some of the site reports that are available in Dreamweaver. You can check for accessibility compliance, alt tags, broken links, and much more.

TOOLS YOU'LL USE
Results panel group, Find and Replace function, Browser check

MATERIALS NEEDED
session11_starterfiles if needed

TIME REQUIRED
45 minutes

Tutorial

» Running a Site Report for Links

In this tutorial, you run a site report for checking broken links in the PDG template as well as for checking the external links site-wide.

1. **Open the DWCC site in the Site panel.**

2. **Double-click the** pdg.dwt **file in the Templates folder.**
   Because all the site's pages are based on the template, you must run several site reports on this page.

3. **Open the Results panel by choosing Window→Results.**
   Notice that the Results panel docks itself below the Property inspector. The Results panel has seven category tabs. Each category has additional options.

4. **Click on the Link Checker tab.**

5. **In the Show drop-down menu, select Broken Links.**

6. **Look in the white field for the report results.**
   In this case, the area is blank because none of the links are broken on this particular page. Now you can check the entire site.

7. **In the Show drop-down menu, select External Links.**
   Again, you should get no results. You can't check orphaned yet because you are currently checking only one file. An orphaned file is one that is not associated with any other files.

8. **Click the arrow near the green arrow icon.**

9. **Click Check Links For Entire Site.**
   What you see may vary from what I get. You may have made different mistakes than I did. Yes, I make mistakes too; we all do. That's what is so nice about tools like the link checker—it'll help us out.

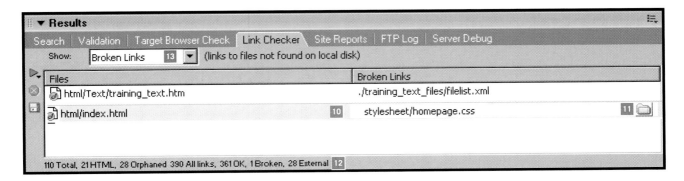

10. **To see the broken link in the page, double-click the file name.**
    This opens the page in the document window with the broken link highlighted in the code.

11. **Now to fix the broken link, click on the entry in the Broken Link section.**
    The name opens for editing. You can either type in the correction or click the yellow folder to navigate to the correct link location. This works for the Library broken link (which should point to the hompage.css file in the stylesheet folder). But the training_text link doesn't exist, so it can't be fixed.

<NOTE>
If you've made any changes, and if that same change is needed in multiple documents, a dialog box opens asking if you want to update all instances of the broken link. Click Yes.

12. **Look along the bottom of the Results panel group.**
    You can see the statistics of the site. Notice that Dreamweaver found 28 orphaned links. This means that these 28 items are not linked to anything.

13. **Click the arrow for the Show field, and then click Orphaned Files.**
    You don't have to be too concerned about the orphaned files; just check and make sure they aren't supposed to be linking to anything. You can double-click any of the icons for the files and see what they are. Some of the orphaned files are for the text files I provided for you to copy and paste. The extra background images that I included in the background folder show up as orphans, as well as the forms we made in Session 9.

Tutorial
» Checking Site Reports

In this tutorial, you run a few site reports for the Palmetto Design Group.

1. **Click the Site Reports category tab in the Results panel.**

2. **Click the green arrow.**
   The Reports dialog box opens.

3. **Click the Report On field arrow, and select Entire Current Local Site.**

4. **Click Untitled Documents to select it.**
   Seeing Untitled Document in a browser's title bar is very annoying. Run this check to assure that you didn't miss naming any of your pages.

5. **Click Run.**

6. **Double-click on an item in the report with no title.**
   The page opens.

7. **The Property inspector is open with the Title field displayed; enter a title and save the page.**

8. **Repeat Step 7 for all pages without a title except for the library item. Do *not* give this a page title.**

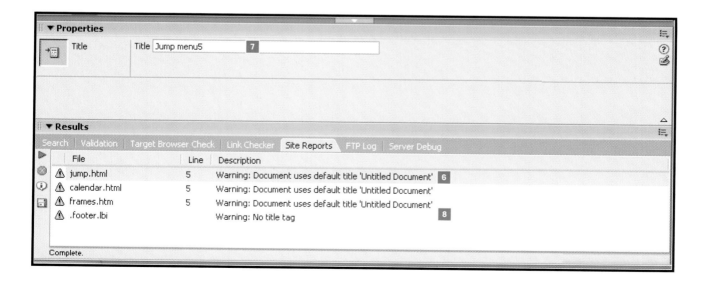

9. **Click the green arrow again to run a new report.**

10. **This time, click Missing Alt Text.**

11. **Click Run.**

    Line 37 on several files is in the head of the document and
    not an image, so disregard that one. But if you find a missing
    alt tag, do Step 12.

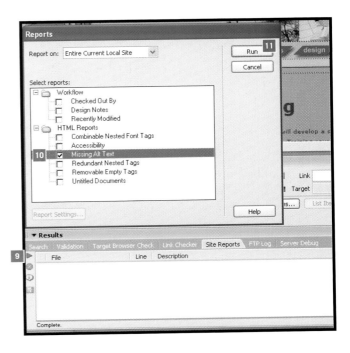

12. **Double-click any file that has a missing alt tag. The code shows
    up, but so does the Property inspector. Add the alt text.**

    For example, I had one missing alt tag in training.html.
    It was a missing alt tag for a spacer image. To fix this, select
    <empty> from the alt field drop-down menu in the Property
    inspector. The highlighted code helps you locate the image
    with the missing alt tag. You may need to select it in the docu-
    ment, and then add the alt text in the Property inspector.

13. **Fix any other missing tags.**

    Your missing tags will most likely vary from mine.

<NOTE>

Clicking on line 44 in the pdg.dwt code selects all four of the
images in the cell. You'll need to check each image for the missing
alt tag. Only one is missing for the palm trees in the pdg.dwt
template file and a missing <empty> alt tag for a spacer.gif.

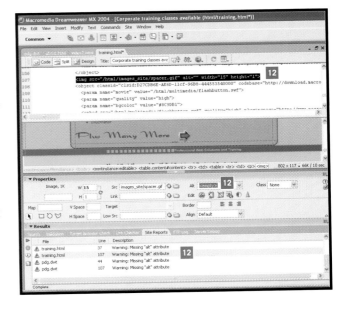

<NOTE>

If you've made changes to the template page, you are asked if you want to update. Click Update.

14. **Continue running different checks if you desire.**

    Most of the options, such as Redundant Nested Tags and Removable Empty Tags, all return no errors because we let Dreamweaver do the coding. These options come in handy when checking your own coding.

15. **Save and close all open pages.**

16. **Click the Results Options pop-up menu, and then click Close the Results panel.**

Accessibility Tests

I didn't have you run the Accessibility test because all kinds of things are shown. Although we added blank Alt text values for the spacer images, the Dreamweaver accessibility test results show them all. Another issue that appears in the Dreamweaver report is all the tables. A more effective way to test for accessibility is to use the full version of the program named Lift (www.usablenet.com). This program gives you all kinds of options to customize the checks such as how to handle your tables and other nonvital images. With Lift, you can also fix each error as it is discovered. If you need to make a totally accessible site, you should definitely read up on the issues involved. The Alt text we've been using is one major part of the accessibility guidelines, but lots of other issues exist as well.

Tutorial
» Using Find and Replace

In this tutorial, you learn how to use the Find and Replace function. You don't really have anything to replace, but this is a tool that you will need to use in the future, and it's important to understand how powerful it really is.

1. **Double-click the** `training.html` **page to open it.**

2. **Highlight the words Palmetto Design Group in the first paragraph.**
   When you highlight words prior to searching for them, they appear in the Search field. A selection is not required, however.

3. **Click Edit→Find and Replace.**
   The Find and Replace dialog box opens. The highlighted text appears in the text field. If you were going to make a change to the company name, you would type it in the Replace box.

4. **Click the arrow for the Find In field, and select one of the options.**
   Notice that you can search the current document, the entire site, a specified folder, and specified files.

5. **Look at the Search field.**
   You can search the code, text, text (advanced), or for a specific tag. In this example, you are searching text.

6. **If you are looking for specific words with capitalization, check the Match Case option.**
   It's a good idea to leave the Ignore Whitespace option checked. This option looks for a phrase without regard to spacing differences.

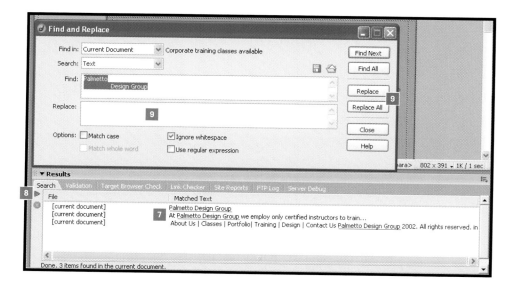

<NOTE>
This dialog box is different from most of the Dreamweaver windows because it stays open while you continue working. Most dialog boxes must be closed to continue working.

<NOTE>
Regular expressions (a list can be found in the Dreamweaver Help) are useful in performing wildcard searches and are more flexible than searching for exact strings.

7. **Click the Find All button.**
   The Results panel group now displays the results of the search. You can double-click each entry to check them if you like.

8. **Click the green arrow to open the Find and Replace dialog box again.**

9. **You would fill in the Replace field and click either Replace or Replace All if you were actually changing this text.**
   You can either close the dialog box now or leave it open for the next tutorial.

Saving Queries

You can develop some pretty complex queries using wildcards with the Find and Replace function and using regular expressions. If you find yourself reusing functions consistently, you can save them by clicking the disk icon in the Find and Replace dialog box.

The settings are saved with a . DWR file extension. You can reuse a saved query by clicking the yellow folder to the left of the disk icon. Just navigate to the location and open the file.

Tutorial
» Doing Browser Checks

You can either do browser checks from the Results panel or keep an eye on them as you develop your site. I haven't paid much attention to them up to this point. Most of the errors in this site are related to Netscape 4. They aren't errors so much as they are incompatibilities. A word of caution—the Dreamweaver browser checks tell you what is or isn't compatible with specific browsers, but they are not necessarily "standards compliant." This means that you may code something to standards, but an error is still shown in Dreamweaver because a particular browser may not recognize the standard.

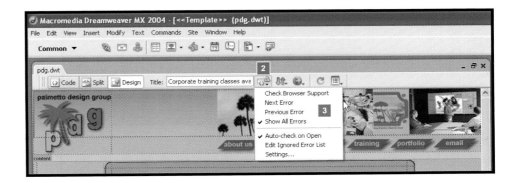

1. **Open the pdg.dwt template file.**

2. **In the Document toolbar, click the Browser icon. (It has a yellow caution image on it.)**
   Notice the various options.

3. **Select Show all errors, if it isn't already selected.**
   The errors are displayed in the Results panel. Take a look at them. Notice that it is primarily Netscape-related.

4. **Click the Browser icon again, but this time select Settings.**

5. **Uncheck Netscape because they have discontinued making new versions at this point.**

6. **Click the down arrow for Internet Explorer, and select 6.0.**

7. **Click OK.**
   Notice that most of the errors are not really errors; rather, they are instances of Internet Explorer not supporting a specific attribute.

<NOTE>
If you happen to be good at coding, you can customize your error report by clicking the Browser icon and selecting Edit ignored error list option. The exception.xml file opens so you can add your own exceptions. But this feature is far more advanced than the scope of this book.

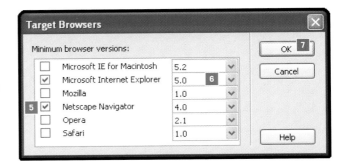

» Session Review

I know that you didn't have many things to fix in this site, but hopefully some of the site reports available to you make more sense now. Test yourself now to see how much you can recall. The answer to each question is in the tutorial or discussion noted in parentheses.

1. How do you access the various reports that you can run? (See "Tutorial: Running a Site Report for Links.")

2. How do you view the results of various reports? (See "Tutorial: Running a Site Report for Links.")

3. What is the full-featured program called that is recommended for those who are serious about accessibility issues? (See "Tutorial: Checking Site Reports.")

4. What is unique about the Find and Replace dialog box? (See "Tutorial: Using Find and Replace.")

5. Name two things for which you can search. (See "Tutorial: Using Find and Replace.")

6. Can you reuse queries that you have developed? (See "Tutorial: Using Find and Replace.")

7. How do you change which browsers are included in the browser check? (See "Tutorial: Doing Browser Checks.")

Getting Your Web Site Online

Discussion: **Finding a Host**

Tutorial: **Setting FTP Preferences**

Tutorial: **FTPing Files to Your Host**

Tutorial: **Synchronizing the Local and Root Folders**

Session Introduction

In this session, you upload your site to a Web server using FTP, which stands for *File Transfer Protocol*. This is how you get your completed site from your computer to the Internet. Prior to uploading your files, you need to get a domain name if you want one and a hosting service or an Internet Service Provider (ISP), which rents space on a computer.

In order to complete this session, you need space on a Web server, or you can use a free service to practice with until you are ready to secure your own domain name and server space.

TOOLS YOU'LL USE
Files panel, Put files, Synchronize

MATERIALS NEEDED
session12_starterfiles if needed

TIME REQUIRED
60 minutes

Discussion

Finding a Host

This discussion is a bit different. I can't really take you through all the steps of setting up a hosting account, but I can list some of the things you should think about before purchasing space on a Web server.

1. **Do you need or want a domain name? Do you want a unique Web address?**
   If so, you have to register a domain name.

2. **Register the name you want (or the closest that is available).**
   Notice that Nexpoint is offering a free domain name with their service.

3. **Do you need a database? If so, what type?**
   If you use ASP, ColdFusion, PHP, or other technologies, be sure that the hosting service you are considering supports that technology.

4. **What kind of support is available?**
   If you are experienced, online help may be enough. If you are new to the game, talking to a live person makes it much easier to set up your first site, especially when a database is involved.

5. **Is support free? Is there a toll-free number?**
    I'd recommend asking a few questions and then sitting back to see how long it takes for a response. If it takes too long prior to ordering a service to get a response, imagine how long it may take after the provider gets your money. Also, by checking up on service ahead of time, you can discover if the provider communicates in a way that you understand.

Registering a Domain

You can register a domain name in many places. Some time ago, you had to register through Network Solutions, but now many other companies offer the same service, often for less money. The hosting services that offer domain registration would like for you to also use their hosting services, but many don't require that you do so. In fact, the ones I've used have very reasonable registration fees and allow you to park the domain name, which means that you can register the name but not use it, and the hosting company doesn't charge you. Parking is free until you are ready to move the domain to a Web server of your choice. You can normally register names for about $15. Crystaltech offers $10 domain registration when you sign up with them for hosting. After you decide on your hosting service, transferring your domain name is pretty easy. Often, the hosting service does it for you. If not, the host supplies you with the information you need to make the transfer. If this part is scary to you or causes you some trepidation, ask your potential host if this service is provided.

6. **How much bandwidth is included with the service?**

   Some servers have no limitations on bandwidth—the amount of data transfer—and others do. Quite often, you get a limit on bandwidth and then pay an additional fee for extra usage.

7. **How much space are you allowed on the server: 10, 20, 50MB? More or less?**

   Often, this is a very large determining factor when choosing a hosting service. If you have very little space requirements, then your options at a reasonable price are vast. If you require a great deal of space, the price of hosting usually increases dramatically. Things that will add to your bandwidth are large databases, large graphics or files available for download.

8. **Carefully compare the different service plans of several hosting services.**

   On the CD-ROM is a page with links; there are several services listed there. Nexpoint is my favorite low cost service but Chrystaltech is my all time favorite for larger sites needing more resources. It's my favorite because of superb customer service and the control panel on the site that I can set up my own DSN name, email aliases, special ftp accounts, etc.

9. **Are Web statistics included?**

   Sometimes, the site stats are available at no additional charge, and sometimes, a fee is charged. The statistics can help you determine which browsers people use to view your site, which pages are mostly frequently visited, which entry pages are being used the most (how people are accessing your site), and many other statistics. Armed with this information, you can tweak your site to best serve your audience.

10. **Do you need a shopping cart? Does the server provide one? What is the cost?**

    If your site sells merchandise and/or needs to be secure, you'll want to have a shopping cart.

11. **How many e-mail accounts are included?**

12. **How do you manage your site? Is it easy to upload and make changes? How do you set up your e-mail, forwarding, auto responders, and the like?**

13. **Do you have access to a CGI-BIN folder for online forms?**

Tutorial
» Setting FTP Preferences

In this tutorial, you'll set up the DWCC site to send the files to a remote server. You can follow along if you have a hosting server or use this tutorial as a reference when you do get one.

1. Click the Files panel to make it active.

2. From the Site drop-down menu, select Manage Sites.

3. Click the site that you defined for this course (DWCC), and then click the Edit button.

4. Select the Advanced tab if it isn't already selected, and click the Local Info category.

5. Type your domain name or Web address in the HTTP Address field. I typed http://www.palmettodesigngroup.com.

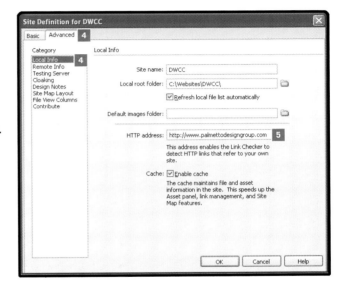

Choosing a Hosting Service

You must consider many determining factors when purchasing server space. For example, the server I chose cost me a bit more, but I worked with this company previously and I'm comfortable with the customer service. Not only can I speak with a real person, but a toll-free number is also available. I think these two things alone more than justify the extra dollars I spend compared to my second choice. You need to take the time to determine what your needs are and what your budget is, and then you can look around for a service that meets your needs.

Free hosting services are also available. These are great for personal sites or for beginners to use as a testing platform. Normally, you can't have your own domain name with a free service, and you usually have to put up with banner ads. You have to determine what you are willing to sacrifice in order to get free space. Please be aware that if you plan on using a free service to host a business site, you may lose a great deal of credibility with potential clients.

Your ISP (the service you use for dial-up accounts) often gives you a small amount of space for a small Web site. You won't be able to use a domain name, but it is a great way to practice or to host a personal site.

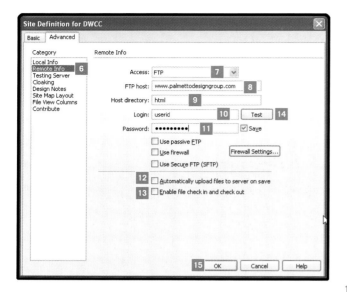

6. **Click the Remote Info category.**

7. **Click the down arrow in the Access field, and click FTP if you are using a dial-up connection.**
   If you are using a network cable, choose Local/Network Server Access. After you click the Access drop-down menu, you can see that there are various other options for transferring your files. You may need to ask your Network Administrator how to upload to a network server.

8. **Type the FTP Host information.**
   You may need to type the IP address numbers or the host name. Check with your host to determine what is required.

9. **If you are FTPing to a specific directory, type that directory into the Host Directory field as well.**
   Again, your hosting service should give you this information. For example, for one host, I have to put my site inside a directory called Public; for another host, I put my files into a directory called httpdocs.

10. **Enter your login name.**
    This is the user name that your hosting service gives you.

11. **Enter your password.**
    Whether you need to check the Use Passive FTP, Use Firewall, or Use SSH encrypted options depends on your server and/or your personal security settings. These are unchecked by default.

12. **Click Automatically upload files to server on save if you want to utilize this feature.**
    If you make lots of changes or save frequently, you may not want to use this feature.

13. **Click Enable File Check In and Check Out if you are working with others who will use the same files.**

14. **Click the Test button to see whether you can connect to the server.**

15. **Click OK, and then click Done to close the Edit Sites dialog box.**

Tutorial
» FTPing Files to Your Host

Now you upload your files to a server. You must either have a Web host or have acquired one of the free services to continue with this session. I've used my host for the figures in this tutorial (of course, I don't use my real FTP information). You, on the other hand, must send your files via FTP from within Dreamweaver. You will be sending the entire site via FTP.

1. **Open the Files panel, and right-click (Ctrl+click) the forms folder.**

2. **Pass your mouse over Cloaking, and select Cloak.**
   This cloaks the folder from being uploaded.

3. **Repeat Steps 1 and 2 for the Library, source, and Templates folders.**
   A message opens for the Library and Templates folders letting you know that cloaking will not hinder any batch operations you want to perform on the folders.

4. **In the Files panel, be sure that the site you want to upload is selected and that you have an Internet connection.**
   Notice that the field next to the site name says Local view. These are the files as seen on your computer.

5. **Select your root folder.**

6. **Click the Connects to Remote Host button.**

7. **Click Put Files.**

8. **Click OK in the dialog box that opens asking you if you are sure you want to put the entire site.**
   Now you just wait for the transfer of files to finish.

9. **Click the Expand/Collapse icon to see the remote and local sites.**
   You have just made an exact mirror of your local site to the remote server. By having a mirror, you can easily manage your site and any changes to it. Although the files on the remote server are the same, they are not in the same order.

10. **Choose Site→Synchronize Files.**

11. **Select Entire "DWCC" Site from the Synchronize drop-down menu.**
    Notice the options in the Direction field. You can choose to just upload newer files, or you can also choose to delete files from the remote server if they aren't present in the local folder.

12. **Click Preview.**
    A dialog box says that no synchronization is necessary. No files have been replaced, but the folders and files now are in the same order as your local view. The remote server is now laid out the same as the local site. What happens if you make changes to the local folder? Let's move some things around and see.

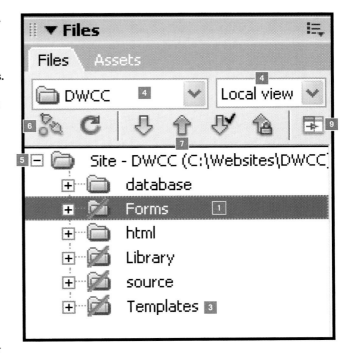

Tutorial

» Synchronizing the Local and Root Folders

In this tutorial, you learn how you can make changes to your local site and then automatically make the same changes to the remote server.

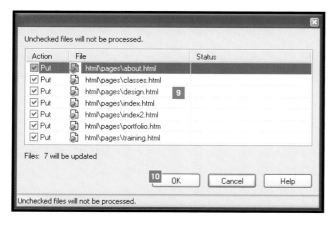

1. Click the Expand/Collapse icon if the Site panel isn't open to view the Remote and Local views.

2. Right-click the root folder, and click New Folder (Local View).

3. Name the folder Pages.

4. Click and drag all the .html files, and drop them into the Pages folder.

5. Click Update to update all the files and their links.

6. Click the Reconnect button if you've lost your connection.

7. Choose Site→Synchronize, and click the entire site.

8. Click the Delete remote files not on local drive option to select it.

This deletes the .html files after they are placed in the Pages folder.

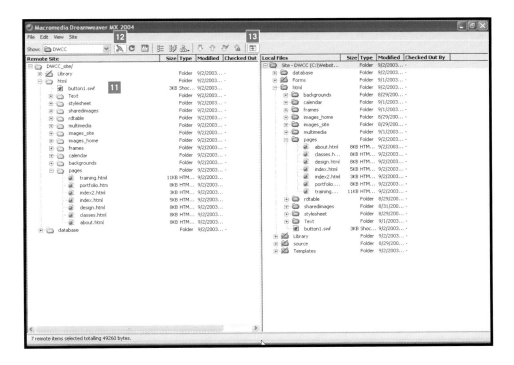

9. **Check the report that opens. Leave everything checked.**

   You could uncheck anything you didn't want to upload, but in this case, you want to upload everything that changed as a result of moving pages into a folder.

10. **Click OK.**

11. **When it's finished synchronizing, you can choose to save a log and/or click Close when you are done.**

   Notice that the Remote site folder now looks just like the Local view folder with the Pages folder and all the .html pages inside.

12. **Click the Disconnect from Remote Host icon.**

13. **Click the Expand/Collapse icon to return to the workspace.**

14. **Double-click training.html to open it.**

   Notice that all the images are still intact, even though the file moved. That's because Dreamweaver updated all the links to images when you moved them. If you did this outside your root folder, all the image links would be broken.

» Session Review

If you have an Internet connection and a hosting service, this session was a breeze for you. Test yourself to see how many of the powerful FTP features of Dreamweaver you can recall. The answer to each question is in the tutorial or discussion noted in parentheses.

1. What must you do if you want a unique Web address? (See "Discussion: Finding a Host.")

2. Name three important things to consider when looking for a hosting service. (See "Discussion: Finding a Host.")

3. What is one drawback to a free hosting service? (See "Discussion: Finding a Host.")

4. Can you transfer files from your computer to a remote server by any means other than FTP? (See "Tutorial: Setting FTP Preferences.")

5. How do you get the information you need (such as FTP host, directory, and so on) when setting up FTP access? (See "Tutorial: Setting FTP Preferences.")

6. Can you automatically upload any new files that you've added to the local directory? (See "Tutorial: Setting FTP Preferences.")

7. Do you need a separate FTP program to transfer your site files to a remote host? (See "Tutorial: Setting FTP Preferences.")

8. What does cloaking do? (See "Tutorial: FTPing Files to Your Host.")

9. Can you make changes to the local directory and have those changes reflected in the remote directory? If so, how? (See "Tutorial: Synchronizing the Local and Root Folders.")

NEXPOINT TECHNOLOGIES

ABOUT US   PRODUCTS & SERVICES   CUSTOMER CARE   CONTACT US   SIGN UP NOW!

domain search

```
[              ]
            GO!
```

control panel

username:
```
[              ]
```
password:
```
[              ]
```
COMING SOON!

news & events

Aug 04, 2003:
Nexpoint Technologies awarded "Top 15" and ranked 12th as a Global Leader in Web Hosting!

Aug 01, 2003:
Windows 2003, Plesk 6, Ensim Pro debut as dedicated server solutions!

driving the web **further.**

NEXPOINT provides shared, dedicated and managed web services for dynamic solutions that will separate your business from the rest of the pack. State-of-the-art technology, reliability that you can trust, and a heavy accent on technical support will help take your venture to the next point.

2000 SPECIAL

- 500 MB Storage
- Unmetered Bandwidth
- Unlimited Email Accts
- Frontpage, ASP & More
- Free Domain Name!

More Info ->

$99/YEAR

ASP.NET SPECIAL

- 500 MB Storage
- Unmetered Bandwidth
- Unlimited Email Accts
- Frontpage, ASP .NET &
- Free Domain Name!

More Info ->

$12/MONTH

$99 DEDICATED

- Intel 1.2Ghz Processor
- 256 MB RAM
- 60GB 7.2K IDE Drive
- Unlimited Domains
- 100GB Data Transfer

More Info ->

$99/MONTH

Part V:
Working with
a Data Source

Session 13 **Setting Up a Database Connection**

Session 14 **Building a Web Application**

Setting Up a Database Connection

Tutorial: **Installing a Personal Web Server (Windows 98)**

Tutorial: **Installing IIS**

Tutorial: **Defining a Dynamic Web Site**

Tutorial: **Setting Up a DSN Name**

Tutorial: **Setting Up a Local DSN Connection**

Tutorial: **Setting Up a Remote DSN Connection**

Tutorial: **Setting Up a Connection String (DSN-less)**

Tutorial: **Using the MapPath Method**

Session Introduction

A good Web site is one that provides meaningful and current content with a minimum of effort. However, updating a site on a daily basis just isn't feasible. In this project, you learn to build a small Web application with pages that support a database designed to collect and store contact information from the Palmetto Design Group Web site.

A Web application is a collection of static and dynamic pages. Static pages contain fixed content and are served up without change when requested by visitors. A dynamic page contains partly or entirely undefined content. When the page is requested from the Web server, final content based on the visitor's actions is added.

Web applications can be used to collect, save, and analyze data, provide search functionality for page or site content, and/or dynamically update the content of a page.

This session walks you through the process of setting up your site and creating a connection to the contact database. This Web application is an intranet site for Palmetto Design Group.

TOOLS YOU'LL USE
Site panel, Application panel group, Databases panel

MATERIALS NEEDED
The DatabaseChapter folder from the CD-ROM. Copy this to your hard drive, but not in your DWCC folder.

Web server software, PC with Microsoft PWS (Personal Web Server) or IIS Internet Information Services or a Web hosting service with database and ASP (Active Server Pages) 2.0 support. Windows XP Home can't use any Web server software, so you'll need a Web connection.

If you use an online service, you need an active Web connection.

TIME REQUIRED
90 minutes

Tutorial
» Installing a Personal Web Server (Windows 98)

In this tutorial, Windows 98 users install Microsoft Personal Web Server (PWS, a scaled-down version of IIS), which runs on Windows 98 and NT Workstation, if it isn't already installed. This is not the same as the Personal Web Server that ships with FrontPage.

To make dynamic pages, you must have a Web server and some sort of application server. To develop ASP pages, you need an application server that supports Microsoft Active Server Pages 2.0. Microsoft PWS runs on Windows 98 and NT Workstation; IIS runs on Windows 2000 and Windows XP.

Sun Chili!Soft ASP may be used on Windows, Linux, and Solaris platforms. Macintosh users should use a Web hosting service with ASP 2.0 support or should install IIS or PWS on a remote (Windows) computer. Macintosh users must (and Windows users may) use a Web hosting solution. Look for a company that supports ASP 2.0 and Access database.

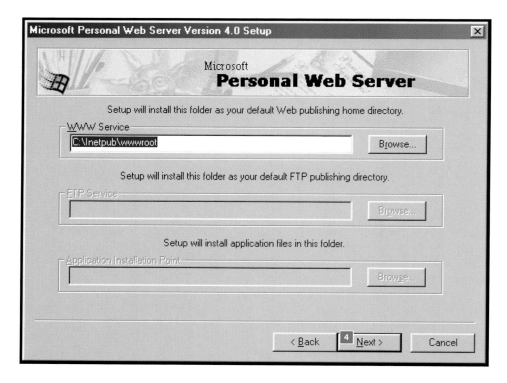

1. **Check your C and/or D drives to see whether you can find an Inetpub folder.**
   If not, you need to install PWS or IIS, or opt to use a hosting service.

2. **Double-click the PWS installation file on the Windows 98 CD. Or double-click the file downloaded from the Microsoft Web site.**

3. **Follow the installation wizard directions.**

4. **When asked for the default Web publishing home directory, accept the default C:\Inetpub\wwwroot.**

5. **Click Finish to end the installation.**

Tutorial
» Installing IIS

In this tutorial, Windows 2000 and Windows XP Professional users install Microsoft IIS, which comes with Windows NT Server, Windows 2000, and Windows XP Professional.

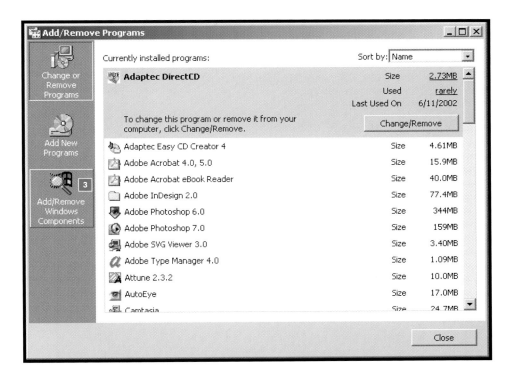

1. **Check your C or D drives to see if you can find an Inetpub folder.**

   If not, you need to install PWS or IIS, or opt to use a hosting service.

2. **In Windows 2000 and Windows XP, choose Start→ Settings→Control Panel→Add/Remove Programs.**

3. **Choose Add/Remove Windows Components.**

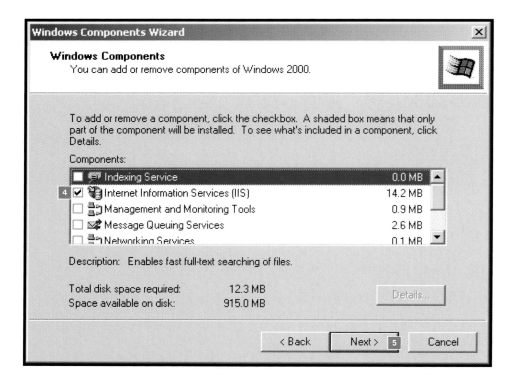

4. **Select the IIS box.**

5. **Click Next.**

6. **Follow the installation steps.**

Dynamic Pages

Dynamic pages require a connection to a Web server and a data source. There are many data source types (ASP, ColdFusion, etc.); which one you use depends upon the nature of the pages that you plan to build. It will also determinte the type of Web server needed to host your pages. The Web server contains special application software that is used to process the scripts contained in a Web page. The software reads the code, and then removes it from the page and passes the page on with the processed results. When users receive the page, all they see is the resulting HTML.

For all this to work, you must first set up the correct information in your Site Definition. Until now, you have worked only with the local information when defining a site. Dynamic pages require a live connection; this means that you must set up the proper access to a Web server with support for your application technology. Because this project uses ASP and an Access database, your local Web server or your provider's Web server must have the latest Microsoft Access Drivers (4.0) and allow a connection to a database.

You need the latest MDAC drivers from Microsoft. You can download MDAC 2.5 and 2.6 for free. Be sure to install 2.5 first, and then 2.6. Windows 2000 with service pack 2 and Windows XP contain the latest drivers.

Tutorial

» Defining a Dynamic Web Site

This step-by-step exercise should have you ready to build a dynamic site in no time! You define a new site for the data-driven portion of the Palmetto Design Group intranet site. To build a Web application, you generally start with HTML and then write server-side scripts or tags to make the page dynamic. The users (visitors) never see the scripts because the Web server processes the code to provide the requested content, which is then sent to the users. The scripting or tags used are based on your choice of server technologies; you have many options. Dreamweaver can work with CFM (ColdFusion), ASP (Active Server Pages), ASP.NET (next generation ASP .NET pages), JSP (Java Server Pages), and PHP (Hypertext Preprocessor) pages. The scope of this chapter does not allow for in-depth discussion of all these solutions. When you decide which server technology you prefer, then look for a book that deals with it specifically such as the ColdFusion Bible for ColdFusion. There are books that deal specifically with ASP.NET and so on.

1. **PC users: Copy and paste the DatabaseChapter folder from the CD-ROM to your hard drive.**

2. **Mac users: Option+drag to copy and paste the folder to your hard drive.**

3. **PC users: If you are testing locally (PWS or IIS), you should also copy the same set of files to C:\Inetpub\wwwroot folder.**

4. **Open Dreamweaver MX 2004, and click Site→Manage Sites→New→Site.**

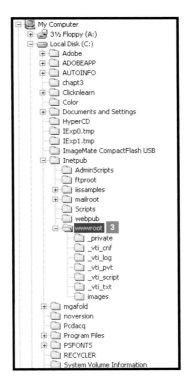

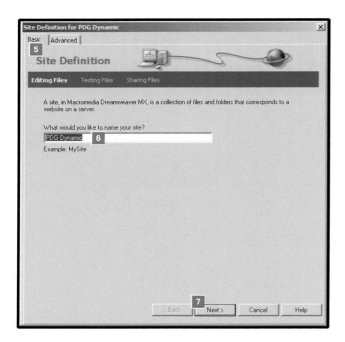

5. **Click the Basic tab.**

6. **Type** PDG Dynamic **for the site name.**

7. **Click the Next button.**
   The Editing Files, Part 2 dialog box opens.

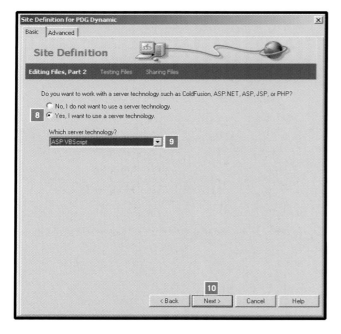

8. **Select the Yes I want to use a server technology option in the Editing Files, Part 2 dialog box.**

9. **Choose ASP VBScript as the server technology.**

10. **Click the Next button.**
    The Editing Files, Part 3 dialog box opens.

    For all Mac users and those PC users testing on a remote machine, skip to Step 22 now.

11. **If you have PWS or IIS, choose Edit and Test Locally.**

<N O T E>

This is your development environment. For those using PWS or IIS, this is a temporary testing location. For Mac users or PC users who prefer to work with a hosted server, this may be either the final location for your files or a special testing folder set up just for development purposes.

12. **Click the folder icon to tell Dreamweaver where you want to store the files on the testing (or application) server.**

13. **Navigate to the location where you saved your DatabaseChapter folder, and select it.**

    You should navigate to the wwwroot folder of inetpub. Open it, and select the DatabaseChapter folder that you copied there.

14. **Click the Next button.**

    The Testing files dialog box opens.

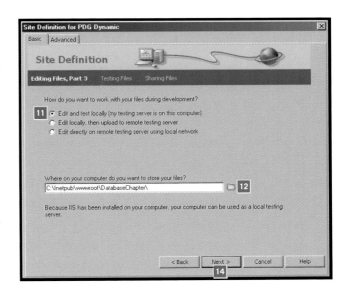

15. **For PC users testing locally, the URL shown in the Testing Files panel should read http://localhost/DatabaseChapter.**

<T I P>

If your computer is on a network with multiple machines, you may need to use the workstation name instead of Localhost.

<N O T E>

For those using a hosted solution, the URL prefix may be set incorrectly by Dreamweaver, because the program appends any directory paths after the host name. In some cases, this may include a folder like wwwroot, which wouldn't be correct for the URL prefix but is correct for FTP. If in doubt, try to think of what the URL would be to get to this site folder using your browser. You may upload to yourdomain.com/wwwroot, but you surf to the site at www.yourdomain.com.

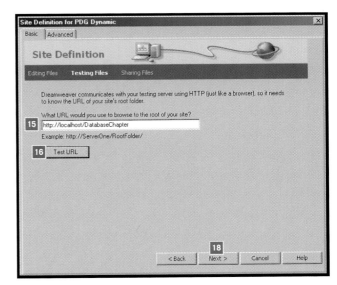

16. **Click the Test URL button to test your connection.**

17. **Click OK on the URL Prefix Test was successful pop-up.**

18. **Click Next.**

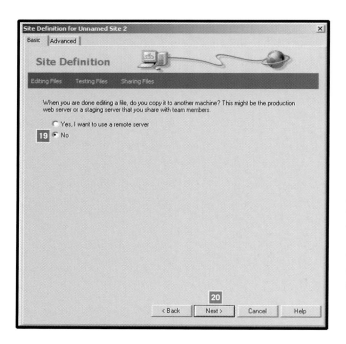

19. Click the **No** radio button option because you are going to test locally only.

<NOTE>

If you are going to be using a remote server, you see how to do the remote settings using the Advanced tab in the "Setting Up a Remote DSN Connection" tutorial.

20. Click the **Next** button.

A Summary dialog box opens showing you the settings that you chose.

<NOTE>

You can access the choices in the Summary dialog box at any time through the Advanced Setup. You should take a look at the various Local, Remote, and Testing categories in the Advanced Setup to familiarize yourself with where all the information you supplied is placed. The Advanced Setup is much faster to use, but more complex, requiring you to understand what goes where.

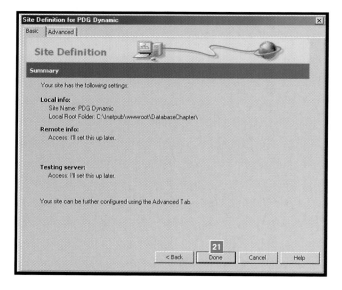

21. Click **Done.**

With your Web and application server setup complete, you are ready to begin working with the pages inside the DatabaseChapter sample folder. Because this session is all about working with a database, you need to set up a connection to that database. Several types of connections are possible, and which you use depends on your setup.

You can now skip to the next tutorial unless you are using a remote server.

22. **This step continues from step 10 for Mac and PC users using a Remote server and FTP to connect. Click Edit directly on remote testing server using FTP or RDS.**

23. **Enter the path to a local file on your computer to which you want to save.**

24. **Uncheck Automatically upload files to my server every time I save. Click Next.**
    You don't have to uncheck this option. I prefer to upload when I'm finished working, but you may prefer to upload automatically.

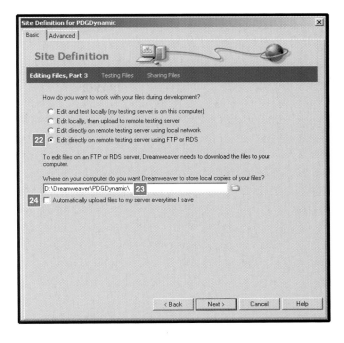

25. **Click FTP in answer to the How do you connect to your testing server? question.**

26. **Enter your domain address.**

27. **Enter the folder to which your database is being uploaded.**
    You might need to get that information from your hosting service. A database is usually kept in a secure location away from the main site.

28. **Enter your username and password. Click the Test Connection button, and then click Next.**
    If you have everything set up properly, the test is successful. If not, check the path to the database.

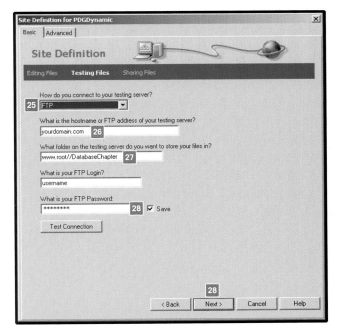

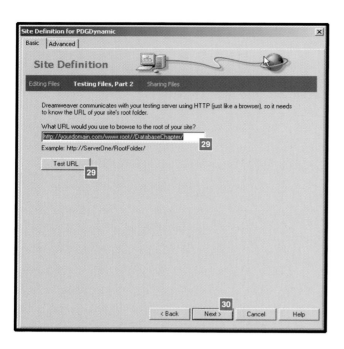

29. **Enter the path to the root of your site, and then click the Test URL button.**

30. **Click Next.**

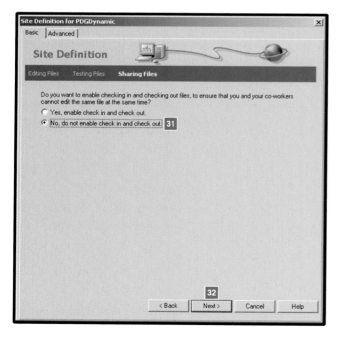

31. **Check the No, do not enable check in and check out option.**
This option depends on how you work, but I'd suggest checking it unless you need it.

32. **Click Next.**
You are now presented with a summary of your options.

33. **Click Done.**
You are now ready to connect to your remote server where your site files will be uploaded to.

Tutorial
» Setting Up a DSN Name

Do this tutorial only if you choose to test locally or remotely using a DSN connection. With Dreamweaver, you can use a data source name (DSN) or a connection string to connect to the database. You learn how to do both, but first you have to set up the DSN name to test locally using a DSN.

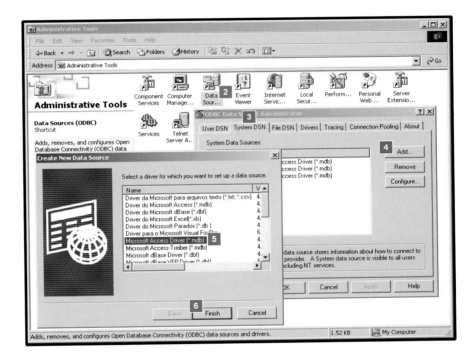

1. **Open Dreamweaver, and be sure that your PDGDynamic folder is the active defined site.**

2. **Choose one of the following options (the figures show Windows 2000):**

   » Windows 98: Click Start→Settings→Control Pane, and then select ODBC Data Source (32 bit).

   » Windows NT: Click Start→Settings→Control Panel, and then click the ODBC icon.

   » Windows 2000: Click Start→Settings→Control Panel, open Administrative tools, and click the Data Sources (ODBC) icon.

   » Windows XP (classic view): Click Start→Settings→ Control Panel, open Administrative tools, and click the Data Sources (ODBC) icon.

3. **Click the System DSN tab.**

4. **Click the Add button.**
   An ASP application must connect to a database through an open database connectivity (ODBC) driver or an object linking and embedding database (OLE DB) provider. You use an ODBC Microsoft Access Driver.

5. **Click the Microsoft Access Driver.**

6. **Click Finish.**

7. **Type** PDG **in the Data Source Name field.**

8. **Type** PDG database for contacts **in the Description field.**

9. **Click the Select button in the Database section of the ODBC Microsoft Access Setup dialog box.**

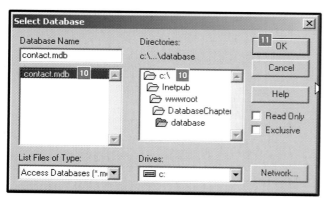

10. **Navigate to the C:\InetPub\wwwroot\DatabaseChapter\database folder, and click** contact.mdb.

11. **Click OK.**

12. **Click the Options button.**

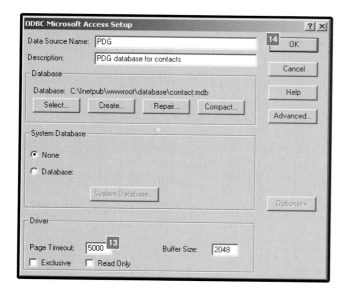

13. **Type** 5000 **in the Page Timeout field.**

14. **Click OK.**

    The ODBC Data Source Administrator dialog box now shows the contact database you added.

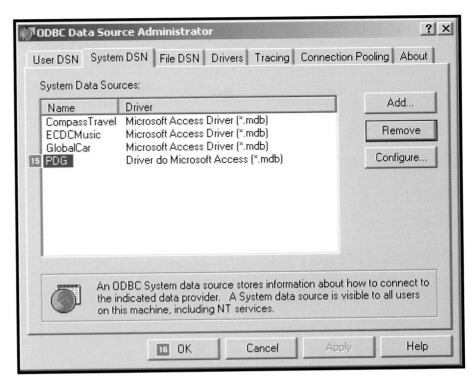

15. **Click PDG.**

16. **Click OK to complete the setup.**

A Note Before You Proceed . . .

The next four tutorials are methods that set connections named connPDG. USE ONLY ONE of the methods, or use different names. Each method uses the same name in the tutorials because that is the connection used by the project. The following are the choices:

» Setting up a local DSN connection—PC only. This tutorial should be done by Windows users who want to test on their local machine using PWS or IIS.

» Setting up a remote DSN connection—PC or Mac. This tutorial is used when you have a remote server that has the DSN set by the Web host.

» Setting up a connection string (DSN-less)—PC or Mac. This tutorial should be done by users who have a remote hosting service and cannot or prefer not to use a DSN connection. With this method, you don't have to rely on the host to set up the DSN for you (but permissions for the folder do need to be set).

» Using the MapPath method—PC or Mac with a remote hosting service. MapPath determines the full path of your database if, for some reason, your hosting service didn't provide it for you.

Perform the "Setting up a DSN Name" tutorial only if you choose to test locally or remotely using a DSN connection. The "Setting Up a Connection String (DSN-less)" and the "Using the MapPath Method" tutorials don't need a DSN name defined.

Tutorial

» Setting Up a Local DSN Connection

In this tutorial, you set up a connection to connect to your local Web server (PWS or IIS). It assumes that you have already set up a DSN for the database named PDG.

A DSN works like an alias—it is a one-word identifier that points to the database and contains information needed to connect to it, such as driver information and path structures and, in some cases, an ID and password.

To use a DSN Connection, the proper ODBC driver must be installed on your machine. PC users will have created a local DSN in their system's registry.

Mac and PC users opting for a hosted Web server may need to request that their provider create a DSN at the remote system using a specific name. Or, if that is not allowed, they must substitute the name the provider gives when working through this tutorial. If that all seems too complicated, you may opt to use a connection string instead (a DSN-less connection).

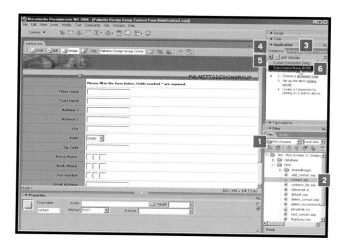

1. **Open your defined site for PDG Dynamic in the Files panel.**

2. **Open the html folder, and double-click** contact.asp **to open it.**

3. **Click the Application panel to open it.**

4. **Click the Databases tab to make it the active panel.**

5. **Click the Add (+) button.**

6. **Click Data Source Name (DSN).**

7. **Type** connPDG **in the Connection Name field.**

8. **Click the down arrow for Data Source Name (DSN), and click PDG.**
   If that is not an available option, you may need to click the DSN button and determine whether your DSN name appears.

9. **Click the Using Local DSN radio button to select it.**

10. **Click the Test button.**

11. **Click OK to close the dialog box.**
    The connection provides access to the tables, views, and/or stored procedures of the data source. For this project, you work only with a data table.

12. **Click the plus sign (+) next to connPDG in the Databases panel to see what is available.**

<NOTE>

Sometimes, databases can be corrupt or get corrupted in the transferring to CD process. If this happens, there is a zipped version in the DatabaseChapter database folder.

Tutorial

» Setting Up a Remote DSN Connection

If you have a Web server and want to test on the remote site, you want to do this tutorial. This is the most complex part of setting up a dynamic site, because the information needed varies in structure from service to service. The examples shown here presume that PDG owns a domain and hosts it with a provider.

1. **Open your defined site for PDG Dynamic in the Site panel.**

2. **Click the site definition down arrow, and click Manage Sites.**
   You now set up the Remote and Testing servers.

3. **Click PDG Dynamic.**

4. **Click Edit.**

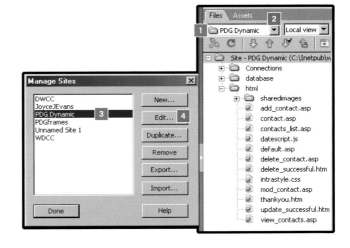

5. **Click the Advanced tab.**

6. **Click the Remote Info category.**

7. **Click the arrow for Access, and click FTP.**

8. **Type your FTP Host connection information in the FTP Host field.**

9. **Type the directory of your database files.**
   Where your files are stored may depend on your server. Most virtual domain NT servers serve the public Web from the www-root directory.

10. **Enter your login and password information.**

11. **Do not check the Enable file check in and check out option.**
    This is an option generally used when working in a team environment and is designed to lock files in use by other developers.

12. **Click the Test button.**
    If your test fails to connect to your server, you'll need to check all your connections such as the FTP address, an opening directory, username, and password.

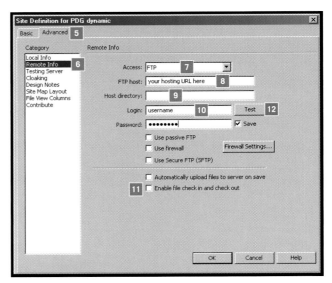

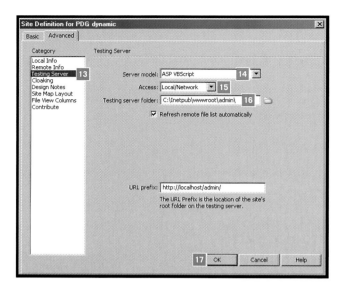

13. **Click the Testing Server category.**

14. **Click the down arrow for the Server Model field, and click ASP VBScript.**
    This is the server technology that is being used to communicate with the database. Notice the other server models available to you.

15. **Select the type of Access you need. For locally, select the Local/Network option.**

16. **Enter as the URL prefix the path to your DatabaseChapter folder.**
    Think of it as the path that a browser would use to find your folder. In other words, if your site uses a wwwroot or some other administrator type of folder, that part would not go into the URL prefix, just the domain name and the path to the folder.

17. **Click OK and Done.**
    You are now ready to make the remote connection.

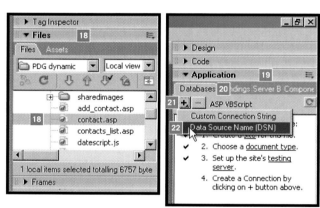

18. **In the Files panel, double-click** contact.asp **to open it.**
    It's in the html folder.

19. **Click the expander arrow of the Application panel group to open it.**

20. **Click the Databases tab to make it the active panel.**

21. **Click the Add (+) button.**

22. **Click Data Source Name (DSN).**

23. **Type** connPDG **in the Connection Name field.**

24. **Click the radio button for Using DSN on Testing Server option.**
    Mac users do not see this option.

25. **Type** PDG **into the Data Source Name (DSN) field.**

26. **You do not need to fill in the User Name and Password fields.**

27. **Click the Test button.**
    Be sure that you are online prior to pressing the Test button.

28. **Click OK to close the dialog box.**
    The connection provides access to the tables, views, and/or stored procedures of the data source. For this project, you work only with a data table.

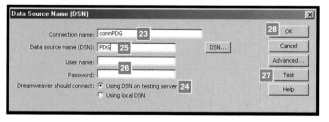

Tutorial
» Setting Up a Connection String (DSN-less)

Using a DSN-less connection, your hosting server doesn't have to set up a DSN name for you, but you should ask for the full path to your database. This tutorial uses a connection string to connect, but you may easily substitute a DSN if you are able to set it up. If you do not or cannot use a DSN connection, you have to set up a custom connection string to provide the database driver and path structure information to Dreamweaver and the browser. The easiest way to determine the path to your database after you upload the site folder is to ask your service provider's technical support person. An alternative option is to use the MapPath method (explained in the next tutorial).

Your provider must also set the correct permissions for the DatabaseChapter\database folder to allow Dreamweaver and browser pages to access your database. Because you specifically have the contact.mdb database in a different folder, you have to ask your provider to set the proper permissions for your folder.

1. **Open** contact.asp **from the sample folder using the Site panel.**

2. **Click the Application panel to open it. Click the Databases tab to make it the active panel.**

3. **Click the Add (+) button.**

4. **Click Custom Connection String.**

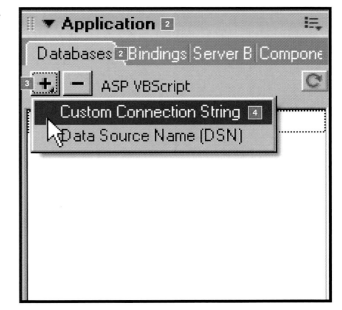

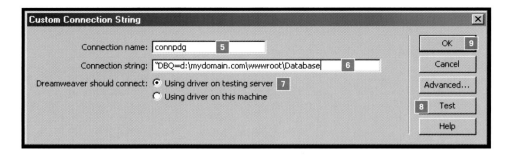

<NOTE>

If your domain name is www.mydomain.com, your host server is mydomain.com, and your provider tells you that you must place your Web pages in a directory at wwwroot. Therefore, your structure may look something like: D:\mydomain.com\wwwroot\DatabaseChapter\database\contact.mdb. When you have the proper path structure, you add it to the driver information to create a custom connection string.

<NOTE>

You would replace mydomain.com with your domain name. You might also have to replace other parts of this structure to match the path given to you by your service provider.

<NOTE>

Be sure that you are connected to the remote server first. Dreamweaver should return a success message. If not, you need to check your string for errors and/or verify with your service provider that it has the latest Microsoft Access Drivers (4.0). If your connection is successful, you are ready to begin developing dynamic pages.

5. **Name your connection** connpdg.

6. **In the Connection String field, add the following (all in one line including quote marks!):**

   ```
   "DBQ=d:\mydomain.com\wwwroot\Database
   Chapter\database\contact.mdb;DRIVER=
   {Microsoft Access Driver (*.mdb)}"
   ```

   This is the path to your database and the driver to be used. This next string is the same but in reverse. You may find that one works better for you than the other. With database connections, it may take some practice and lots of testing.

   ```
   "DRIVER={Microsoft Access Driver (*.mdb)};
   DBQ=d:\mydomain.com\wwwroot\DatabaseChapter\
   database\contact.mdb"
   ```

7. **Select the Using Driver On Testing Server option.**
   Mac users do not see this option.

8. **Click the Test button.**

9. **Click OK.**

<NOTE>

A *connection string* is a hand-coded line of text that does the same thing as a DSN connection, but it is often faster and uses fewer system resources. When you use a DSN, you are looking up the alias to find out the same information contained in a connection string. Connection strings are sometimes called DSN-less connections.

Tutorial
» Using the MapPath Method

If you know the virtual path to your database folder (supplied by the hosting service), you can determine the physical path using the MapPath method. When you have uploaded your DatabaseChapter files to the remote server, your files end up in a folder structure for that server. For example, on a server running MS IIS, the path or folder structure to the database could look like this:

`C:\Inetpub\wwwroot\accounts\users\yourfolder\DatabaseChapter\database\contact.mdb`

This is a physical path to your file. But the URL to access a file doesn't use the physical path. Most, if not all, service providers are set up to use the name of the server or domain, followed by a virtual path, such as the following:

`http://www.mydomain.com/yourfolder/DatabaseChapter/database/contact.mdb`

A virtual path is a "shortcut" for the physical path. Host providers use this method for security and convenience, because it hides the true path and eliminates writing the longer URL. Your provider typically gives you a URL to view your pages on the Internet using the virtual path.

1. **Upload your files to the remote server, and make a note of the virtual path.**

2. **Be sure that you are connected to the remote server and that you know the virtual path.**

3. **Open the** `contact.asp` **page from the local site root folder using the Site panel.**

4. **Click the Databases panel in the Application panel group.**

5. **Click the Add (+) button.**

6. **Click Custom Connection String.**

7. **Name this connection** connpdg.

8. **In the Connection String field, add the following:**
   "DRIVER={Microsoft Access Driver (*.mdb)};DBQ=" & Server.MapPath("yourfolder\DatabaseChapter\database\ contact.mdb")"

9. **Select the Using Driver On Testing Server option.**
   Mac users do not see this option.

10. **Click the Test button.**

11. **If the connection is successful, close the dialog box by pressing OK.**
   If not, check the virtual path and the rest of your string to be sure that all quotation marks, ampersands, and such are in place.

< N O T E >

This code is entered all on one line! The format of this book doesn't provide space to show it to you that way.

< N O T E >

Using MapPath is less desirable than a DSN or connection string that uses the physical path, because it requires an extra step to the process each time the database is requested. Most host providers give you the proper path to your database.

» Session Review

You may not be able to answer all these questions depending on which option you chose for testing—local or remote—but go ahead and see how you do. The answer to each question can be found in the tutorial noted in parentheses.

1. How can you tell whether PWS has been installed on your machine? (See "Tutorial: Installing a Personal Web Server (Windows 98).")

2. Can Windows XP Home users install IIS? (See "Tutorial: Installing IIS.")

3. Where do you place your database files on a PC for testing locally? (See "Tutorial: Defining a Dynamic Web Site.")

4. What does DSN stand for? (See "Tutorial: Setting Up a DSN Name.")

5. Which panel do you access to add connection information? (See "Setting Up a Local DSN Connection.")

6. How does the URL prefix differ from the host directory? (See "Tutorial: Setting Up a Remote DSN Connection.")

7. Why would you want or need to use a DSN-less connection? (See "Tutorial: Setting Up a Connection String (DSN-less).")

8. What does a custom connection string do? (See "Tutorial: Setting Up a Connection String (DSN-less).")

9. Do you enter the custom string containing the driver information and the path information on two lines? (See "Tutorial: Setting Up a Connection String (DSN-less).")

10. When would you use the MapPath method? (See "Tutorial: Using the MapPath Method.")

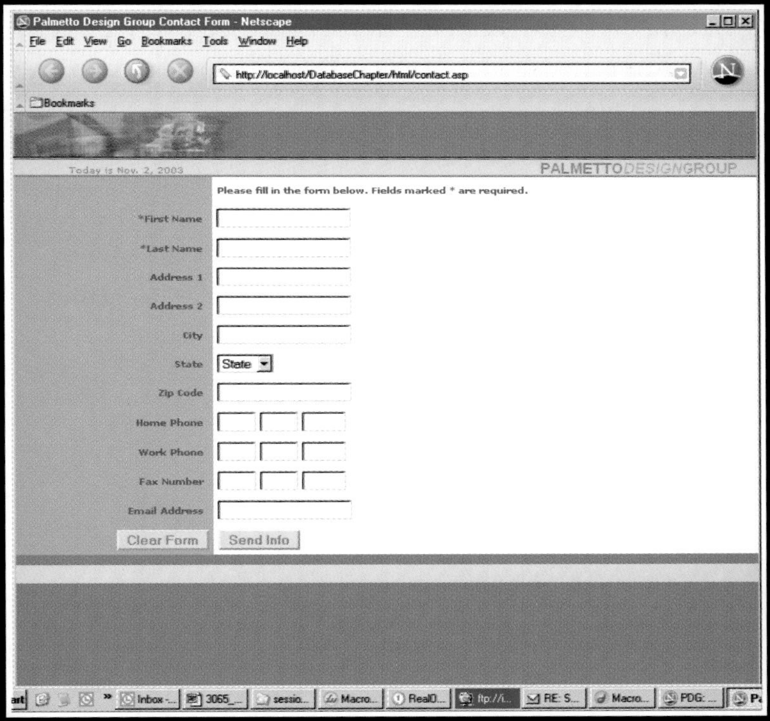
Palmetto Design Group Contact Form - Netscape
File Edit View Go Bookmarks Tools Window Help
http://localhost/DatabaseChapter/html/contact.asp
Bookmarks
Today is Nov. 2, 2003
PALMETTODESIGNGROUP
Please fill in the form below. Fields marked * are required.
*First Name
*Last Name
Address 1
Address 2
City
State
State
Zip Code
Home Phone
Work Phone
Fax Number
Email Address
Clear Form
Send Info

Building a Web Application

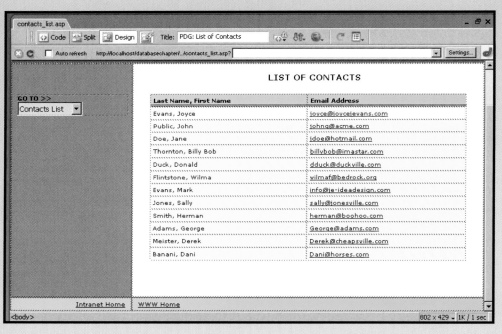

Tutorial: **Adding a Recordset**

Tutorial: **Using Repeating Regions**

Tutorial: **Using Insert Record on Forms**

Tutorial: **Validating Your Forms**

Tutorial: **Building Update Pages**

Tutorial: **Inserting a Recordset Navigation Bar**

Tutorial: **Building Delete Pages**

Tutorial: **Making Master Detail Pages**

Session Introduction

Now that your connection is in place and you can successfully connect to your database, you are ready to begin using Dreamweaver to build dynamic pages. In this session, you explore the basics of manipulating a data source (the database) to provide dynamic Web content.

Dreamweaver contains many useful tools and functions to set up, connect, and script your pages. In this session, you learn to bind data and add server-side logic to the site pages to collect, view, and modify information obtained from a contact form and database.

The building block of your Web application is the record. In a database, records are stored in related blocks of information, formatted in tables. Each piece of information in a record is called a field. A collection of records that share the same fields is called a table because the information is easily presented in table format; each column represents a field and each row a separate record. In fact, you can substitute the words column for field and vice versa. The same is true for row and record. Throughout this session, you use column/field information and display rows/records dynamically.

TOOLS YOU'LL USE
Site panel; Application panel group; Databases, Bindings, and Server Behaviors panels; Live Data view; Property inspector; Insert bar; and the StatePostalABR extension available from the Macromedia Dreamweaver Exchange

MATERIALS NEEDED
Session 13 must be completed before attempting this session. The session14_starterfiles are for PC users testing locally if you want to use them. Web Server software (PC with PWS or IIS or a Web hosting service with database and ASP 2.0 support). If you use an online service, you need an active Web connection.

TIME REQUIRED
120 minutes

Tutorial
» Adding a Recordset

Your first dynamic page takes the information from a contact database and displays it on a list of contacts page. This project uses Active Server Page (ASP) technology, so the name of each page uses the extension .ASP. The .ASP extension tells the Web server to process the page prior to serving it via the Web browser. In this tutorial, you run a database query. A query consists of search criteria relating to the requested subset (table) of the database. The result of the query is a recordset. A recordset consists of data returned by a database query that is temporarily stored in the application server's memory for faster data retrieval.

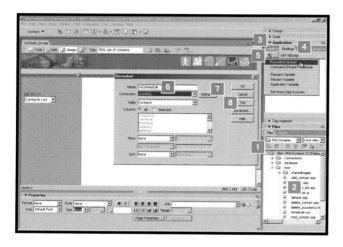

1. **Be sure that you are online and connected to your server if you're using a remote service provider.**

2. **Double-click** `contacts_list.asp` **in the Files panel for the PDG Dynamic site.**

3. **Click the Application panel group to open it.**

4. **Click the Bindings panel tab to make it active.**
   You may need to set up the Testing Server at this time if you haven't already. Refer to Steps 13 through 17 of the "Setting Up a Remote DSN Connection" tutorial in Session 13.

5. **Click the Add (+) button, and select Recordset (Query).**
   The Add button is grayed out if you haven't set up the Testing Server yet.

6. **Set the recordset name to** rsContactList**.**

<NOTE>
Most developers use a naming convention when working with recordsets. If you use rs for a recordset, when you see rs(name of set) in your code, you may be certain that it is a reference to your recordset.

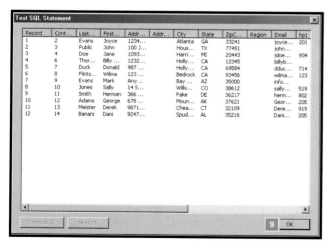

7. **From the Connection menu, choose connpdg.**
   Selecting the connection populates the Table menu and gives you access to a table in your database. This database contains one table, so the menu lists only the Contacts table. The columns (data fields) in the table populate the columns list.

8. **Click the Test button.**
   You should see all the present contacts in this table.

9. **Click OK to close the Testing dialog box; click the OK button on the Recordset dialog box to close it as well.**
   Now you build a table to hold the dynamic data.

10. **Place your cursor into the main (white) area of the page, and press Enter (Return).**

11. **Click the Insert Table icon (Common category of the Insert bar), and add a new table with the following settings:**

    » Rows: **2**

    » Columns: **2**

    » Width: **90%**

    » Border: **0**

    » Padding: **5px**

    » Spacing: **0**

12. **Type** Layout table **in the Summary field, and click OK.**

13. **Type** Last Name, First Name **into the first cell of the top row.**

14. **In the second cell of the top row, type** Email Address.

15. **Select the `<tr>` tag; in the Property inspector, set the height (H) to 20. Repeat this step for the second row.**

16. **Place your cursor into the first cell of the top row.**

17. **Right-click (Ctrl+click) the `<tr>` tag in the Tag Selector to apply the class tabletop.**
    The stylesheet (intrastyle.css if you want to look at it) for this site has been supplied for you.

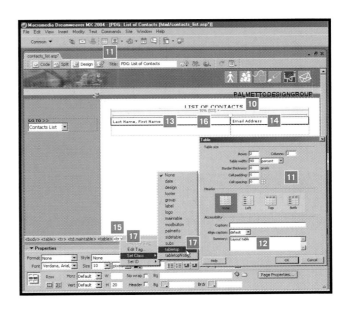

<NOTE>

To create a dynamic page, you place dynamic fields that refer to specific columns or data fields in the rsContactList recordset. Dreamweaver provides several methods for placing the code. You can drag and drop from the Bindings panel or select a data field and use the Insert button at the bottom of the panel.

18. **From the Bindings panel, open click the plus sign next to the recordset name Recordset (rsContactList) to reveal the data fields within.**

19. **Locate LastName in the rsContactList recordset.**

20. **Select and drag LastName to the first column of the second table row, and release the mouse.**

21. **Place your cursor after the LastName dynamic field, and add a comma, followed by a space.**

22. **Insert the FirstName data field the same way (drag and drop, or select and click the Insert button).**

23. **Drag Email from the Bindings panel, and drop it into the second cell of the second row.**

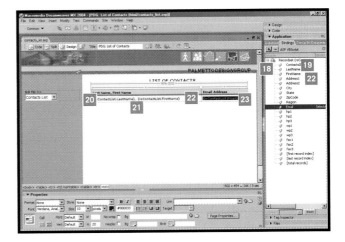

<NOTE>

Depending upon your computer setup and your Web server settings, previewing may require a save or auto-save. In all cases, it's a good idea to add the saved page to the remote server. You can press the Live Data View button to see how your page looks with one set of data, but you are not able to test the functionality of the dynamic link and subject line unless you preview in the appropriate browsers.

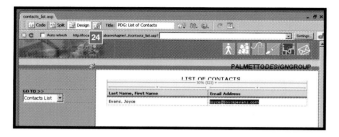

24. **Save the page, and click the Live Data View button in the Document bar.**
    You must be online if you're using a remote application server (but not if you are using PWS or IIS). Live Data View displays the first record of the Contacts table in the database. The e-mail address is displayed, but it is not active. Next you add a mailto: link and then add a dynamic data field in the href of the mailto: link.

<NOTE>

If you get a message that the file is in use and can't be accessed, try closing Dreamweaver, opening it again, and then clicking Live View again. I don't know why, but this has happened before.

25. **Select the Email dynamic field (the one that now displays** joyce@joycejevans.com **in Live Data View).**

26. **In the Link field of the Property inspector, type** mailto: **and press Enter (Return).**

27. **Select the** <a> **tag using the Tag Selector.**

28. **Click the Split View icon, and locate the opening anchor tag** (<a href="mailto:").

29. **Insert your cursor just after the colon in the tag.**

30. **Go to the Bindings panel, and drag and drop the Email data field just after the colon. The code now appears as follows:**
    ```
    <a href="mailto:<%=(rsContactList.Fields.
    Item("Email").Value)%>"><%=
    (rsContactList.Fields.Item("Email").Value)%><
    /a>
    ```

31. **Place your cursor just after the dynamic data field to provide a subject line to the e-mail sent by this link.**
    Place the cursor after Value)%> **(in front of** "><%...)

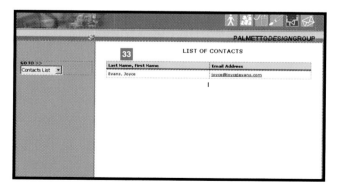

32. **Add** ?subject=From Palmetto Design Group **before the ending quote. Now the code for the cell appears as follows:**
    ```
    <td><a href="mailto:<%=(rsContactList.Fields.
    Item("Email").Value)%>?subject=From Palmetto
    Design Group "><%=(rsContactList.Fields.Item
    ("Email").Value)%></a></td>
    ```

33. **Save and preview your work by clicking Live View. Notice the underline under** joyce@joycejevans.com; **it is now a working link.**

Tutorial
» Using Repeating Regions

In this tutorial, you learn how to use the Repeat Region server behavior to display all records in the data table on this page of your site. To display all records of the data table in this page, you use the Repeat Region server behavior. A server behavior is predefined server-side logic that adds specific functionality and interaction through application logic. The application server processes server-side logic before it is sent to the browser. Dreamweaver server behaviors give you powerful logic without your having to write any ASP code.

1. **Open** contacts_list.asp **if you closed it, and select the second row by clicking its** <tr> **tag.**

2. **Click the Server Behaviors tab in the Application panel group.**

3. **Click the Add (+) button, and choose Repeat Region from the menu.**

4. **Enter these settings:**

   » Recordset: **rsContactList**

   » Show: **All Records**

5. **Click OK.**

6. **To test locally: Press the Live Data View button to view all records in your page. (If you are testing remotely, skip to Step 9.)**
   The Repeat Region code adds a new row for each record in the data source. The dynamic fields display the last and first names and the e-mail addresses, and create a live e-mail link for each, complete with subject line.

7. **Click the Live Data View button again to turn off the view. Be patient; it takes awhile for Live Data View to show the results.**

8. **Save your page.**
   You can use the keyboard shortcut File→Save.

9. **To test remotely: Go to the Files panel, and click**
   `contacts_list.asp`.

10. **Click the Put button (you must be online with a remote server in order to access this button).**
    Alternatively, you can click the File Management icon and select Put from that menu.

11. **For either remote or local testing, test in the browser (F12), and click one of the e-mail links. The user's e-mail client opens with the subject line added and the e-mail field filled in.**

< N O T E >

When using Repeat Region to display dynamic data, carefully set up the HTML structure to make it easily repeated. Paragraphs and table rows are very easy to repeat. Individual columns are not.

12. **Close the page; you won't need it for the next tutorial.**

Tutorial

» Using Insert Record on Forms

The Palmetto Design Group Contact Form collects information to add to the Contacts database. In this tutorial, you use the Insert Record server behavior to bind the form fields to the data columns.

The Palmetto Design Group contact form is accessed by the Web site and used by PDG's clients. The PDG intranet site maintains a link to the form for adding contact information that is received by mail.

Forms work by creating name-value pairs. A named form object collects a value, supplied either by the author of the page or by the user in a Web browser session. Submitting the form adds a record to the database, matching named form fields to data fields (columns).

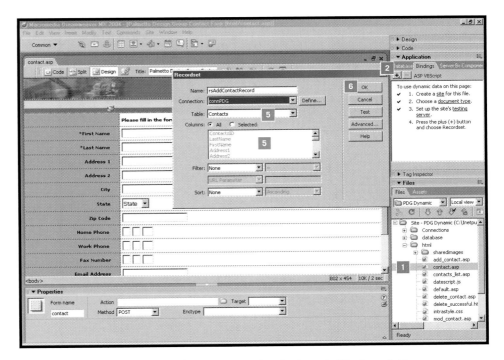

1. **In the Files panel, double-click the** `contact.asp` **page to open it.**
   This page contains a prepared form that needs application logic to make it useful.

2. **Click the Add (+) button in the Bindings panel of the Application panel group to add a recordset.**

3. **Click Recordset (Query).**

4. **Type** rsAddContactRecord **in the Name field.**

5. **Use these settings for the rest of the Query fields:**

   » Connection: **connPDG**

   » Table: **Contacts**

   » Columns: **All**

   » Filter: **None**

   » Sort: **None**

   You might need to be patient while the connection loads the database table(s). If your database contained multiple tables, you would need to select the correct table from the Tables menu. In this case, it does not.

6. **Click OK to close the dialog box.**   > **273**

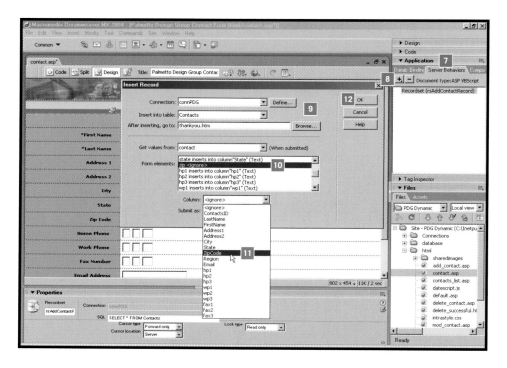

7. **Click the Server Behaviors panel to make it active.**

8. **Click Add (+) Insert Record.**

9. **In the dialog box, use these settings:**

   » Connection: **connPDG**

   » Insert into Table: **Contacts**

   » After Inserting, Go To: **thankyou.htm**

   Look in the Form elements list at the bottom of the dialog box. After the table information loads, the first few fields find a matching column, but some fields don't. When a form field's name and a column's name match, the Insert Record server behavior is smart enough to see the relationship. The Column menu is used to match form fields to data columns.

10. **To set the zip code, simply highlight it in the list.**

11. **From the Column list, select and set the zip element to ZipCode.** Be very careful to add this only once. The rest of the form objects match database columns and are already set.

12. **Click OK to close the dialog box.**

13. **Save the page.**

14. **For remote testing, upload this page to test in the appropriate browsers.**

15. **Preview the page in a browser for local testing.**

16. **Fill in the form, and add a record to the database.**

17. **Keep the page open because you use it in the next tutorial.**

<NOTE>
Upon submitting the form, you are redirected to the thank-you page.

Tutorial

» Validating Your Forms

In this tutorial, you learn how to validate your forms, checking to be sure that the required information has the proper format on specific areas of a form.

1. Open the `contact.asp` page if you've closed it.

2. Click the Send Info button.

3. Click the Tag Inspector panel, and select the Behaviors panel to make it active.

4. Click the Add (+) button.

5. Click the Validate Form behavior.

6. In the Validate Form dialog box, highlight or select the text "first-name" in the form "contact".

7. Set this value as required.

8. Leave the default Anything radio button selected.

9. Repeat for the text "lastname" in the form "contact".

10. Go through the phone and fax number fields, and set each to Number.

11. Set the Email field as Required, and choose the Email Address option.

12. Click OK to close the dialog box.

13. Save and test your page.

14. Close the file.

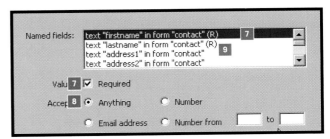

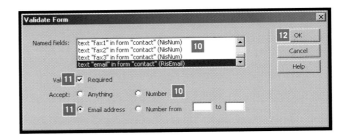

Validation

The process of adding information to a database should have some sort of validation process to be sure that the required information has the proper format. Some fields are required (by the database and the form), and others are not. To be sure that the page does not return errors from the database, a form validation script runs to catch any empty required fields prior to sending the page to the application server. The validation script is written in JavaScript and is processed client-side, as opposed to the server-side logic of ASP. Client-side scripts are processed by the user's Web browser.

Tutorial

» Building Update Pages

Occasionally, it's necessary to update the information in the contact database. Rather than add a new contact, it's better to modify the original entry to change information. The Update Record server behavior adds this complex application logic with a minimum of effort!

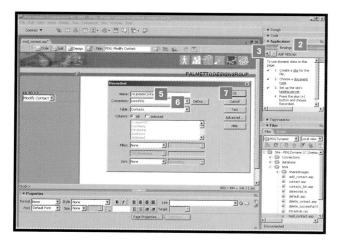

1. Double-click the `mod_contact.asp` **page to open it.**

2. **Open the Bindings panel in the Application panel group.**

3. **Click the Add (+) button.**

4. **Click Recordset (Query).**

5. **Type** rsUpdateContacts **in the Name field.**

6. **Select the** connpdg **connection.**

7. **Click OK to close the dialog box.**

8. **Place your cursor to the right of the page heading (Modify Contact).**

9. **Add a paragraph return by pressing Enter (Return).**

10. **Select Insert→Application Objects→Update Record→ Record Update Form Wizard.**
   Because this page does not contain a form with fields, you insert one to collect a value for every field in the database.

11. **Match these settings:**

   » Connection: **connpdg**

   » Table to Update: **Contacts**

   » Select Record From: **rsUpdateContacts**

   » Unique Key Column: **ContactsID** (uncheck Numeric if it's checked)

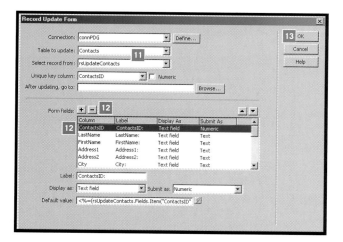

12. **Remove the ContactsID column by selecting it and pressing the Remove (−) button.**
   You remove the ContactsID column because Access takes care of the key. You don't want anyone to be able to modify this field and corrupt the database.

13. **Click OK to set this form.**
   The Label, Display As, and Submit As fields display the information for any selected form field. You can make changes here if needed. For instance, you've done this already in another form for the Zip Code field where it was ignored.

<NOTE>
A Unique Key Column is a special field in the database that is auto-generated by Access (or any other database) to control the data records. Although it is possible to have two records with identical information, it is not possible for each of them to have the same unique key. A primary key is set up when the database is created. This database auto-generates a number value when an entry is added.

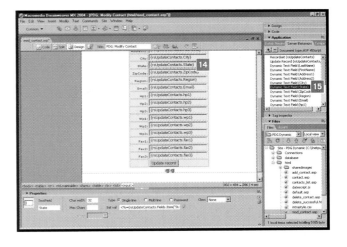

14. **Select the state form object.**
This is a text field.

15. **Look at the Server Behaviors panel.**
You should see Dynamic Text Field (State).

16. **Double-click the entry to take a look at the details of this behavior.**

17. **Close the entry when you're done.**

18. **Because it is possible to set the specifics of the Update behavior, select the State field from the form and delete it.**
Don't worry about deleting this field; you add a list of states here instead.

19. **Save this file.**
You need to download and install the StatePostalABR extension now if you haven't done so already. If you've already installed the extension, skip to Step 26.

20. **Click Help→Dreamweaver Support Center. Pass your mouse over the Downloads link at the top of the page, and select Exchange. At the top of the right column, select Search Exchanges.**

21. **Type** StatePostalABR **into the Search Exchange field, and click the Search button.**

22. **Download the extension into your Downloaded Extensions folder (inside the Dreamweaver MX 2004 application folder).**

23. **Click Commands→Manage Extensions.**

24. **Click the Install New extension icon, and select the StatePostalABR from the list.**
If you don't see the list, navigate to the folder in which you saved it, select it, and click Install.

25. **When the installation is complete, close the Extensions Manager. Close Dreamweaver, and restart it.**

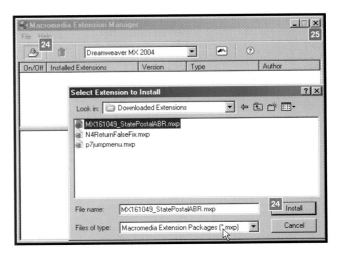

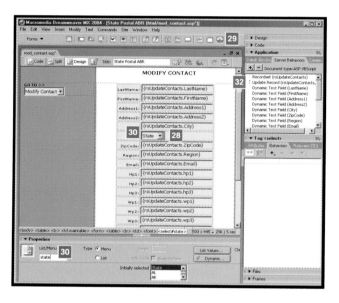

26. **Click the Forms category in the Insert bar.**
Notice that an icon for ABR has been added. The icon looks like an envelope.

27. **Double-click the mod_contact.asp page to open it.**

28. **Be sure that your cursor is in the cell of the recently deleted text field.**

29. **Click the StatePostalABR icon in the forms panel to add the menu to the space.**

30. **Select the state object; in the Property inspector, rename the object** state.

31. **Be sure that the new State object is still selected.**

32. **In the Server Behaviors panel, your Update Record behavior should now have a red exclamation mark next to it.**
It's there because you deleted an item used by this behavior.

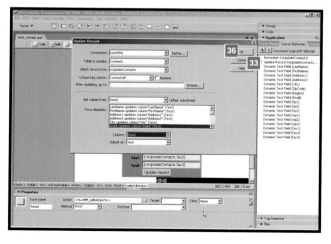

33. **Double-click the server behavior and you get a message stating that the form object cannot be found. Click OK to close the message.**

34. **Use the Form Elements menu in the Update Record dialog box to select state, and choose state from the Columns pop-up menu.**

35. **Give the page a new title of** PDG: Modify Contact.

36. **Click OK to close the dialog box.**

37. **Save your page. Upload it, if needed, and preview it to test.**
The tables generated by Application Objects contain undesirable HTML markup. In the next set of steps, you make some adjustments to the layout of the table and form objects, to make the layout match the rest of the site and to improve the readability of the form.

38. **Click in one of the table fields in the form (such as City), and select its table in the Tag Selector.**

39. **Set the width of the table to** 90%.

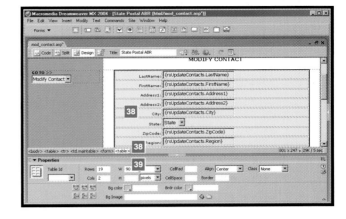

40. **Select all the cells in the left column of the table.**

41. **Right-click (Ctrl+click) on the** `<td>` **tag.**

42. **Set the class to tabletopNobg.**

43. **Adjust the various labels in the left column of the table, adding spaces where necessary to match this list. Where a label is not listed, leave it as the default. Most of the names need a space.**

>> Last Name:

>> First Name:

>> Address 1:

>> Address 2:

>> City:

>> State:

>> Zip Code:

>> Region:

>> Email:

>> Home Phone: (this replaces hp1; ignore hp2 & hp3)

>> Work Phone: (this replaces wp1; ignore wp2 & wp3)

>> Fax: (this replaces fax1; ignore fax2 & fax3)

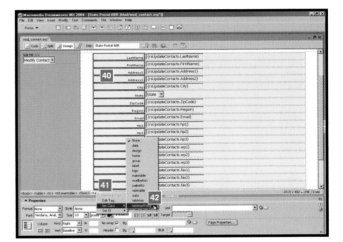

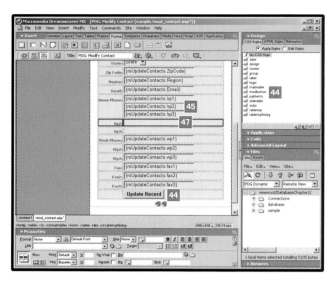

44. **Select the Update Record button. Select the `<input>` tag, right-click (Ctrl+click), and set it to the modbutton class.**

45. **Click and drag the hp2 and hp3 form objects to the right of the hp1 form object.**
    You now have three fields for the phone number: one for the area code, one for the prefix, and one for the suffix.

46. **Select each of the phone number fields; in the Property inspector, change the Char Width and Max Chars. Set the first one to 3, the second field to 3, and the third to 4.**

47. **Select and delete the empty hp2 and hp3 rows. Click the `<tr>` tag to select the row.**

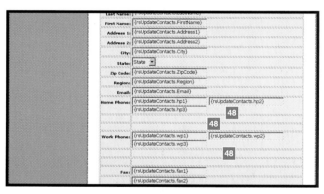

48. **Use the same method to adjust the wp and fax fields, moving the form objects and deleting the extra rows.**

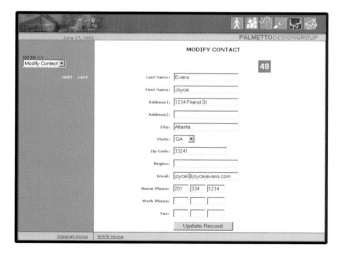

49. **Save and upload your page, and then test it in the appropriate browsers.**
    Your page should list only the first record in the database. Make a small change to see whether your page updates the record and sends you to the success page. Of course, to be useful, you would need to be able to update all the records. In the next tutorial, you learn to add a Recordset Navigation Bar to gain access to each record.

Tutorial

» Inserting a Recordset Navigation Bar

Updating the contact database requires access to all records. In this tutorial, you insert a Recordset Navigation Bar to allow access to all records.

1. **Double-click the** mod_contact.asp **page to open it.**

2. **Click the jump menu in the left side of the page to select it.**

3. **Select the form tag using the Tag Selector, and then press your right-arrow key to move just outside and after the form code.**

4. **Choose Insert→Application Objects→Recordset Paging→ Recordset Navigation Bar.**

5. **Match the following settings:**

   » Recordset: **rsUpdateContacts**

   » Display Using: **Text**

6. **Click OK in the dialog box to close it.**

7. **Select the new navigation table.**

8. **Use the Property inspector to match these settings:**

   » Table Width: **180px**

   » Cell Spacing: **10px**

   » Cell Padding: **0**

   » Border: **0**

   » Align menu: **Default**

9. **Click inside the cells in the row (one at a time) and match these settings:**

   » Width: **30, 50, 30, 30** (four cells, from left to right)

   » Horz Align: **Default** (all)

   » Vert Align: **Bottom** (all)

10. **Place your cursor into the last cell, and tab to add a new row.**

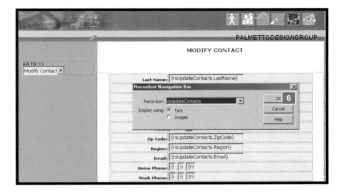

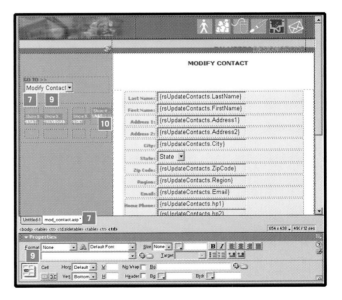

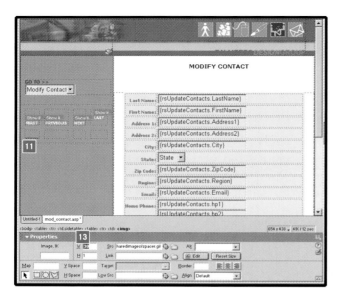

11. **Click inside the left cell of the new row.**

12. **In the Images category of the Assets panel, click** `spacer.gif` **and then click the Insert button.**

13. **Set the size of the spacer to** 30px **(the same width as the cell); set the height to** 1px.

14. **Repeat Steps 11 through 13 for all the cells, but make the second spacer** 50px.

15. **Save, upload, and test the page.**
    When you test in the browser, click the Next link. You see the First and Previous links appear.

16. **When you have tested the page, close it.**
    In the next tutorial, you work in a different page.

The Recordset Navigation Bar Object

The table and link elements may be modified in layout or labeling. Be careful, though, when doing so, because scripting has been applied to the links to cycle through all records in the database. If you look in your Server Behaviors panel, you see that new behaviors have been added to each of the links. As you select each new behavior, Dreamweaver shows you where, on the page, it is applied.

Each link has two behaviors. The first behavior, Show If Not First Record, and the second behavior, Move to First Record, are applied to the first link. When live, this link does not display when the record being viewed is the first in the database. Of course, if the link doesn't display, you are on the first record and don't need to move there!

Tutorial
» Building Delete Pages

Chances are good that you'll want to delete a contact from time to time. With another of Dreamweaver's incredibly useful application objects, you can set this up in a few clicks. This tutorial walks you through this.

1. **Double-click the** `delete_contact.asp` **page to open it.**

2. **Open the Bindings panel.**

3. **Click the Add (+) button.**

4. **Click Recordset (Query).**

5. **Name it** `rsDeleteContact`, **and choose connPDG for the Connection field.**

6. **Click OK in the dialog box.**

7. **Place your cursor just below the page heading, and add a paragraph return.**

8. **Click the plus (+) sign for the** `rsDeleteContact` **recordset in the Bindings panel to see its Columns.**

9. **Select LastName, and click the Insert button at the bottom of the panel.**
You can also drag and drop LastName to the cursor location.

10. **In the document, to the right of the added recordset, add a comma followed by a space.**

11. **Click FirstName in the Bindings panel, and insert it.**

12. **Add a paragraph return.**

13. **Choose Insert→Form→Form.**

14. **Name the form** RemoveRecord.

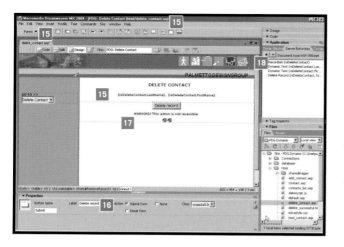

15. **Place your cursor inside the form, and click the Button icon in the Forms category of the Insert bar.**

16. **Label the button** Delete Record. **If you are using Accessibility options, name that label as well.**
    Deleting a record is a serious proposition, because the user doesn't get a confirmation dialog box when he/she clicks the button. To ensure that the user understands this, you add a warning notice below to the button.

17. **After the button, add a paragraph return and type** WARNING! This action is not reversible.

18. **While still inside the form, use the Server Behaviors panel to Add (+) the behavior Delete Record.**

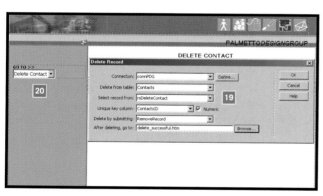

19. **In the dialog box, match these settings:**
    » Connection: **connPDG**
    » Delete from Table: **Contacts**
    » Select Record From: **rsDeleteContact**
    » Unique Key Column: **ContactsID**
    » Delete by Submitting: **RemoveRecord**
    » After Deleting, Go To: **delete_successful.htm**

    Be sure to check the Numeric check box as well.

20. **Now position your cursor just below the jump menu in the left side of the page.**

21. **To navigate through all the records, choose Insert→ Application Objects→Recordset Paging→Recordset Navigation Bar, just as you did for the previous page.**
    Refer to the preceding tutorial (Steps 9 through 14) to format the navigational table. You want to maintain a consistent look for similar page elements.

22. **Save your page.**

23. **Upload this page, and test.**

24. **Close the page.**

Tutorial
» Making Master Detail Pages

The Contacts List page limits the information that you can see about each record. It would be more useful to view a list of names and then select a single contact to view all its details. You could use the existing list page and apply separate bits of logic, but instead you create two new pages and let Dreamweaver do the work! In this tutorial, you use a Master Detail Page Set to do just that.

1. **Double-click the** `view_contacts.asp` **page to open it.**

2. **In the Bindings panel of the Application panel group, click the Add (+) button.**

3. **Click Recordset (Query).**

4. **Name the recordset** `rsContactDetails`.

5. **Choose the connPDG connection; the table and columns load. This should be a familiar routine by now.**

6. **Click OK to close the dialog box.**

7. **Place your cursor in the main content area after the heading, and add a paragraph return.**

8. **Choose Insert➔Application Objects➔Master Detail Page Set.**

9. **The Recordset menu should list rsContactDetails.**

   » Master Page Fields: **LastName, FirstName** [select and remove (–) others]

   » Link to Detail From: **LastName**

   » Pass Unique Key: **ContactsID**

   » Show: **10 Records at a time**

10. **Click the Browse button at the right of the Detail page name text box to find** `details.asp` **in the sample folder.**

11. **Leave everything else at the default, and click OK.**

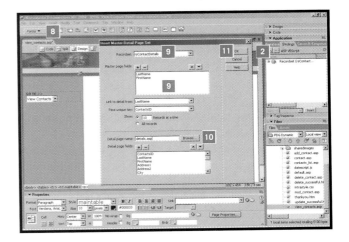

< N O T E >

Dreamweaver inserts code to display one record at a time and provide a navigation bar to access all records. It also opens and adds a details table to the `details.asp` page. However, when you have a preset page layout, Dreamweaver simply adds the new table at the end of the layout, so you have to move the table to the correct location.

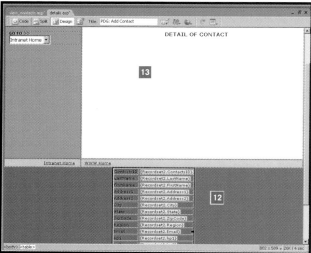

12. The details.asp page opens and the table is inserted below the design at the bottom of the page. In details.asp, select the newly inserted table and press Ctrl+X (⌘+X) to cut it.

13. Place your cursor in the main cell after the heading, and press Ctrl+V (⌘+V) to paste it.

14. Save the page.
    The layout of the table needs some work because the phone numbers are displayed inconveniently.

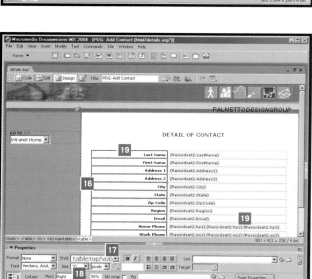

15. Select the table, and match these settings:
    » Table Width: **90%**
    » Cell Spacing: **0px**
    » Cell Padding: **5px**
    » Border: **0**
    » Align menu: **Default**

16. Shift-select all the cells in the left column.

17. In the Property inspector click the Style drop-down list and select tabletopNobg to apply it.

18. Set the cell Horz Align to Right.

19. Re-label and rearrange the form objects as you did in the earlier exercise to put the phone and fax numbers together in single cells.

20. Delete empty rows where necessary.

21. **Save and upload this page.**

22. **Click the** `view_contacts.asp` **page to open it.**
    This page could use a little formatting as well.

23. **Select the first row of the table, and merge both cells by clicking and dragging across the cells to select and then right-clicking (Ctrl+clicking) and selecting Table→Merge Cells.**

24. **Place a comma and space between LastName and FirstName, and add spaces between the words as well.**
    The Repeat label obstructs the view of the word, LastName. You can use your arrow key to position the cursor and press the spacebar to add a space, or do it in Code View.

25. **Select the merged cell, and apply the tabletop class by selecting it from the Style drop-down list in the Property inspector.**

26. **Set the cell's height to 20px.**

26. **Select the table, and make the border 0 and 400px wide.**

27. **Save and upload the page.**

28. **Preview and click a link to view the details.**

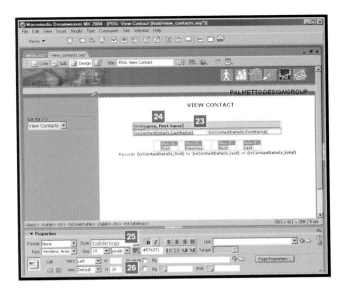

Where to Go from Here

The future of Web sites is data-driven. With the frantic, content-now pace of today, you just don't have time to maintain static Web pages with content that changes from day to day. Dreamweaver provides an easy introduction to the world of Web application development with built-in server behaviors and auto-generated forms, but you've barely begun to scratch the surface in this session!

Unlike HTML, you cannot simply view the source to see how your favorite site accomplished that very cool new feature. If you are drawn to the development end of Web design, you need to explore

different technologies, such as ColdFusion and ASP.NET. Some great free and inexpensive options are available as well, such as MySQL, PostgreSQL, and PHP. Increase your knowledge of how a database functions. You can find many good books on all these subjects.

Also, Dreamweaver Help includes information for readers from a variety of backgrounds, from novice to expert. Be sure to read *Absolute Beginner's Guide to Databases* and *Database Design for Mere Mortals* if you are new to using a database or need to develop your own.

» Session Review

You just made your site dynamic! It's amazing how much power Dreamweaver gives you even with little knowledge of coding. Test your newly learned knowledge with these questions. The answer to each question is in the tutorial or discussion noted in parentheses.

1. What type of server technology did you use for this session? (See "Tutorial: Adding a Recordset.")

2. What is a recordset? (See "Tutorial: Adding a Recordset.")

3. Which panel do you use to add a recordset? (See "Tutorial: Adding a Recordset.")

4. What does a repeating region do? (See "Tutorial: Using Repeating Regions.")

5. When a recordset shows a column with <ignore> by it, how do you fix it? (See "Tutorial: Using Insert Record on Forms.")

6. How do you make sure that parts of a form are filled in correctly? (See "Tutorial: Validating Your Forms.")

7. What is Unique Key Column? (See "Tutorial: Building Update Pages.")

8. How do you install an extension? (See "Tutorial: Building Update Pages.")

9. After you added the recordset navigation and tested it, you saw only two of the four links. Why? (See "Tutorial: Inserting a Recordset Navigation Bar.")

10. After a record is deleted, can you change your mind and undo it? (See "Tutorial: Building Delete Pages.")

11. When you added the table to the details page, what happened to it? (See "Tutorial: Making Master Detail Pages.")

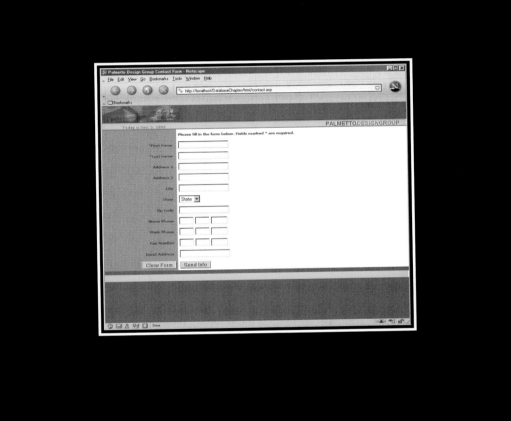

Part VI:
Extra Features

Session 15 **Making a Pop-Up Menu**

Session 16 **Building a Frame-Based Site**

Making a Pop-Up Menu

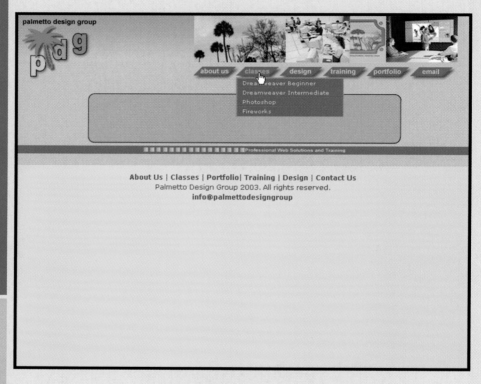

Tutorial: **Adding the Show Pop-Up Menu Behavior**

Tutorial: **Setting the Menu's Appearance**

Tutorial: **Setting the Advanced Settings**

Tutorial: **Setting the Menu's Position**

Tutorial: **Adding the Rest of the Menus**

Tutorial: **Making a New Template Page**

Session Introduction

Pop-up menus, drop-down menus, DHTML menus, fly-out menus—they are all basically the same concept but with different names. Dreamweaver MX 2004 ships with a very cool pop-up menu behavior that enables you to make pop-up menus with little effort. Sure, you can make your own without this behavior, and for certain effects, you might want to. But this new behavior, which first appeared in Fireworks 4, is a fantastic timesaver.

Now when your client asks for a DHTML menu, you can say "no problem" and whip one up in no time at all. Just don't tell anyone how easy it was!

TOOLS YOU'LL USE
Show Pop-Up Menu behavior

MATERIALS NEEDED
session15_starterfiles if needed

TIME REQUIRED
90 minutes

Tutorial
» Adding the Show Pop-Up Menu Behavior

In this tutorial, you add the Show Pop-Up Menu behavior and configure the menu for the About Us link.

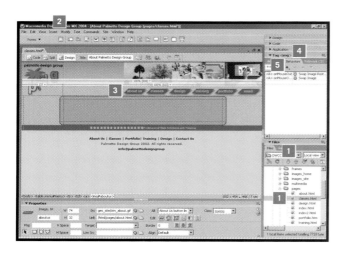

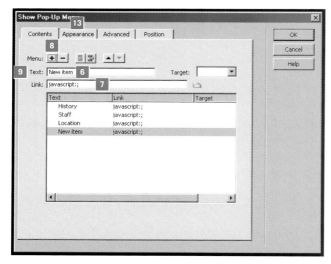

1. **Select the DWCC defined site, and then double-click the** classes.html **file to open it.**

2. **Click Modify→Templates→Detach from Template.**
   Because the Show Pop-Up Menu behavior won't work in the template file, you add it to this page just to learn how to make this menu. If you decide that this is the type of menu you want, make it prior to making the template or add the menu to the template file.

3. **Click the About Us button to select it.**

4. **Click the Tag inspector, and then select Behaviors to make it the active panel.**

5. **Click the plus sign (+), and click Show Pop-Up Menu.**
   The Show Pop-Up Menu dialog box opens.

6. **In the Text field, type** History**.**

7. **In the Link field, type** Javascript:;**.**
   If you recall, this is a null link, which you can change at any time.

8. **Click the plus sign (+) to add the menu item.**
   Notice that the first menu item is in the Text field in the main window. A New Item is listed and will be replaced with the next entry.

9. **In the Text field, highlight New Item and type** Staff**.**

10. **Click the plus sign (+).**
    You could change the link field now if you knew the name of the link page.

11. **Highlight New Item, and type** Location**.**

12. **Click the plus sign (+).**

13. **Click the Appearance tab.**
    So far you've added just the link text that will be seen in your pop-up menu when a user passes over the About Us button.

Tutorial
» Setting the Menu's Appearance

In this tutorial, you determine the appearance of the menu items.

1. **Click the down arrow in the first field.**
   Notice that you have two options: the Vertical Menu and the Horizontal Menu. Leave the default of Vertical Menu selected.

2. **Click the down arrow for the Font field, and click Verdana, Arial, Helvetica, sans-serif.**

3. **Highlight the Size, and type** 10.

4. **Click the B icon if you want the text to be bold and the I icon if you want the text to be italic.**
   In this example, I didn't select either one.

5. **Look at the preview in the lower portion of this dialog box to see how the text looks.**
   The preview is approximate.

6. **Leave the default alignment at left-align.**

7. **Click the color box for the Up State Text field.**

8. **With the Eyedropper tool, click a gold color.**
   The color clicked here is the second gold color from the right of the seventh row from the top, Hex #FFCC00. You can also click on the System Color Picker for more color options.

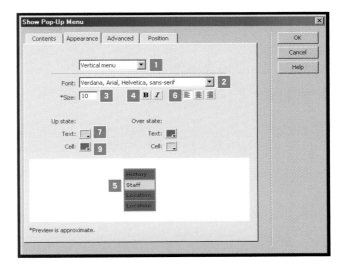

<NOTE>
If you've ever used the Fireworks Pop-Up Menu, you may know that you can type in a Hex number. You can't do that in Dreamweaver.

9. **Click the color box of the Cell field in the Up State, and click a blue color.**
   The color selected in this example is the blue from the About Us button.

10. **Repeat for the Over State, but reverse the colors.**
    Sample the colors with the Eyedropper from the Text and Cell boxes that you selected in the Up State.

11. **Click the Advanced tab.**

12. **Leave the dialog box open.**
    Now you've set up the colors and the appearance of your menu links.

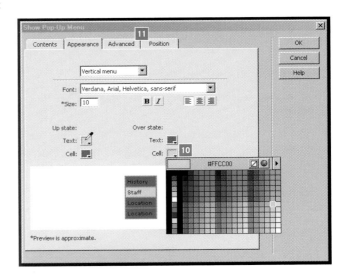

Tutorial
» Setting the Advanced Settings

In this tutorial, you set the width and height of the cells as well as the border and shadow properties.

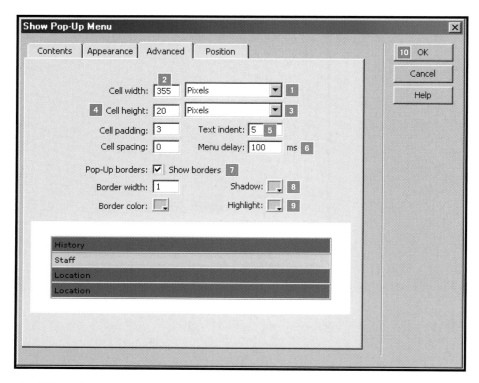

1. **Click the down-pointing arrow of the Cell Width field, and click Pixels.**

2. **Type** 355 **for the Cell Width amount.**

3. **Click the down-pointing arrow of the Cell Height field, and click Pixels.**

4. **Type** 20 **for the Cell Height.**
   You can see the changes in the Preview part of the window.

5. **Type** 5 **for the Text Indent.**
   This indents the text by five pixels from the left of the menu's edge.

6. **Delete the last 0 in the Menu Delay to change the number from 1000 to 100.**
   This setting determines how fast the menu closes when you move your mouse off the menu.

7. **Leave the Show Borders box checked.**

8. **Click in the Shadow color box, and click the symbol for no.**

9. **Click in the Highlight color box, and click the symbol for no.**

< N O T E >

Determining the size of the cells may take some trial and error. You can click OK at any time and preview in a browser. To continue editing, you simply select the About Us button again and double-click the Show Pop-Up Menu behavior to open the Show Pop-Up Menu dialog box.

10. **Click OK.**

11. **Preview your work in the appropriate browser(s).**

12. **Mouse over the About Us button.**
    As you can see, the menu isn't positioned properly and it's too long.

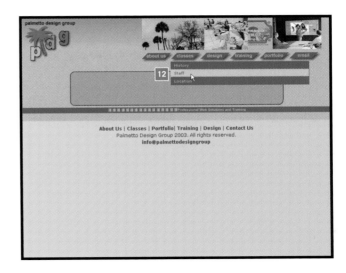

13. **Open the Behaviors panel (Tag Inspector panel group).**

14. **Double-click on the Show Pop-Up menu behavior.**

15. **Click on the Advanced tab in the Show Pop-Up Menu dialog box.**

16. **Change the Cell Width to** 65.
    The position will still be wrong but you'll fix that in the next tutorial.

17. **Save the file, but keep it open.**

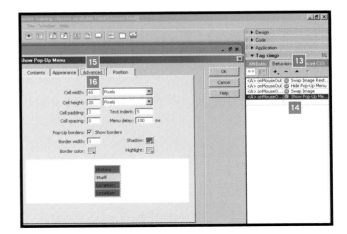

Submenu Items

Because we align this table to the right of the document window, you don't use submenus. You might at some point want to have a menu system with submenus. A submenu item is added the same way as you just inserted the first three items. To make a submenu entry, type the name in the text field, click the plus sign (+), select the entry, and click the Indent Item button. The item appears indented. Be sure to add the submenu items below the associated menu item. If you add a menu item and it appears indented, be sure to click the Outdent Item button.

Tutorial
» Setting the Menu's Position

In this tutorial, you set the menu's positioning. You set the position relative to the trigger button, which in this case is the About Us button.

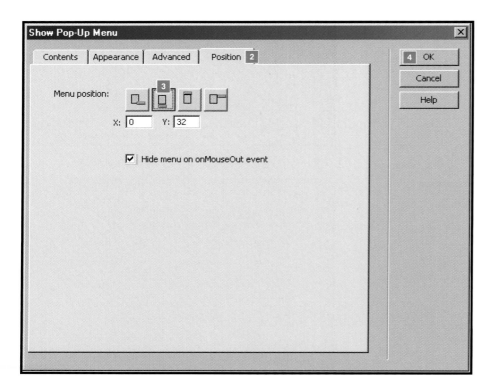

1. **Click the About Us button.**

2. **In the Show Pop-Up Menu dialog box, click on the Position tab.**

3. **Click the second icon from the left.**
   It places the menu below and at left edge of trigger, which is the About Us button. The position will be x: 0 and y: 32. The bottom-right corner position is selected by default. The x and y coordinates are set automatically, but you can adjust these values if needed.

4. **Click OK.**

5. **Preview your work in the appropriate browser(s).**

Personally I like the menu a tad closer to the button.

6. **Double-click the Show Pop-Up Menu behavior in the Behaviors panel.**

7. **Select the Position tab and change the y coordinate to** 27. **Click OK.**

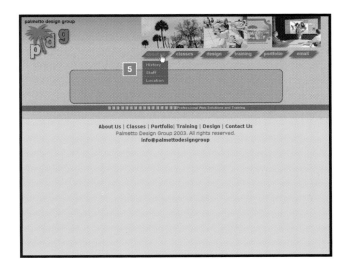

8. **Preview again.**

I like this better.

9. **Save the file, but keep it open.**

You've added a menu just to the About Us button. Now you'll add the rest of them.

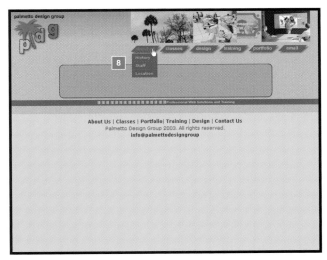

Tutorial
» Adding the Rest of the Menus

In this tutorial, you add the rest of the menus. The process is the same as you've done for the About Us button, just the positioning and sizes will change.

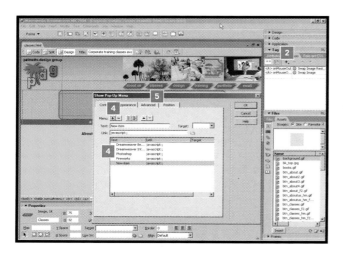

1. **Click the Classes button.**

2. **Click the plus sign (+) in the Behaviors panel.**

3. **Click on the Show Pop-Up Menu.**

4. **Add the following menu items (using a null link) as you did in the "Adding the Show Pop-Up Menu Behavior" tutorial:**

   » Dreamweaver Beginner

   » Dreamweaver Intermediate

   » Photoshop

   » Fireworks

5. **Click on the Appearance tab.**
   The settings are the same as the last time you used this tab. But if by some chance they aren't correct, use the same settings that you did in the "Setting the Menu's Appearance" tutorial.

6. **Click on the Advanced tab.**

7. **Leave the Cell width and Cell height set to Automatic.**

8. **Set the Indent to 5.**

9. **Set the Shadow to none again.**
   For some reason this setting is not retained between uses.

10. **Set the Highlight back to none.**

11. **Click on the Position tab.**

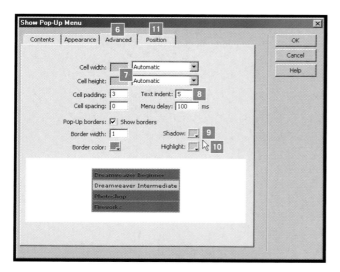

12. **Click the second icon from the left again to line the menu up with the left of the classes button.**

13. **Change the y coordinate to 27 so it's the same level as the About Us menu.**

14. **Click OK.**

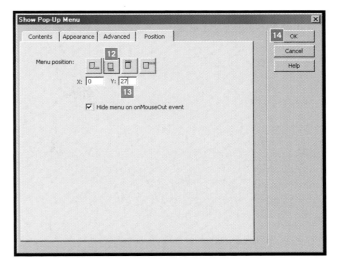

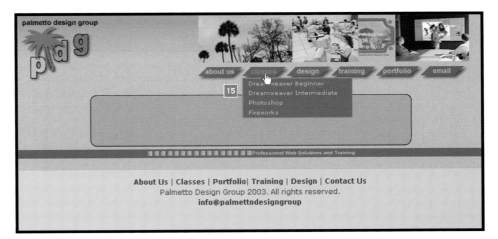

15. **Preview your work in the appropriate browser(s).**

16. **Save the document.**

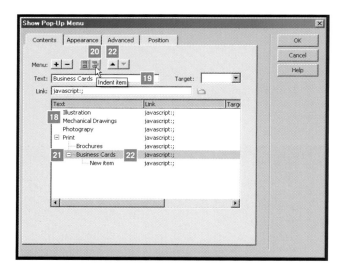

17. **Click the Design icon, and add the Show Pop-Up Menu behavior.**
    The Portfolio and Training buttons don't need menus, so you can skip those two.

18. **Add these menu items:**

    » Illustration

    » Mechanical Drawings

    » Photography

    » Print

19. **Type** Brochures **in the Text field and click the Add (+) button.**

20. **Click the Indent icon.**
    Use the Indent icon for submenus. To make an item a main menu, it shouldn't be indented. If it is, click the Outdent button.

21. **Add Business Cards and indent it as a submenu.**

22. **Select Business Cards and click the Up arrow.**
    This moves Business Cards above Brochures.

23. **Click on the Advanced tab, and set these settings:**

    » Shadow: **None**

    » Highlight: **None**

24. **Click on the Position tab, click the second from the left icon again, and change the y coordinate to** 27.

25. **Click OK.**

26. **Preview your work in the appropriate browser(s).**

27. **Mouse over the Design button.**
    Notice the little arrow next to Print. This indicates there is a submenu.

28. **Now for the best part: Make the browser window larger, and mouse over the menus.**
    Look at that! The menus are still aligned properly because they are positioned relative to the trigger.

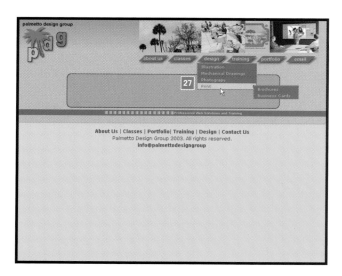

Tutorial
» Making a New Template Page

You now make another template. This one can be used if you want to have pop-up menus on your pages. Instead of applying pdg.dwt, you would apply this template to any pages on which you want the pop-up menu to appear. Normally, you wouldn't have more than one menu system on a Web site. This template page gives you options when you design your own site.

1. **With** classes.htm **still open, click File→Save as Template.**

2. **Type** popup **in the Save As field.**

3. **Click Save. Click Yes to update links.**

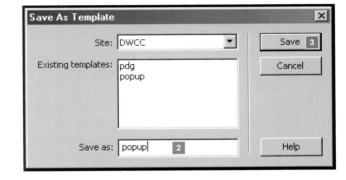

4. **Click in the area outside the rounded table area.**

5. **In the Common category of the Insert bar, click on the arrow for the Template menu.**

6. **Select Editable Region.**

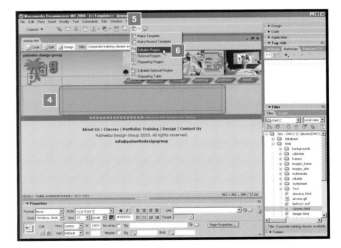

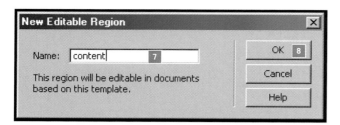

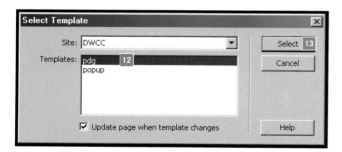

7. **Name it** content.

8. **Click OK.**

9. **Save the template.**
   You get a message about updated pages linked to the template. That's okay; only classes change, and you take care of that in a moment. You now have a template that supports pop-up menus available to use if you'd rather use it than pdg.dwt.

10. **Double-click** classes.htm **to open it.**
    It's no longer open because it was changed to popup.dwt. You now return this file to the original template.

11. **Click Modify→Templates→Apply Template to Page.**

12. **In the Select Template dialog box, click PDG.**

13. **Click Select.**
    You reapply the original template to classes.htm; you used it only to make the alternative menu template.

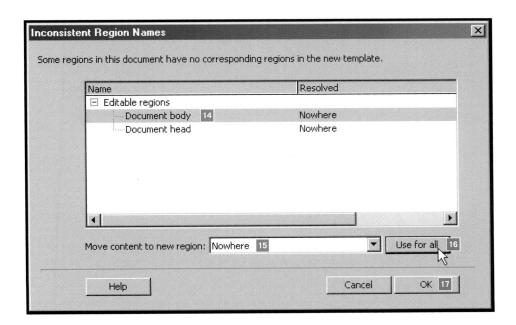

14. **Click Document body.**

15. **In the Move Content to New Region menu, click Nowhere.**

16. **Click on the Use for All button.**

17. **Click OK.**

18. **Save and close the page.**
    You now have a template to use for a site using the pop-up menus as an alternative to the original template design you made for PDG.

» Session Review

In this session, you learned how to add layers that could be used for a layout instead of tables. In the process, you learned lots of layer basics such as sizing and positioning. You also nested a layer inside the content layer. On the `training.htm` page, you added a layer with content. This layer is unseen in the final file because we placed it above the page content. It was lowered for this illustration.

Aren't these menus fun? The best part is they are so quick to do and you have tons of flexibility. Test yourself now and see how much you retained. The answer to each question is in the tutorial or discussion noted in parentheses.

1. How do you add a null link? (See "Tutorial: Adding the Show Pop-Up Menu Behavior.")

2. What do you do if you want to add a submenu item? (See "Tutorial: Adding the Show Pop-Up Menu Behavior.")

3. Can you change the color of the menu cells? (See "Tutorial: Setting the Menu's Appearance.")

4. What are the two options for the menu types in the Appearance category? (See "Tutorial: Setting the Menu's Appearance.")

5. What are the two options for the Cell Width and Height? (See "Tutorial: Setting the Advanced Settings.")

6. How did you make the menu go over the design title? (See "Tutorial: Setting the Advanced Settings.")

7. Which position icon do you click for a custom x or y setting? (See "Tutorial: Setting the Menu's Position.")

8. How do you designate a submenu item? (See "Tutorial: Adding the Rest of the Menus.")

9. What happened to the classes.html page after you made it into a template? (See "Tutorial: Making a New Template Page.")

» Other Projects

Try making a menu using submenus. You couldn't do so in this design because of the position of the buttons.

1. Type a few text links for navigation, or start with a few buttons.

2. Add the Show Pop-up Menu behavior.

3. Add the menu items, and use the indent button for the submenu items.

4. Set the Appearance of your menus. Try changing the border or adding a shadow and highlight.

5. Set the Advanced settings for the menu size to Automatic.

6. Choose the positioning you like.

7. Test your new menu.

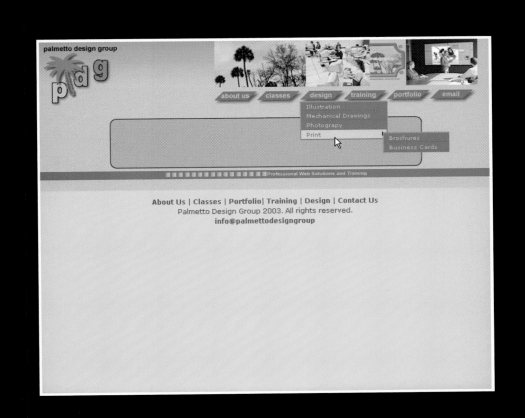

palmetto design group

about us   classes   design   training   portfolio   email

Illustration
Mechanical Drawings
Photograpy
Print
                              Brochures
                              Business Cards

Professional Web Solutions and Training

About Us | Classes | Portfolio| Training | Design | Contact Us
Palmetto Design Group 2003. All rights reserved.
info@palmettodesigngroup

Building a Frame-Based Site

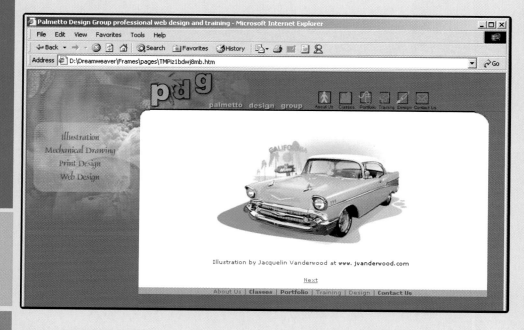

Tutorial: **Building the Frameset**

Tutorial: **Naming the Frames**

Tutorial: **Adding a Nested Frame and Saving the Frameset**

Tutorial: **Adding Content to the Frames**

Tutorial: **Linking the Navigation**

Tutorial: **Adding Multiple Links**

Tutorial: **Coding for Search Engines**

Tutorial: **Adding a Specialized Jump Menu**

Session Introduction

Using frames to design a site is an extremely controversial topic. Designers usually either love them or hate them. I list some of the pros and cons later in this session. But you may be thrilled to discover that most of the cons are addressed and converted into pros in this session.

The best argument and solutions I've seen for developing frame-based Web pages comes from Al Sparber and Gerry Jacobsen of Project VII (www.projectseven.com). They developed an extension for a special jump menu that works wonderfully with frames.

In this session, you create an alternative Web site design. It isn't linked to the main project in any way except that you use some of the image resources. I felt it would be an injustice to you not to show you how to develop a frame-based site. Of course, all the issues surrounding frame-based sites can't be covered, but the major issues and the basics can get you started if you want or need to build a frame-based site.

TOOLS YOU'LL USE
Property inspector, Behaviors panel, Jump menu extension,
Frames panel

MATERIALS NEEDED
The PDGFrames folder on the CD-ROM. Save the folder to your
hard drive, but not in the DWCC root folder.

TIME REQUIRED
90–120 minutes

Tutorial

» Building the Frameset

In this tutorial, you build the frameset structure. I have supplied a few new images for a new design, added some pages for the site, and attached the `pdg.css` style sheet.

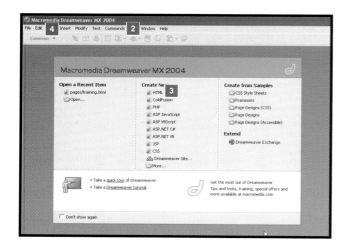

1. **Copy the PDGFrames folder from the CD-ROM to your hard drive.**
   You can copy it anywhere but in the DWCC folder.

2. **In Dreamweaver, define a new site by choosing Site→ Manage Sites→New and name it PDGFrames.**
   This new site contains images, a style sheet, and enough files to learn how to put together and link a frame-based Web page. I didn't make a new home page or fill in all the content, but it's a great start for you to practice some of your new skills.

3. **Click HTML in the New category on the Start page to open a new blank document, but don't save it yet.**

4. **Choose View→Visual Aids, and click Frame Borders.**
   Frame Borders are not turned on by default. While designing the frameset, you need to see the borders.

5. **Press Shift+F2 to open the Frames panel.**
   You can also access it from the Window menu.

6. **Click the Layout category in the Insert bar.**
   You insert a simple frame, and then I show you how to make the frameset more complex.

<NOTE>

The icons that show three frames with both horizontal and vertical areas are actually nested frames. Instead of using one of these, I show you how to nest the frames yourself visually. Doing so equips you with more knowledge of how to customize a frameset to meet your needs.

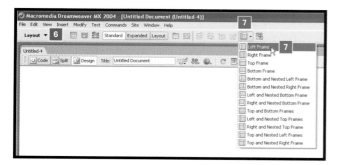

7. **Click the Frames icon to access the frames list, and select the Left Frame icon.**
   You can now see the frame in the document. You can also see the new frame in the Frames panel.

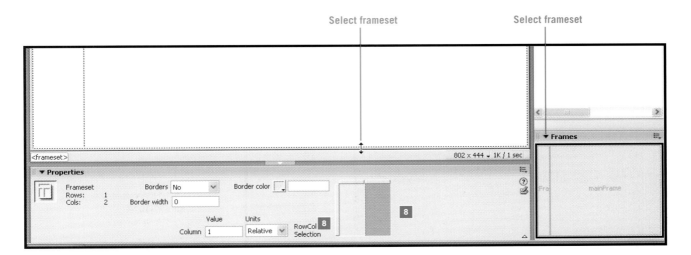

Select frameset   Select frameset

8. **Look in the Property inspector.**
   Notice that this is a frameset; you can set the borders for the frameset, which affects all the frames. You can also set a specific column width. You also see a visual representation of the two frames on the right side of the Property inspector. This frameset consists of three documents: the frameset document and the two individual frame documents.

9. **Click inside the left frame, and look in the Tag Selector.**
   Do you see the <body> tag? This shows you that it is a separate page with its own <body> tag. You can access each frame from the Frames panel as well.

10. **Leave the page open for the next tutorial.**
    That's all you need to do to add a frame to a page. Simple, huh?

<NOTE>

If you don't see the frameset information in the Property inspector, you need to select the frameset. An easy way to do this is to click the outside border of the frameset in the Frames panel. Another way is to pass your mouse over any of the outside edges of the document until you see a double arrow. When the arrow is present, click to select the entire frameset.

Tutorial
» Naming the Frames

In this tutorial, you set the properties of each frame and name them with meaningful names.

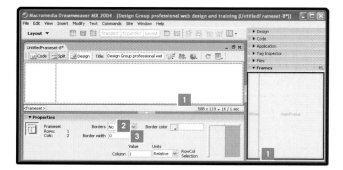

1. **Click on the outer border in the Frames panel or on one of the edges in the document to select the frameset.**
   When you click the outer border of the frameset, you are working with the frameset document, which is actually three pages right now.

2. **In the Property inspector, set Borders to No.**

3. **Set the Border Width to 0.**
   Remember, you have to type zero; a blank is not interpreted as zero.

4. **In the Title area of the document, type** Palmetto Design Group professional web design and training.
   You don't need to title the individual frame pages because only the title from the frameset appears in the user's browser.

5. **Select the left frame by clicking inside the frame in the Frames panel.**

6. **In the Property inspector, name it** sidebar.
   Always give your individual frames meaningful names that describe their function.

7. **Leave No Resize checked.**
   If unchecked, this option allows the user to resize the frame.

8. **Set Scroll to No.**
   Be extremely careful when you select No for scroll. Because this navigation area is small, I know it fits in any browser without scrolling.

9. **Select the right mainFrame, and name it** content.

10. **Set the Scroll to Auto.**
    This frame has an undetermined amount of content, so it is set to scroll if needed.

11. **Click No Resize.**
    You've just named our frames; now it's time to customize the frame arrangement and then to name all the pages.

Tutorial

» Adding a Nested Frame and Saving the Frameset

In this tutorial, you add a frame inside the top content frame to act as the top navigation and logo frame. This is called a nested frame. You then save the frameset and the three individual frames.

1. **Click in the content frame in the Frames panel.**
   Clicking in the content frame in the document does not select it. The easiest way to select the appropriate frame is by using the Frames panel.

2. **In the document window, drag the top border of the content frame down to about ¼ of the space.**

3. **Select the new frame, and name it** topnav.

4. **Set the Scroll to No, and click No Resize to select it.**

5. **Pass your cursor over the inside sidebar border in the document window, and drag a bit larger, about ¼ of the document window.**
   When you place the cursor over the inside border, you see a double arrow; click and drag to the new position.

6. **Click the outer border of all the frames to select the frameset. Look in the Tag Inspector; the** <frameset> **tag is highlighted.**

7. **Click File→Save Frameset As.**

8. **Name it** index.html, **and save it in the Pages folder. You should see lots of other pages that I saved for you to use in this session.**

9. **Click inside the sidebar frame.**

10. **Click File→Save Frame As, and name it** sidebar.html. **Save it in the Pages folder.**

11. **Click inside the topnav frame.**

12. **Click File→Save Frame As, and name it** topnav.html. **Save it in the Pages folder.**

13. **Click inside the content frame.**

14. **Click File→Save Frame As, and name it** content.html. **Save it in the Pages folder.**
   Now that you've named all your frame pages and added pages to use with your frames, you are now ready to add content to the frames.

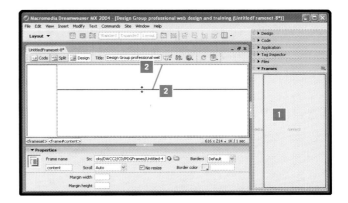

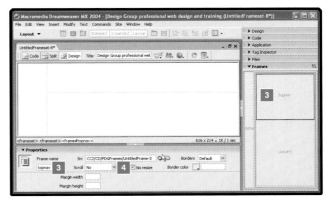

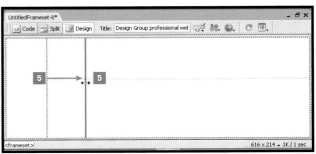

Tutorial
» Adding Content to the Frames

In this tutorial, you insert the `.HTML` files that load into the `index.html` file whenever it opens. I have supplied the pages for you to use for this practice.

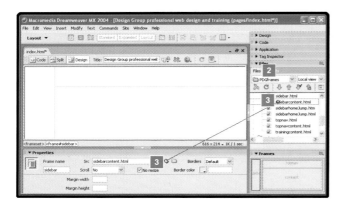

1. **Click the sidebar in the Frames panel.**
   Be sure that you can see the name sidebar in the Property inspector. Another way to tell if you've got the frame selected is to check the Tag Selector. `<frame#sidebar>` is highlighted.

2. **Open the Files panel, and open the Pages folder.**

3. **In the Property inspector, click and drag the Point to File icon to the right of the Src field and drag to the `sidebarcontent.html` page in the Pages folder.**
   The frame may be too small or too large for the content. You can click and drag the border to fit, but you can be more precise in the Property inspector.

<CAUTION>
At the time of this writing Dreamweaver generated the improper link code. Check the Link field in the Property inspector; the link should be `sidebarcontent.htm` (delete /pages/ if you see it).

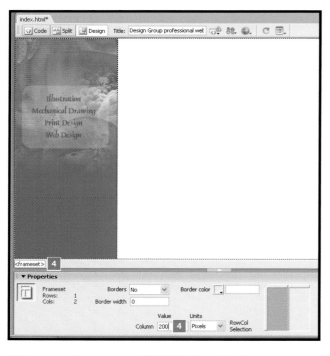

4. **Click the frameset border and change the Column size to** 200, **and press Enter (Return).**

5. **Select the topnav frame; `<frame#topnav>` is highlighted.**

6. **Use the Point to File icon and drag the Point to File icon to the Pages folder and release the mouse on `topnavcontent.htm`.**

<CAUTION>
Again, delete the /pages/ part of the link if you see it.

7. **In the Frames panel, select the topnav frame.**

8. **In the Status bar, select** `<frameset>` **in front of the**
   `<frame#topnav>` **tag.**

9. **In the Property inspector, be sure that the top row is selected. You
   can use the frame selector in the Property inspector.**

10. **Set the Row value to** `71` **and the Units to Pixels.**

11. **Select the content frame.**

12. **Use the Point to File icon and drag the Point to File
    icon to the Pages folder and release the mouse on**
    `contenthome.htm`.

<CAUTION>

Delete /pages/ from the link in the Link field of the
Property inspector.

13. **In the Column area of the Property inspector, click the bottom row
    in the little image.**

14. **Set the Row Value to** `2` **and the Units to Relative.**
    This setting expands this column based on the browser
    window size.

15. **Choose File→Save All.**
    You now have content in your frames. Now you need to add
    links to access all the pages in the site.

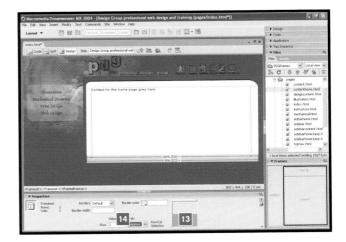

Tutorial
» Linking the Navigation

In this tutorial, you add links to the sidebar navigation, which open pages in the content area. Then you click a link in the content area, which opens a document in the same area.

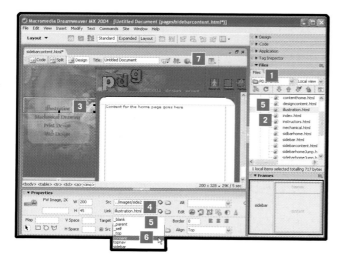

1. **Open the Files panel.**

2. **Open the Pages folder, and double-click on** `index.html` **if you closed it.**

3. **Click the Illustration image in the document sidebar.**

4. **In the Property inspector, drag the Point to File icon to the right of the Link field to the** `illustration.htm` **file and release the mouse. Delete /pages/ from the Src field in the Propety inspector.**

5. **Click the down arrow for Target.**

6. **Click content as the target from the drop-down menu.**

7. **Choose File→Save All. Preview in your default browser.**
   Use the Preview/Debug icon to select a browser to preview in, or use the keyboard shortcut of F12 to preview in your default browser.

<NOTE>
If you don't save before trying to preview, a warning dialog box opens. Click OK, and it saves for you and continues with the preview.

8. **In the browser, click the Illustration button.**
   The image of the Bel Air loads in the content area.

9. **Repeat Steps 3 through 6 for Mechanical Drawing and Print Design.**
   There is no file for Web Design, so you can use a null link or just skip it.

10. **In the browser, click the Mechanical Drawing link.**

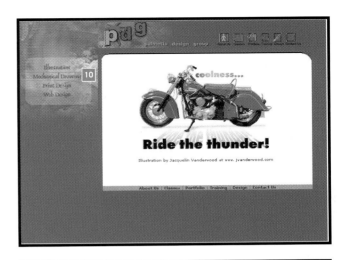

11. **Click on the Print Design links.**
    Notice that the content area expands to fit the different sized images.

12. **Double-click the** `illustration.htm` **file to open it, and highlight the word Next.**

13. **Drag the Point to File icon for the link to the** `mechanical.htm` **file, and release the mouse.**
    If this were a real site, you probably would have more samples under the illustration link. Because we don't, you simply use the next category for the next link.

14. **Click the arrow for the Target.**

15. **Click** `_self`.
    This opens the link on top of the current page. Therefore, it replaces the current page.

16. **Preview your work in the appropriate browsers. Click the Illustration link, and then click the Next link.**

17. **Repeat for** `mechanical.htm` **and** `print.htm`. **Link Print Design to** illustration.htm **to make a loop.**

18. **Save your file.**
    Now when you click the Illustration, Print, and Mechanical buttons, a new page loads in the content area.

<NOTE>

The drawings were provided by Jacquelin Vanderwood of www.jvanderwood.com.

Tutorial
» Adding Multiple Links

In this tutorial, you still work with the frameset you've built so far. The previous tutorials used the content for the sidebar that goes to the design link. You change that content to an empty sidebar, so you can see that clicking on the Design icon not only brings up content in the content area but changes the sidebar as well.

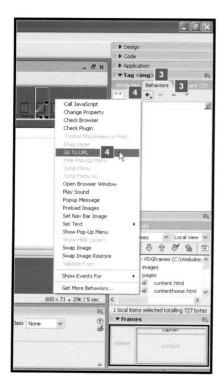

1. **In the Frames panel, select the sidebar. Drag the Point to File icon to the** `sidebarhome.htm` **page. Press F12 to preview; notice that the sidebar is just an image.**

2. **Click the Design icon (second from the right). Check the Property inspector to be sure it shows properties for an image.**

<TIP>

Maintaining focus is sometimes a problem in Dreamweaver; it's a good idea to always check the Property inspector to be sure the focus is where you want it. For instance, when selecting the icon after a frameset, you may have to select it twice to make the image active.

3. **Click the Tag inspector, and then click Behaviors to activate the Behaviors panel.**

4. **Click the plus sign (+), and click Go to URL.**
   The Go to URL dialog box opens. This is a pretty neat feature.

5. **In the Open In field, select frame "sidebar"*.**

6. **Click the Browse button, and navigate to the Pages folder.**

7. **Click** `sidebarcontent.htm`.
   If you recall, this is the page to which we linked the Illustration, Mechanical Drawing, Print Design, and Web Design links.

8. **In the Open in field, select frame "content"*.**

9. **Click the Browse button.**

10. **Navigate to the Pages folder, click** `designcontent.htm`, **and click OK.**

11. **Click OK to close the Go to URL dialog box.**
    You simply repeat these steps for other links. Isn't that easy?

12. **In the Behaviors panel, click the Event on the right side of the behavior name (probably onLoad), and then click the down arrow.**

13. **Select onClick.**

    You can use any one of the options that you see listed in the menu. You can even have the sidebar and content both load onLoad if you like.

<NOTE>

If you don't see the onClick option, click the Plus button and select Show Events For→IE6.

14. **Click File→Save All.**

15. **Preview your work in the appropriate browsers.**

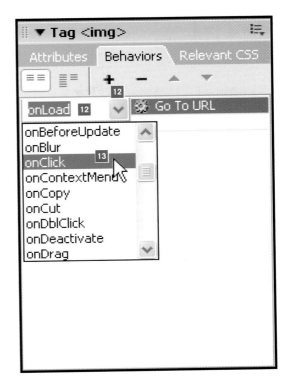

16. **In the browser, click the Design icon.**

    Notice that the sidebar and the content window change; isn't that cool? The sidebar now has links, and the content area says that design content goes here to distinquish that the page did in fact change.

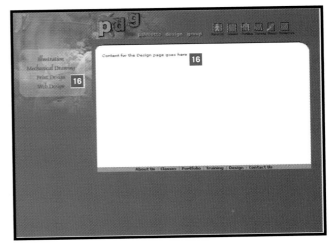

Tutorial
» Coding for Search Engines

One of the greatest arguments for not using frames is the fact that they are difficult to index in a search engine. If you code your page properly, you can overcome this drawback. Of course, I show you how to do that now.

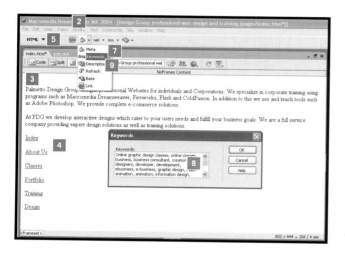

1. Open the index.htm file if it isn't open.

2. Select the frameset and choose Modify→Frameset→Edit NoFrames Content.

3. In the blank window that opens, type a description of your site.

<NOTE>

This is the window that appears in browsers that don't support frames. It is also the information that the search engine uses to index your site, so use keywords and phrases in your description. I filled in this one using as many keywords as I could, but I'm not a copywriter. For these kinds of things, you might want to consult with someone who is really good at writing these sorts of descriptions. This and your metatags are some of the most important things to be found in search engines.

4. Add links to every page that you'd like a search engine to index. Type the text names for the links. When you add the actual link in the Property inspector, use an absolute URL.
   I used http://www.palmettodesigngroup.com and then added each file name to the end—for example, http://www.palmettodesigngroup.com/training.html.

5. Switch to the HTML category of the Insert bar.

6. Click the Head tab in the Insert bar.
   If you haven't used this icon yet, it is called the Head: Meta icon. Otherwise, the icon is whatever you used last from the list.

7. Click the Keywords icon.

8. Enter the keywords that you want to use, and click OK.
   I just copied the ones used in the PDG site that we've already done.

9. Click the Description icon from the Head list in the Insert bar.

10. Type a description, and click OK.

11. Choose File→Save All, and close the document.

Tutorial
» Adding a Specialized Jump Menu

This is an enhanced jump menu that is great for using with frames. It doesn't fit with the sample design because you can't have multiple links, so you build it in a new page.

1. **Open the Goodies folder in the Session16 folder on the CD-ROM.**

2. **Copy the extensions in it, and paste them into the Downloaded Extensions folder in the Dreamweaver MX 2004 program files.** For Windows XP, the path is: Program files\Macromedia\ Dreamweaver MX 2004\Downloaded Extensions.

3. **Double-click each extension to install it. Or you can use the Extension Manager (Commands→Manage Extensions), click the Install icon (with green arrow), select extension name, and click the Install button.**

4. **After you accept the licensing agreement, the extension is installed and displays a message saying that it has successfully installed.**

5. **In Dreamweaver, open the PDGFrames site and double-click the** sidebarhomejump.htm **page to open it.**

6. **Click the layer named jumpmenu.** If you can't tell where the layer is, press F2 to open the Layers panel and select it there. You can close the Frames panel now if you like.

7. **Place your cursor inside the layer, and click the Forms icon in the Forms bar of the Insert bar.** This field is required for this menu to work in Netscape 4X.

8. **Click inside the form field in the sidebar frame.**

9. **Click Insert→StudioVII→PVII Jump Menu Magic.**

10. **In the text field, type** Choose A Destination.

11. **Click the plus sign (+) to enter the menu item.**

12. **In the Text field, type** About Us.

13. **Click the Browse button, and select the** aboutus.html **page in the Pages folder.**

14. **Click the Select Target arrow, and select frame: "content".**

15. **Type** Main Navigation **in the Menu Name field.**

16. **Click the Select First Item After URL Change option.** This option returns the Choose A Destination item to the menu. You don't need to add any links yet because this is just the beginning item that the users see.

< N O T E >

Extensions don't have to be saved in the Downloaded Extensions folder. You can put them anywhere you like. This is just a handy storage place, but it's not required.

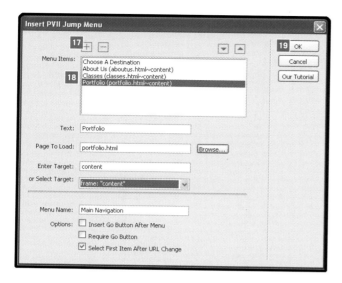

17. Click the plus sign (+).

18. Repeat Steps 11 through 14 for Classes and Portfolio.

19. Click OK to close the dialog box.

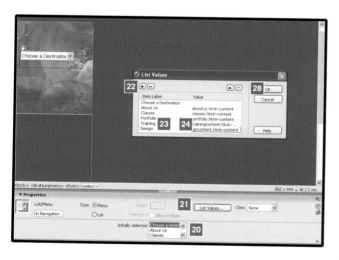

20. In the Initially Selected field of the Property inspector, select Choose a Destination.

    If you want to add more items to the menu, you can do so from the Property inspector, which you do next. You add a couple pages with some real content now.

21. Click the List Values.

22. Click the plus sign (+).

23. Type Training in the Item Label field.

24. Type trainingcontent.html~content into the Value field.

    You need to know your links when you use this method of adding menu items.

25. Click the plus sign (+).

26. Type Design in the Item Label field.

27. Type designcontent.html~content into the Value field.

28. Click OK to close the dialog box.

29. Save and close the file.

    You need to add this new sidebar to your frameset in order to preview it, which you do next.

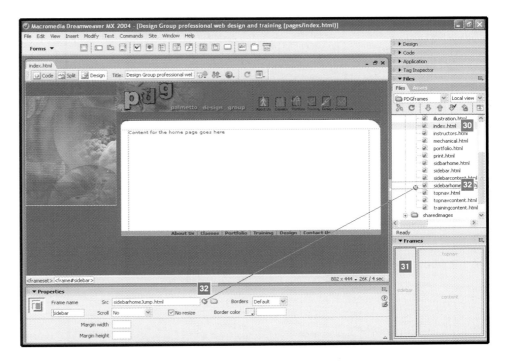

30. **Open the** `index.html` **page.**

31. **Select the sidebar frame in the Frames panel.**

32. **Drag the Point to File icon for Src to the**
    `sidebarhomeJump.htm` **file, and release the mouse.**

33. **Preview your work in the appropriate browsers. Click Training, and then click Design.**

34. **Click File→Save All.**
    You can now test out your new specialized jump menu.

» Session Review

It's time to test yourself again to see how much of the frames information you retained. You may have to work with frames a bit more to have it really sink in. You may want to repeat this session if you find you can't answer the majority of these questions. The answer to each question can be found in the tutorial listed in parentheses.

1. Name one way to insert a frame. (See "Tutorial: Building the Frameset.")

2. What is a frameset? (See "Tutorial: Building the Frameset.")

3. How do you select a frameset? (See "Tutorial: Naming the Frames.")

4. How do you add a nested frame? (See "Tutorial: Adding a Nested Frame and Saving the Frameset.")

5. How do you add content to the individual frames? (See "Tutorial: Adding Content to the Frames.")

6. When adding links, what is different about linking in a frame to open in another frame? What is this type of frame called? (See "Tutorial: Linking the Navigation.")

7. What method is used that enables you to link multiple frames to one link? (See "Tutorial: Adding Multiple Links.")

8. How do you save all the frameset files at one time? (See "Tutorial: Adding Multiple Links.")

9. Name two important features that allow search engines to index your site even if it's framed. (See "Tutorial: Coding for Search Engines.")

10. Must you have a Go button with a jump menu? (See "Tutorial: Adding a Specialized Jump Menu.")

» Other Projects

If you want to practice some more, you can add some content to one of the other categories.

1. Open the `sidebarhome.htm` file on the CD-ROM (not the one that you just saved).

2. Save the file in your Pages folder as `portfolio.htm`.

3. Add a jump menu (a Dreamweaver or PVII one).

4. Use any names you want for the menu items.

5. Add a portfolio content page with identifying text in it (such as a content page for portfolio). This helps you identify whether it works properly when you test it.

6. Link the Portfolio icon to open the new sidebar and content onClick.

7. Add a content page or two to correspond to your menu item links.

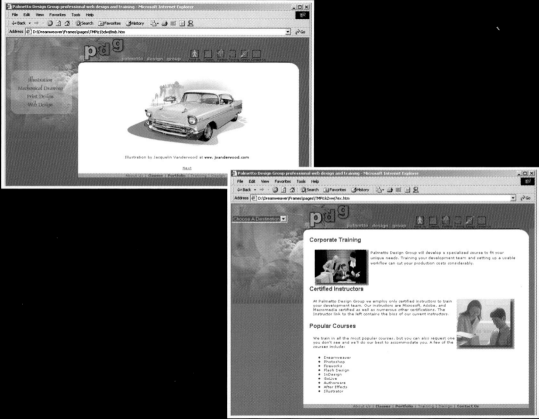

What's on the CD-ROM

This appendix provides you with information on the contents of the CD-ROM that accompanies this book. For the latest and greatest information, please refer to the ReadMe file located at the root of the CD-ROM. Here's what you will find:

» System Requirements

» Using the CD-ROM wtih Windows and Macintosh

» What's on the CD-ROM

» Troubleshooting

System Requirements

Make sure that your computer meets the minimum system requirements listed in this section. If your computer does not match up to most of these requirements, you may have a problem using the contents of the CD-ROM.

System requirements for Microsoft Windows:

» An Intel Pentium III processor or equivalent, 600 MHz or faster, running Windows 98, Windows 2000, Windows XP, or Windows Server 2003

» Version 4.0 or later of Netscape Navigator or Microsoft Internet Explorer

» 128MB of RAM (256MB recommended) plus 275MB of available disk space

» A 256-color monitor capable of 800 x 600 pixel resolution or better

» A CD-ROM drive

System requirements for Apple Macintosh:

» A 500MHz Power Macintosh running Mac OS X 10.2.6 and later, 10.3

» Version 4.0 or later of Netscape Navigator or Microsoft Internet Explorer

» 128MB of RAM (256MB recommended) plus 275MB of available disk space

» A 256-color monitor capable of 800 x 600 pixel resolution or better

» A CD-ROM drive

Using the CD-ROM with Windows

To install the items from the CD-ROM to your hard drive, follow these steps:

1. Insert the CD-ROM into your computer's CD-ROM drive.

2. The interface will launch. If you have autorun disabled, click Start→Run. In the dialog box that appears, type **D:\setup.exe**. Replace *D* with the proper letter if your CD-ROM drive uses a different letter. (If you do not know the letter, see how your CD-ROM drive is listed under My Computer.) Click OK.

3. A license agreement appears. Read through the license agreement, and then click the Accept button if you want to use the CD. After you click Accept, you will never be bothered by the License Agreement window again.

4. Click anywhere on the Welcome screen to enter the interface. This next screen lists categories for the software on the CD.

5. For more information about a program, click the program's name. Be sure to read the information that appears. Sometimes a program has its own system requirements or requires you to do a few tricks on your computer before you can install or run the program, and this screen tells you what you might need to do, if necessary.

   If you do not want to install the program, click the Back button to return to the previous screen. You can always return to the previous screen by clicking the Back button. This feature allows you to browse the different categories and products and decide what you want to install.

6. To install a program, click the appropriate Install button. The CD interface drops to the background while the CD installs the program you chose.

7. To install other items, repeat Steps 5 and 6.

8. When you have finished installing programs, click the Quit button to close the interface. You can eject the CD now. Carefully place it back in the plastic jacket of the book for safekeeping.

Using the CD-ROM with the Macintosh OS

To install the items from the CD-ROM to your hard drive, follow these steps:

1. Insert the CD-ROM into your computer's CD-ROM drive.

2. Double-click the icon for the CD-ROM after it appears on the desktop.

3. Double-click the License Agreement icon. This is the license that you are agreeing to by using the CD. You can close this window after you have looked over the agreement.

4. Most programs come with installers; for those, simply open the program's folder on the CD-ROM and double-click the Install or Installer icon. *Note:* To install some programs, just drag the program's folder from the CD-ROM window and drop it on your hard drive icon.

What's on the CD-ROM

The following sections provide a summary of the software and other materials that you'll find on the CD-ROM.

Tutorial Files

All the tutorial files that you use when working through the tutorials in this book are on the CD-ROM in the folder named "Tutorial Files." Within the Tutorial Files folder are subfolders containing the tutorial files for each session. In each session subfolder, you can find all the files referenced in that session, including a starter file to use with that session if you need it.

Copy the DWCC folder to your hard drive: This is the starter file for building your site. You'll be instructed on how to define a site. Use this folder as your root. As you progress through the book, if you have a problem with a session or decide to skip a session, then begin that session with the starter file in its folder. To use a starter file, simply copy it to your hard drive and define it as a new root folder. You could, of course, paste it into the DWCC folder and overwrite your files if you want to.

Software

The following applications are on the CD-ROM:

» Dreamweaver 2004 trial version—the best darn HTML editor and layout designer around.

» Fireworks 2004 trial version—the premiere image editor what works hand-in-hand with Dreamweaver.

» WebSpice Objects demo version—a nifty program that contains 3,000 high-quality buttons, labels, borders, and other art to give the professional look to your Web pages.

» Xenofex 2 demo plug-in has 14 effects and hundreds of presets. You can simulate natural phenomena such as lightning and clouds and distortions such as Flag, Television, and Rip Open. You can transform your photos into jigsaw puzzles, constellations, and intricate mosaics with a single click. The hundreds of presets make adding effects very quick and easy.

» Mystical Lighting demo version of Mystical Lighting plug-in is an easy way to add realistic lighting and shading effects to digital images. There are 16 visual effects with over 400 presets. Mystical Lighting also includes features such as layers, unlimited undos, visual presets, masking, and dynamic effect controls.

» Mystical Tint and Color demo version of Mystical Tint Tone and Color plug-in is a suite of 38 color effects. The effects are applied by brushing on or removing the effect from the desired area. Mystical Tint Tone also has unlimited undo and redo, layers, visual presets, and a robust set of tools.

» Wild FX is a fully functioning demo of the Wild FX Flash Text Animator. The demo does not allow you to save your files, and the preview contains a watermark. You can easily make Flash text including over 400+ effects including 40+ customizable effects.

» WebAssist PayPal is a fully functioning extension to add a shopping cart to your site.

Trial, demo, or evaluation versions are usually limited either by time or functionality, such as being unable to save projects. Some trial versions are very sensitive to system date changes. If you alter your computer's date, the programs "time out" and are no longer functional.

Troubleshooting

If you have difficulty installing or using any of the materials on the companion CD-ROM, try the following solutions:

» Turn off any antivirus software that you may have running. Installers some-times mimic virus activity and can make your computer incorrectly believe that a virus is infecting it. Be sure to turn the antivirus software back on later.

» Close all running programs. The more programs you are running, the less memory is available to other programs. Installers also typically update files and programs; if you keep other programs running, the installation may not work properly.

» Reference the ReadMe file. Please refer to the ReadMe file located at the root of the CD-ROM for the latest product information at the time of publication.

If you still have trouble with the CD-ROM, please call the Wiley Publishing Customer Care phone number: (800) 762-2974. Outside the United States, call 1(317) 572-3994. You can also contact Wiley Publishing Customer Service by visiting our Web site at www.wiley.com/techsupport. Wiley Publishing provides technical support only for installation and other general quality control items; for technical support on the applications themselves, consult the program's vendor or author.

Resources

Resources List

This appendix contains recommendations for tools that you may find useful. When designing a Web site, you often need other resources to enhance the design or to help make your development time more productive. None of these products is required; I just wanted to give a little input and help in finding things that you may need or want. I have not included a list of links to Dreamweaver resources because they are included on the CD-ROM.

Products

The products listed here are some I've found useful. I thought that you might be interested in some of them.

Web Assist

www.webassist.com

Web Assist provides a free plug-in that adds a PayPal shopping cart to your Web site. Web Assist also has a much more robust version with many more features available for sale. I use this plug-in for a quick shopping cart solution.

Smart Draw

www.smartdraw.com

SmartDraw.com features more than 50,000 symbols, images, and templates, as well as easy drag-and-drop drawing. I found this application extremely easy to use, much easier than the competing major product. SmartDraw is intuitive and imme- diately usable with no training, no manuals, and practically no learning curve.

Color Schemer

www.colorschemer.com

Color Schemer is an application that helps you come up with a color scheme. Some of the features include multiple color-matching modes, drag-and-drop colors, saved colors schemes that you can easily navigate, and pre-made color schemes that you can sample. You can customize various schemes and change color values.

ColorWrite

www.adaptiveview.com/cw

ColorWrite is a color chooser with an integrated CSS/HTML code generator. It allows you to define colors using RGB, HSV, CMY, and CMYK, and makes using Web-safe colors easy. ColorWrite runs on Macintosh (OS X), Linux, Solaris, and Windows systems.

Camtasia Studio

www.techsmith.com

Camtasia Studio records full-motion video of your screen and produces the videos in Flash and streaming formats. You can edit the videos, as well as narrate and annotate with callouts, text boxes, and so on. You can also create Flash menus for your videos with the Theater add-in. Camtasia Studio videos can be used to train, support, and demonstrate the best way to use PC software.

Sorenson Squeeze 3

www.sorenson.com

Sorenson Squeeze 3 is a simple yet powerful software application that provides an interface to Sorenson Media's professional video codecs—Sorenson Video 3.1 Pro, Sorenson Spark Pro, and Sorenson MPEG-4 Pro. The software application simpli- fies the compression process by providing the user with the presets to easily access the advanced features of the codecs. Sorenson Squeeze 3 is available in three versions—Sorenson Squeeze 3 Compression Suite, Sorenson Squeeze 3 for Macromedia Flash MX, and Sorenson Squeeze 3 for MPEG. All three versions are designed to meet the needs of both novice and professional content creators who want to encode and deliver high-quality video.

Wildform

www.wildform.com

The Wildform Resource Center contains numerous Flash tutorials, FLAs, articles, and links, as well as sections on how to create Flash projectors, Flash players, and Flash ads and e-mails. Wildform creates easy-to-use Flash products including the Flix Flash Video Encoders, the Linx Easy Flash Editor, and the SWfX Flash Text Animator. With Wildform products, you can create stunning Flash projects without knowing Flash, including Flash buttons, banners, navigation elements, tutorials, demos, slide shows, and multimedia presentations.

TopStyle Pro

www.bradsoft.com

You can get a trial version of TopStyle Pro at the Web site listed here. Dreamweaver has wonderful new support for CSS, but if you want all the power and flexibility that you can get, try the TopStyle editor. It's reasonably priced at $49 and is Dreamweaver MX-compatible. CSS is actually quite simple, but getting it to work in multiple browsers is a challenge. TopStyle is unique in that it checks your style sheets against multiple browser implementations, letting you know about bugs and incompatibilities that may affect your design. It also provides site management from a CSS perspective, providing you with detailed style information about your entire site.

Proposal Kit and Contracts

www.proposalkit.com

If you need inspiration and templates to write professional proposals and contracts, then check this one out. The best value is the Proposal Kit Pro bundle, which includes all the packages for estimating, contracts, proposals, and more. Each kit includes templates with placeholders to put in your own text as well as completed samples to guide you. This has been one of my better finds. You can find a complete review at my site, www.joycejevans.com/reviews.

Plug-ins to Use with Fireworks

Most Photoshop-compatible plug-ins work with Fireworks. It's the Photoshop native filters after version 5.5 that do not work. But the mainstream third-party plug-ins work great. Here is a sampling of some of my favorites.

Alien Skin Software

www.alienskin.com

Xenofex 2

Xenofex 2 is OS X-compatitble and delivers 14 phenomenal effects. You can simulate natural phenomena such as lightning and clouds, and distortions such as Flag, Television, and Rip Open. You can transform your photos into jigsaw puzzles, constellations, and intricate mosaics with a single click. The hundreds of presets make adding effects very quick and easy.

Eye Candy 4000

Eye Candy 4000 includes 23 prescription-strength special effects. This major upgrade to Alien Skin's award-winning Eye Candy includes five new filters—Marble, Wood, Drip, Melt, and Corona—and many powerful improvements.

Eye Candy 4000 combines practical filters that you'll use every day, such as Bevel Boss, Shadowlab, and Gradient Glow with effects like Chrome, Smoke, and Fire. New features include bevel profile and color gradient editors, a preview that allows you to see underlying layers, perform seamless tiling, undo an unlimited number of actions, and more. You can even trade your favorite settings with others.

Splat!

I love this one; you can make some pretty great edges with it. What I especially like is the expandability of it. You can edit or make your own effects. The things you can do include:

- » **Frame** adds realistic frames and mattes to any photo or other rectangle. Choose from 100 frames, including traditional wood frames, Dover, and geometric borders.

- » **Resurface** adds any of 100 high-resolution surface textures to an object or selection. It adds natural media with only a few clicks, distorting your image to match the surface. Textures include paper, concrete, leather, brick, stone, metal, wood, and more.

» **Edges** adds versatile, decorative edge effects such as halftone dots, torn paper, and pixelated edges. This effect works with any selection and looks great applied to text.

» **Fill Stamp** fills any selection with familiar objects. Choose from more than 100 stamp files, and then scale the objects to fit. Fill Stamp adapts to any shape and works well on text. This effect can be seamlessly tiled and colorized to match your image.

» **Border Stamp** applies the power of Fill Stamp to borders, creating borders from everyday objects such as pebbles, pills, and tickets. Great for themed borders, Border Stamp includes realistic drop shadows and adapts to any shape.

» **Patchwork** re-creates images as mosaics such as light pegs, ASCII art, ceramic tile, and cross-stitch. Simply browse the Patchwork libraries, scale your tiles, and apply.

Image Doctor

This one is new and is in public beta at this writing. It should be available by the time this book is published. It has some really cool editing effects. I've tried some of the effects, such as repairing blocky JPEGs, and it did a wonderful job.

It is an all-new set of powerful image-correction filters for Photoshop, Fireworks, Paint Shop Pro, and other image editors. Image Doctor removes blemishes and defects, repairs over-compressed JPEGs, and replaces unwanted details and objects. Professional and amateur photographers, photo editors, archivists, graphic designers, and Web designers can quickly fix their images with Image Doctor.

Image Doctor delivers these effects in a clean, easy-to-use interface. Users can tweak their effects in a huge preview that includes a before/after toggle, command menus, keyboard shortcuts, and unlimited undo capability.

Image Doctor is the only filter set to offer selection-based image repair. Use the familiar selection tools of your image editor, and then correct large and small areas in one pass. The intelligent pattern matching of Image Doctor makes it the perfect complement to existing photo-editing tools.

Auto FX

www.autofx.com

I don't use plug-ins often, but when I do, I use these sets (and Alien Skin) most often. I provide information only about the few that I like the best, but you can check the vendor's Web site for additional offerings.

Mystical Lighting

Mystical Lighting is an easy way to add realistic lighting and shading effects to digital images. You can choose from 16 visual effects and more than 400 presets. Mystical Lighting also includes features such as layers, unlimited undos, visual presets, masking, and dynamic effect controls.

Mystical Tint Tone and Color

Mystical Tint Tone and Color is a suite of 38 color effects. An effect is applied by brushing on or removing the effect from the desired area. Mystical Tint Tone also has unlimited undo and redo, layers, visual presets, and a robust set of tools.

DreamSuite Gel Series

This series is a fun visual arts tool that lets you create translucent colored artwork and images. DreamSuite Gel Series allows you to add reflective and refractive depth effects. Gel includes advanced brush-based tools to let you paint on depth and translucent reflections, colors, and textures.

Gel effects include Gel, Gel Painter, Liquid Crystal, Crystal Painter, and Gel Mixer.

Each product from Auto FX Software serves as either a stand-alone application or as a plug-in for image-editing programs like Adobe Photoshop, Adobe Elements, Corel PhotoPaint, and Paint Shop Pro.

Clipart and Stock Images

When you need a quick piece of art or an image, clipart and stock images is a great way to go. Here are a few resources that I use.

Getty

www.gettyimages.com

Getty Images is totally focused on producing the most relevant, reflective, and "defining" pictures of today. Getty Images produces, preserves, and markets the largest collection of imagery in the world. You can find images from companies such as Photodisc, Digital Vision, Thinkstock, FoodPix, and many more.

Rubberball

www.rubberball.com

The images used for www.stockimagenation.com (site made in the *Web Design Complete Course* book) were supplied by Rubberball. I love the fun and energetic images. Visit them to see the fun images of people. Rubberball uses silhouette style in themes, photographic angles, and people on white backgrounds.

Rubberball has a 5,000-image picture library. Children, teens, and adults in different environments and roles are portrayed throughout the 47-volume collection.

Hemera Photo-Objects 50,000 Volumes I & II

www.hemera.com

Photo-Objects are photographic images of people, animals, and objects that have been isolated from their original background and pre-masked so they can be quickly and easily dropped into any design. These images are great for business and design professionals. Photo-Objects can enhance everything from presentations and annual reports to marketing collateral such as advertisements and brochures. Each collection of 50,000 Photo-Objects is available for Windows and Macintosh.

The Big Box of Art

www.hemera.com

The Big Box of Art is a digital image collection of great quality and variety that includes Hemera Photo-Objects, clip art, illustrations, professional stock photos, Web graphics, and more.

Photosphere

www.photosphere.com

The images that I used on the training page came from the Office Situations CD collection. PhotoSphere Images is a premiere supplier of professional, royalty-free stock images. Accessing the library of more than 2,800 images is fast and easy. The keyword search engine helps you find specific images quickly. Each of the 30 collections of stock images includes 80 to 100 images.

All images are available online in JPEG format and on CD in Photo CD format. The pricing is very competitive.

Index

»SYMBOLS«

& (ampersand) for nonbreaking spaces ( ), 110

* (asterisk) in title bar, 36

© (copyright symbol), 119

/ (slash) in comments, 54

»A«

<a> (anchor) tags
- keywords in, 66
- overview, 24
- for pseudo-class selectors, 158–159

about.htm file
- applying template to, 173–174
- creating footer Library item from, 178
- detaching the template, 177
- image map link to, 139
- link to, 134, 137

Access Drivers (Microsoft), 248

accessibility. *See also* Alt fields
- Accessibility test, 224
- Lift program for, 224
- preferences, 63

- Section 508 of laws, 5
- standards, 63
- table summary information for, 72
- text links, 12–17

Actions, 185, 189, 197

active link color, 16, 65

Active Server Pages. *See* ASP

Alien Skin Software Web site, 336

Alt fields
- empty, 110
- for image map links, 10–11
- for index.htm images, 8, 84, 85, 86
- for masthead images, 100, 101
- for navbar.gif image, 8
- for navigation table images, 104–105
- overview, 8
- site report on missing alt text, 223

ampersand (&) for nonbreaking spaces ( ), 110

anchor tags. *See* <a> (anchor) tags

Apple Macintosh. *See* Macintosh (Apple)

applying
- custom classes (CSS), 155–157
- template changes to all pages, 176
- templates, 172–174

ASP (Active Server Pages)
application server required for, 246
delete pages, 283–284
master detail pages, 285–287
Microsoft Access drivers for, 248
update pages, 276–280

.ASP file extension, 268

asset availability, determining, 34

Assets panel
alphabetization by, 86
Favorites list, 46
links in, 135
removing Files panel and, 38
using, 46

asterisk (*) in title bar, 36

attaching a style sheet, 150–151

attributes
alignment attributes, 103
setting for <body> tag, 64–65
XHTML versus HTML, 54

audience for your site, 32

Auto FX plug-ins, 337

autostretch tables, 71, 88–89

»B«

background color. *See also* **colors**
for autostretch table, 89
for content table, 92
for custom borders, 80
for `index.htm` page, 7, 65
Layout view and, 95
for navigation table, 90
for rounded table, 112
Snap to Web Safe color and, 141
for tables, 78

text same color as, 67
for Web page, 7, 65

background images, 111, 113

bandwidth with hosting service, 234

`basic.html` **form**
building the form, 186–189
buttons, 190–193
inserting check boxes, 194–195
inserting list, 196–197
inserting text area, 196
jump menu, 198–199

BBEdit keyboard shortcuts, 40

Behaviors panel, 199, 294

Big Box of Art image collection, 339

<body> tag
automatic generation, 23
editing, 152–153
form code in, 187
for frames, 311
setting attributes, 64–65

`books.gif` **image, 86**

borders, 79, 80–81, 296, 310

brightness, adding to images, 209

broken links, 220–221

browsers
adding, 62
browser checks, 227
modes for CSS, 53
preferences, 62
previewing in, 62, 87, 102, 269
primary browser, 62
system requirements, 27, 28, 328
testing templates in, 169
for testing this project, 26

`btn_about4.gif` **image, 108**

`btn_about.gif` **image, 104, 106**

`btn_about3.gif` **image, 107**

`btn_about2.gif` **image, 106**

`btn_aboutus_hm.gif` **image, 86**

`btn_classes_hm.gif` **image, 86**

`btn_design.gif` **image, 104**

`btn_design_hm.gif` **image, 86**

`btn_email.gif` **image, 105**

`btn_email_hm.gif` **image, 86**

`btn_portfolio.gif` **image, 105**

`btn_portfolio_hm.gif` **image, 86**

`btn_training.gif` **image, 104**

`btn_training_hm.gif` **image, 86**

building frame-based sites
adding contents to frames, 314–315
adding multiple links, 318–319
building the frameset, 310–311
coding for search engines, 320
linking the navigation, 316–317
maintaining Dreamweaver focus, 318
naming frames, 312
nested frames, 313
other projects, 324
overview, 306
saving the frameset, 313
selecting the frameset, 311
setting frame properties, 312
specialized jump menu, 321–323

building the site framework
adding design notes, 55–57
adding meta tags, 66–67
choosing a view, 60–61
home page specification, 55
opening a new document, 58
overview, 51

saving a document, 58–59

setting accessibility preferences, 63

setting browser preferences, 62

setting page properties, 64–65

buttons

adding links, 137

adding to `index.htm` page, 86

adding to navigation table, 104–105

Flash buttons, 140–141

for forms, 190–193

Go button for jump menu, 199

image maps versus, 138

rollovers for, 136–137

`byline_text.gif` **image, 105**

»C«

caching

enabling for site, 43

refreshing site list, 107

`calendar.htm` **file, 72–75, 79, 80–81**

Camtasia Web site, 334

Cascading Style Sheets. *See* **CSS styles**

case in XHTML versus HTML, 54

CD-ROM with this book

ConfidenceBuilder folder on, 6

copying files from, 27

DatabaseChapter folder on, 249

Dreamweaver extensions on, 321

Dreamweaver trial version on, 26, 330

DWCC folder on, 27

Fireworks trial version on, 26, 205, 330

Goodies folder on, 321

installing items, 328–329

ReadMe file, 327, 331

software on, 330

system requirements, 327–328

troubleshooting, 331

tutorials on, 329

cells. *See* **tables**

CGI scripts, 197, 234

check boxes for forms, 194–195

Chili!Soft ASP (Sun), 246

`classes.html` **file**

applying template to, 174

image map link to, 139

link to, 134, 137

pop-up menu for, 294–302

Clean Up Word HTML dialog box, 121

Clear button for forms, 190

cloaking folders, 237

`cnr_lbtm.gif` **image, 110**

`cnr_ltop.gif` **image, 109**

`cnr_rbtm.gif` **image, 110**

`cnr_rtop.gif` **image, 109**

Code View, 22, 60

Color Schemer application, 334

colors. *See also* **background color**

choosing, 79

contextual selector for, 162

defining in <body> tag, 152

editing for Fireworks image, 214

for Flash text, 128

for fonts, 123

gradient behind logo, 103

for links, 16, 65

for pop-up menus, 295, 296

same for text and background, 67

Snap to Web Safe color option, 141

for table borders, 81

in tables, 73, 78–79

ColorWrite color chooser, 334

comments, XHTML versus HTML, 54

compatibility, browser checks for, 227

Confidence Builder. *See* `index.htm` **page**

connection string setup, 257, 261–262

`connPDG` **connection**

connection string method, 257, 261–262

local DSN method, 257, 258

MapPath method, 257, 263

overview, 257

remote DSN method, 257, 259–260

`contacts_list.asp` **page, 268–272**

content table, 92

`content.html` **frame, 313**

contextual selectors, 161–163

contrast, adding to images, 209

copying

extensions from the CD, 321

files from the CD, 27

folders from the CD, 6, 27, 249

importing text by, 120

Library items, 179

copyright notice, 118–119

copyright symbol (_), 119

`corporate.gif` **image, 84, 85**

cropping images, 206–207, 215

CSS (Cascading Style Sheet) styles

adding space using, 164–165

advantages, 54, 117

applying custom classes, 155–157

attaching a style sheet, 150–151

background color, 7

browser modes and, 53

class name for footer area, 160

CSS (Cascading Style Sheet)

styles *(continued)*

contextual selectors, 161–163

defining, 13–14

DOCTYPES, 53, 54

editing <body> tags, 152–153

embedded styles, 147

external style sheets, 147

for font information, 117

formatting text for links, 13–14

grouping selector tags, 154

inline styles, 147

Library items, 178–181

overview, 147

preferences, 163

Property Inspector versus, 124

pseudo-class selectors, 158–159

removing embedded styles, 148–149

rules, 153

standards for, 52–53

transitional design and, 52–53

CSS Style Definition dialog box, 13–14

CSS Styles panel, 13–14, 151, 155–157

custom borders for tables, 80–81

custom classes (CSS), 155–157

custom fonts, 123

customizing

keyboard shortcuts, 40–41

workspace, 38–39

»D«

data source name. *See* **DSN**

database connection

choosing a connection method, 257

connection string method, 257, 261–262

defining a dynamic Web site, 249–254

DSN name setup, 255–257

hosting service support for, 232

installing a Web server, 246–248

local DSN method, 257, 258

MapPath method, 257, 263

overview, 245

remote DSN method, 257, 259–260

DatabaseChapter folder on the CD, 249

databases. *See also* **database connection**

adding a recordset, 268–270

building delete pages, 283–284

building master detail pages, 285–287

building update pages, 276–280

Insert Record on forms, 273–274

records overview, 267

Recordset Navigation Bar, 281–282

Repeat Region behavior, 271–272

running a query, 268–270

Unique Key Column, 277

validation, 275

default.htm page, 7

delete pages, building, 283–284

delete_contact.asp page, 283–284

design

modular, 90

previewing in browsers, 62, 87, 102, 269

standards changes for, 52

transitional method, 52–53

design notes, 56–57, 67

Design Notes dialog box, 57

Design panel, 150–151

Design View, 22, 60

designcontent.htm page, 318

design.html file, 134, 137, 139, 174

detaching templates, 177

DHTML menus. *See* **pop-up menus**

docking panels, 39

DOCTYPES, 53, 54

Document toolbar functions, 36

documents. *See also* **files**

creating templates from, 170–171

opening a new document, 58

saving, 58–59

title for, 64

windows, 37, 61

domain name, 231, 232, 233

download time on status bar, 37

DreamSuite Gel Series tool, 338

Dreamweaver Exchange, 47

Dreamweaver MX

complexity of, 26

customizing keyboard shortcuts, 40–41

font groups, 123

further information, 26

HTML and, 21, 23, 24

Macintosh/Windows differences, 28

maintaining focus, 318

opening, 35

overview, 21–22

server models supported, 26

server technologies supported, 249

system requirements, 27–28

trial version on the CD, 26, 330

***Dreamweaver MX 2004 Complete Course* (Evans, Joyce J.)**

audience for, 1–2

logic of, 25–26

overview, 1, 2–4, 25–26

using, 2

Dreamweaver 3 keyboard shortcuts, 40

drop shadow for images, 215

drop-down menus. *See* pop-up menus

DSN (data source name)

    local connection, 257, 258

    remote connection, 257, 259–260

    setting up, 255–257

DSN-less (connection string) setup, 257, 261–262

Duplicate CSS Style dialog box, 158, 159

DWCC folder on the CD, 27

dynamic pages. *See also* Web applications

    creating, 269–270

    defined, 245

    defining a dynamic Web site, 249–254

    overview, 248

    previewing in browsers, 269

    Repeat Region behavior, 271–272

    requirements, 246, 248

» E «

editable region of templates, 170–171

editing

    <body> tags, 152–153

    Library items, 180–181

    shapes, 138

    templates, 175–176

editing images

    adding brightness, contrast, and sharpening, 209

    cropping, 206–207, 215

    Fireworks source images in Dreamweaver, 213–215

    optimizing in Fireworks, 211–212

    overview, 205

    resampling, 208

    using external image editors, 210

e-mail or `mailto:` links. *See also* links

    allowing copy and paste for, 16

    contextual selector for, 161

    for hotspots, 11

    on image maps, 139

    regular links versus, 135

    for text, 16, 134–135

embedded styles, 147, 148–149

empty Alt fields, 110

empty forms, viewing, 186

Evans, Joyce J. (*Dreamweaver MX 2004 Complete Course*), 1–4

external image editor preferences, 210

Eye Candy 4000 plug-in, 336

» F «

Favorites list (Assets panel), 46

file extensions

    .ASP extension, 268

    changing the default, 45

    defaults for Web pages, 6

File Transfer Protocol. *See* FTP

files. *See also specific files*

    adding in Files panel, 45

    on the CD, 329–330

    changing read-only property, 27

    copying from the CD, 27

    importing text from, 120–121

    refreshing local file list, 43

Files panel

    refreshing site list, 107

    using, 38, 44–45

Find and Replace function, 219, 225–226

Fireworks

    defined, 26

    editing images in Dreamweaver, 213–215

    inserting images in Web page, 9

    optimizing images in, 211–212

    system requirements, 27–28

    trial version on the CD, 26, 205, 330

fixed tables, 71, 82–87

Flash (Macromedia), 128–129, 140–141

fly-out menus. *See* pop-up menus

focus, maintaining, 318

folders

    cloaking, 237

    copying from the CD, 6, 27, 249

    local root folder for site, 43

    synchronizing local site with remote server, 238–239

fonts

    CSS styles for, 14, 152, 153, 154

    custom, 123

    defining in <body> tag, 152, 153

    Dreamweaver font groups, 123

    Flash text, 128

    setting page properties, 65

    tags deprecated for, 117

footer area, 160, 161–163, 176

`footer` Library item, 178–181

Form Name attribute, 185, 187

Format Table dialog box, 73

formatting text, 13–14, 122–124

forms

    building a basic form, 186–189

    check boxes, 194–195

    Clear button, 190

forms *(continued)*

jump menus, 198–199, 200

lists for, 196–197

name-value pairs, 273

other projects, 200

overview, 185

Property Inspector settings, 189

radio buttons, 191–193

Submit button, 190

text area for, 196

using Insert Record on, 273–274

validating, 275

viewing empty forms, 186

frames. *See* **building frame-based sites**

Frameset DOCTYPE, 53

frames.htm **file, creating, 58–59**

FTP (File Transfer Protocol)

defined, 231

preferences, 235–236

remote server connection setup, 253–254

synchronizing local site with remote server, 238–239

uploading files to your host, 237

»G«

GET method of forms, 185

getting your Web site online

choosing a hosting service, 232–234, 235

FTPing files to your host, 237

overview, 231

setting FTP preferences, 235–236

synchronizing local and root folders, 238–239

Getty Images Web site, 338

GIF (Graphic Interchange Format) images, 99. *See also* **images**

Go button for jump menu, 199

gradient, creating, 103

»H«

<h1> (heading) tags, 117, 122

hard drive space requirements, 27, 28

<head> tag, 23

heading tags (HTML), 117, 122

Hemera Photo-Objects image collections, 339

home page. *See also* index.htm **page**

adding design notes, 56–57

fixed tables for, 82–87

setting index.htm page as, 55

HomeSite keyboard shortcuts, 40

hosting service

choosing, 232–234, 235

synchronizing local site with remote server, 238–239

uploading files to your host, 237

hotspots, 10–11, 138–139

hovering. *See* **rollovers for links**

.htm **file extension, 6**

.html **file extension, 6**

HTML (HyperText Markup Language). *See also* **tags (HTML)**

defined, 21

Dreamweaver MX for writing, 21

O'Reilly HTML Reference, 118

standards, 23, 24

XHTML versus, 24, 52, 54

<html> tags, 23

hybrid tables, 71

hyperlinks. *See* **links**

»I«

IIS (Microsoft), installing, 247–248

illustration.htm **file, 316, 317**

Image Doctor filters, 337

image editor preferences, 210

image maps, 10–11, 138–139

image tags, 24, 108

images

adding brightness, contrast, and sharpening, 209

adding to Favorites list, 46

aligning in adjacent columns, 105

Alt field, 8

background, 111, 113

clipart and stock images, 338–339

cropping, 206–207, 215

drop shadow for, 215

editing in external image editors, 210

gradients, 103

<img> tags, 24, 108

inserting from Assets panel, 46

inserting in index.htm page, 8–9, 83–86

inserting masthead images, 100–103

inserting navigation images, 104–105

Library items and, 179

optimizing in Fireworks, 211–212

overview, 99

refreshing site list for, 107

replacing, 106–108

resampling, 208

rounded table using, 109–112

spacer, 111, 112

vector graphics, 99

wrapping text around, 125–126

<img> tags, 24, 108

importing text, 120–121

`index.htm` **page**
adding and formatting text, 12–14
adding buttons, 86
Alt fields for images, 8, 84, 85, 86
background color, 7, 65
centering items on the page, 17
`default.htm` page versus, 7
editing `footer` Library item, 180–181
fixed table for, 82–87
inserting `footer` Library item, 179
inserting images, 8–9, 83–86
link to, 15
linking the text, 15–17
making an image map, 10–11
overview, 5, 7
saving, 7
setting as home page, 55
setting page properties, 64–65
setting up, 6–7
title, 7, 64

`index.html` **file.** *See also* **building frame-based sites**
adding content to frames, 314–315
building the frameset, 310–311
linking the navigation, 316–317
nested frame for, 313
saving, 313

`index2.html` **page, 138–139**

Insert bar, 36

Insert Fireworks HTML dialog box, 9

Insert Flash Button dialog box, 140–141

Insert Flash Text dialog box, 128–129

Insert Rollover Image dialog box, 137

inserting
buttons in forms, 190–193
check boxes in forms, 194–195
columns in tables, 75
Flash text, 128–129
images from Assets panel, 46
images in `index.htm` page, 8–9, 83–86
Library items, 179
lists in forms, 196–197
masthead images, 100–103
navigation images, 104–105
Recordset Navigation Bar, 281–282
rows in tables, 75
tables in tables (nesting), 80, 109
tables on pages, 72
text area in forms, 196
text in Web pages, 118–119

installing
CD items, 321, 328–329
Microsoft IIS, 247–248
Microsoft Personal Web Server, 246

Internet Explorer (Microsoft). *See also* **browsers**
setting browser preferences, 62
system requirements, 27, 28, 328
version for testing, 26

Internet resources
Alien Skin Software site, 336
Auto FX plug-ins, 337
Camtasia site, 334
clipart and stock images, 338–339
Color Schemer application, 334
ColorWrite color chooser, 334
keyword information, 66
Lift program, 224
Macromedia Exchange, 140
Proposal Kit Pro bundle, 335
SmartDraw.com site, 334
Sorenson Squeeze 3 application, 334–335
TopStyle Pro editor, 335
Web Assist site, 333
Wildform Resource Center, 335

ISP (Internet Service Provider). *See* **hosting service**

»J«

JPEG (Joint Photographic Experts Group) images, 99. *See also* **images**

jump menus, 198–199, 200, 321–323

»K«

keyboard shortcuts, 28, 40–41

Keyword dialog box, 66

keywords, 64, 66–67, 88

»L«

launching. *See* **opening**

laying the foundation
customizing keyboard shortcuts, 40–41
customizing the workspace, 38–39
defining a site, 42–43
other projects, 48
overview, 31
planning your site, 32–34
setting up the workspace, 35–37
using the Assets panel, 46
using the Files panel, 44–45
using the Start Page, 47

Layout view, 93–95

<li> (list) tags, 117, 122, 127

Library items, 178–181

Lift program, 224

`line_bhorz.gif` **image, 111**

`line_lvert.gif` **image, 112**

links. *See also* **e-mail or** `mailto:` **links**
colors for, 16, 65
e-mail versus regular, 135
fixing broken links, 221

links. *See also* e-mail or `mailto:` links *(continued)*
  frame navigation, 316–317
  to Home page, 15
  for image map, 11
  in jump menus, 198–199
  navigational, 132–142
  rollovers for, 136–137
  site report for broken links, 220–221
  text for, 12–14
  for `training.html` page, 134–135
  using, 135

list tags (HTML), 117, 122, 127

lists for forms, 196–197

Live Data View, 269, 270, 271

local DSN connection, 257, 258

local root folder, 43, 238–239

`logo.gif` image, 8, 83–84

`logo_top.jpg` image, 89

`logo2.gif` image, 91

M

Macintosh (Apple)
  default Web page file extension, 6
  system requirements, 28, 328
  Windows differences, 28

Macromedia Dreamweaver MX Bible, 26

Macromedia Exchange site, 140

Macromedia Flash, 128–129, 140–141

`mailto:` links. *See* e-mail or `mailto:` links

maintaining focus, 318

MapPath method, 257, 263

margins, setting, 65

master detail pages, building, 285–287

masthead images, 100–103

MDAC drivers (Microsoft), 248

`mechanical.htm` file, 317

menu bar, 36

menus, jump, 198–199, 200, 321–323

menus, pop-up. *See* pop-up menus

merging table cells, 77

meta tags (HTML), 66–67

Microsoft. *See also* Windows (Microsoft)
  Access Drivers, 248
  ASP, 246
  IIS, installing, 247–248
  Internet Explorer, 26, 27, 28, 62, 328
  MDAC drivers, 248
  PWS, installing, 246
  Word, importing text from, 121

mock up for site, creating, 33–34

`mod_contact.asp` page, 276–282

modular design, 90

Mozilla browser. *See* browsers

`mycalendar.html` file, 79

Mystical Lighting demo on the CD, 330, 338

Mystical Tint Tone and Color demo on the CD, 330, 338

N

names
  class name for footer area, 160
  for custom classes (CSS), 155
  domain name, 231, 232, 233

DSN name setup, 255–257
  for frames, 312
  for image maps, 138
  `index.htm` page title, 7
  login name for FTP, 236
  recordset naming conventions, 268
  for site, 43
  XHTML versus HTML and, 54

`navbar.gif` image, 8, 10–11

navigation bar, 8, 10–11, 281–282

navigation options, evaluating, 34

navigation table, 90–91, 104–105, 136–137, 137

`navigation.htm` file, 9

nested frames, 313

nesting tables, 80, 109

Netscape browser. *See also* browsers
  setting browser preferences, 62
  spacer images for, 111
  supporting, 53
  system requirements, 27, 28, 328
  versions for testing, 26

New Document dialog box, 47, 58–59

Nexpoint hosting service, 232

O

objective for your site, 32

ODBC driver, 258

opening
  Dreamweaver MX, 35
  files from Start Page, 47
  image editor from Assets panel, 46
  Macintosh/Windows differences, 28
  new document, 58

Opera browser. *See* browsers

optimizing images in Fireworks, 211–212

O'Reilly HTML Reference, 118

organizing your files, 27

»P«

<p> (paragraph) tags, 24

Page Properties dialog box
    index.htm page settings, 65
    picking background color, 7, 65
    setting background image, 113
    setting link colors, 16, 65
    Tracing Image settings, 94
    training.html page settings, 88

panels, 37–39. *See also specific panels*

paragraph tags, 24

parchment_bk.gif **image, 113**

password for FTP login, 236

PayPal (Web Assist) plug-in on the CD, 330, 333

pdg.css **style sheet, 150–151, 158–159, 160**

pdg.dwt **template, 220–221, 227**

Personal Web Server (Microsoft), installing, 246

Photosphere image collection, 339

planning your site, 32–34

PNG images, 99. *See also* images

pop-up menus
    adding more menus, 300–302
    advanced settings, 296–297
    appearance settings, 295
    making template page for, 303–305

    other names for, 293
    other projects, 306
    overview, 293
    positioning, 298–299
    Show Pop-up Menu behavior, 294
    submenu items for, 297, 306

popup.dwt **template, 303–305**

portfolio.html **file, 134, 137, 139, 174**

POST method of forms, 185

preferences
    accessibility, 63
    browser, 62
    CSS styles, 163
    external image editor, 210
    FTP, 235–236
    workspace, 36

previewing in browsers, 62, 87, 102, 269

primary browser, 62

print.htm **file, 317**

processor requirements, 27, 28, 328

Property Inspector. *See also* Page Properties dialog box
    Alt field, 8
    applying custom classes (CSS), 156
    centering tables or content, 73, 82, 83, 89
    changing cell padding and spacing, 74
    changing image size and, 112
    changing table colors, 78–79
    collapsing table column to fit image, 84
    context-sensitivity of, 37
    form settings, 189
    formatting text with, 123–124
    Layout view and, 95
    moving with gripper, 39
    overview, 37

    positioning cell contents to top, 83, 91, 92
    Rectangular Hotspot tool, 10
    rounded table settings, 109, 110
    setting column width, 84, 89, 91, 92

Proposal Kit Pro bundle, 335

pseudo-class selectors, 158–159

PWS (Microsoft Personal Web Server), installing, 246

»Q«

queries. *See* recordsets

»R«

radio buttons for forms, 191–193

RAM (random-access memory) requirements, 27, 28, 328

ReadMe file on the CD, 327, 331

read-only files, 27

Record Update Form wizard, 276

Recordset Navigation Bar, 281–282

recordsets
    adding, 268–270
    defined, 268
    Insert Record on forms, 273–275
    naming conventions, 268
    Repeat Region behavior, 271–272

registering a domain name, 233

regular expressions for Find and Replace, 226

Relevant CSS panel, 151

remote DSN connection, 257, 259–260

Repeat Region behavior, 271–272

replacing
Find and Replace function for, 219, 225–226
images, 106–108

Reports dialog box, 222

resampling an image, 208

resources. *See also* **Internet resources**
clipart and stock images, 338–339
Fireworks plug-ins, 336–338
products, 333–335

rollovers for links
adding, 136–137
color for, 16, 65, 162

Rubberball image collection, 339

rules (CSS), 153

running. *See* **opening**

»S«

saving
changes to files, 59
documents, 58–59
Find and Replace queries, 226
framesets, 313
`index.htm` page, 7
templates, 171, 303
your work, 9

search engines
coding frames for, 320
Flash and, 140
keywords for, 64, 66–67, 88

Section 508 of accessibility laws, 5

selecting
framesets, 311
in Layout view, 95

table elements, 73, 74, 76–77
tables, 74, 76, 77
views, 60–61

shapes, editing, 138

sharpening images, 209

shopping cart for your site, 234

Show Pop-Up Menu behavior, 294

Show Pop-Up Menu dialog box
Advanced tab, 296–297
Appearance tab, 295
Contents tab, 294
Position tab, 298–299

`sidebarcontent.html` **page, 314, 318**

`sidebar.html` **frame, 313, 314**

Site Definition dialog box, 42–43

site reports
Accessibility test, 224
for broken links, 220–221
checking, 222–224
on entire current local site, 222
on missing alt text, 223
updating template after, 224

sites. *See also* **getting your Web site online; Internet resources**
defining, 42–43
local root folder for, 43
page properties, 64–65
planning, 32–34
screen size for, 61
Web statistics, 234

slash (/) in comments, 54

SmartDraw.com Web site, 334

Sorenson Squeeze 3 application, 334–335

space, adding using CSS, 164–165

spacer images, 111, 112

spamming, keywords and, 67

span tags, 157

spelling, checking for text, 126

Splat! plug-in, 336–337

Split View, 60

splitting table cells, 75

Start Page, using, 47

starting. *See* **opening**

static pages, 245

status bar, 37

Strict DOCTYPE, 53

submenu items for pop-up menus, 297, 306

Submit button for forms, 190

Sun Chili!Soft ASP, 246

support, hosting service, 232–233

`survey.html` **file**
inserting check boxes, 194–195
inserting radio buttons, 191–193
inserting text area and list, 196–197

SWF vector images, 99. *See also* **images**

synchronizing local site with remote server, 238–239

system requirements
for Apple Macintosh, 28, 328
for CD-ROM items, 327–328
for Microsoft Windows, 27–28, 328

»T«

Table dialog box
  autostretch table settings, 89
  basic form settings, 187
  content table settings, 92
  custom borders settings, 80
  database table settings, 269
  fixed table settings, 83
  layout table settings, 72
  navigation table settings, 90
  nested table settings, 80, 109
  radio button form settings, 191
  rounded table settings, 109

<table> tags (HTML), 24

tables
  aligning images in adjacent columns, 105
  autostretch, 71, 88–89
  for basic form, 187–189
  basics, 72–75
  building home page using, 82–87
  building interior pages using, 88–89
  cell padding and spacing, 72, 74
  centering, 73, 82, 83
  changing colors, 78–79
  for check boxes form, 194–195
  collapsing column width to fit image, 84
  content table, 92
  creating, 72
  custom borders, 80–81
  entering text in cells, 73
  expanded view, 74, 100
  fixed, 71, 82–87
  fluid columns in, 111
  formatting columns in color, 73
  hierarchy in, 71

  hybrid, 71
  inserting columns, 75
  inserting rows, 75
  Layout view for, 93–95
  merging cells, 77
  navigation table, 90–91
  nesting, 80, 109
  overview, 71
  positioning cell contents to top, 83, 91, 92
  for radio buttons form, 191–193
  rounded, using images, 109–112
  selecting elements, 73, 74, 76–77
  selecting entire table, 74, 76, 77
  splitting cells, 75
  tags (HTML), 24

Tag selector on status bar, 37

tags (HTML). *See also specific tags*
  anchor tags, 24, 66
  font tags, 117
  heading tags, 117, 122
  image tags, 24
  list tags, 117, 122, 127
  meta tags, 66–67
  overview, 23–24
  paragraph tags, 24
  span tags, 157
  table tags, 24
  Tag selector on status bar, 37
  XHTML versus HTML, 54

<td> (table cell) tags, 24

technical support for the CD, 331

templates
  advantages, 169
  applying, 172–174
  applying changes to all pages, 176

  creating for pop-up menus, 303–305
  creating from existing documents, 170–171
  detaching, 177
  editing, 175–176
  multiple templates for sites, 177
  overview, 169
  pdg.dwt template, 220–221, 227
  setting editable region, 170–171
  on Start Page, 47
  testing in multiple browsers, 169
  updating after site reports, 224

text
  adding for navigation, 12–14
  checking spelling, 126
  entering in tables, 73
  Flash text, 128–129
  formatting, 13–14, 122–124
  importing, 120–121
  inserting in Web page, 118–119
  linking, 15–17
  lists, 127
  overview, 117
  same color as background, 67
  wrapping around images, 125–126

text area for forms, 196

tiled background images, 111, 113

time for downloading on status bar, 37

title bar, 36

<title> tag, 23

titles
  for documents, 64
  for index.htm page, 7, 64
  keywords in, 64, 66
  for training.html page, 88

top_classes.jpg image, 101

`top_corp.jpg` **image, 101**

`topnavcontent.htm` **page, 314**

`topnav.html` **frame, 313, 314–315**

TopStyle Pro editor, 335

`top_trees.jpg` **image, 100**

<tr> (table row) tags, 24

`trainingcontent.html` **file**

    adding brightness, contrast, and sharpening images, 209

    cropping images in, 206–207

    editing Fireworks image in Dreamweaver, 213–215

    optimizing images in Fireworks, 211–212

    resampling an image, 208

`training.html` **page**

    adding links, 134–135

    adding space using CSS, 164–165

    applying custom classes, 155–157

    applying template to, 172–173

    attaching a style sheet, 150–151

    autostretch table for, 89

    content table for, 92

    contextual selectors, 161–163

    copyright notice in, 118–119

    creating template from, 170–171

    description, 88

    editing the <body> tag, 152–153

    Find and Replace function in, 225–226

    footer area, 160–163

    grouping selector tags, 154

    image map link to, 139

    inserting masthead images, 100–103

    inserting text, 118–119

    keywords, 88

    link to, 137

    list in, 127

    navigation table for, 90–91, 104–105, 136–137

    pseudo-class selectors, 158–159

    removing embedded styles, 148–149

    replacing images, 106–108

    title, 88

    wrapping text around images, 125–126

`training.jpg` **image, 125**

`training2.jpg` **image, 126**

`training.txt` **file, importing, 120**

transitional design method, 52–53

Transitional DOCTYPE, 53

`trees.gif` **image, 86**

troubleshooting the CD, 331

tutorials on Start Page, 47

»U«

<ul> (unordered list) tags, 127

undocking panels, 38

update pages, building, 276–280

Update Pages dialog box, 176

Update Record behavior, 276, 277

Update Template Files dialog box, 176

»V«

validating forms, 275

vector graphics, 99. *See also* **images**

`view_contacts.asp` **page, 285–287**

visited link color, 16, 65, 162

»W«

Web applications

    adding a recordset, 268–270

    building delete pages, 283–284

    building master detail pages, 285–287

    building update pages, 276–280

    Insert Record on forms, 273–274

    overview, 267

    Recordset Navigation Bar, 281–282

    Repeat Region behavior, 271–272

    static versus dynamic pages in, 245

    technologies for developing, 287

    validating forms, 275

Web Assist PayPal extension on the CD, 330, 333

Web hits, keywords and, 66

Web servers, 246–248

Web sites. *See* **Internet resources; sites**

Web statistics, 234

WebSpice Objects demo on the CD, 330

Wild FX demo on the CD, 330

wildcards for Find and Replace, 226

Wildform Resource Center, 335

Wiley Publishing Customer Care, 331

windows, 37, 61. *See also* **documents**

Windows (Microsoft)

    ASP support, 246

    default Web page file extension, 6

    IIS for, 247–248

    Macintosh differences, 28

    making read-only files usable, 27

    PWS for, 246

    system requirements, 27–28, 328

Word (Microsoft), importing text from, 121

workspace
changing workspaces, 36
customizing, 38–39

Designer versus HomeSite/Coder, 35
setting up, 35–37

wrapping text around images, 125–126

W3C (World Wide Web Consortium), 23, 63

Xenofex 2 demo plug-in on the CD, 330, 336

XHTML, 24, 52, 53, 54

About Seybold Seminars and Publications

Workflow
Media Te
Creation C
Manageme
Digital As
Fonts an
Digital M
Content I
Managem
Workflow
Media Te
Creation I
Manageme
Digital Ac
Fonts at
Digital M
Content
Managem
Workflow
Media T
Creation
Managem

Seybold Seminars and Publications is your complete guide
to the publishing industry. For more than 30 years it
has been the most trusted source for technology events,
news, and insider intelligence.

Produced by

Key3 Media Group

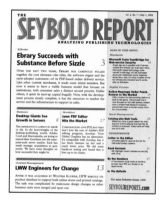

PUBLICATIONS

Today, Seybold Publications and Consulting continues to guide publishing professionals around the world in their purchasing decisions and business strategies through newsletters, online resources, consulting, and custom corporate services.

○ ***The Seybold Report: Analyzing Publishing Technologies***
The Seybold Report analyzes the cross-media tools, technologies, and trends shaping professional publishing today. Each in-depth newsletter delves into the topics changing the marketplace. *The Seybold Report* covers critical analyses of the business issues and market conditions that determine the success of new products, technologies, and companies. Read about the latest developments in mission-critical topic areas, including content and asset management, color management and proofing, industry standards, and cross-media workflows. A subscription to *The Seybold Report* (24 issues per year) includes our weekly email news service, *The Bulletin,* and full access to the seyboldreports.com archives.

○ ***The Bulletin: Seybold News & Views on Electronic Publishing***
The Bulletin: Seybold News & Views on Electronic Publishing is Seybold Publications' weekly email news service covering all aspects of electronic publishing. Every week *The Bulletin* brings you all the important news in a concise, easy-to-read format.

For more information on **NEWSLETTER SUBSCRIPTIONS,** please visit **seyboldreports.com**.

CUSTOM SERVICES

In addition to newsletters and online information resources, Seybold
Publications and Consulting offers a variety of custom corporate services
designed to meet your organization's specific needs.

○ **Strategic Technology Advisory Research Service (STARS)**
The STARS program includes a group license to *The Seybold Report* and
The Bulletin, phone access to our analysts, access to online archives at
seyboldreports.com, an on-site visit by one of our analysts, and much more.

○ **Personalized Seminars**
Our team of skilled consultants and subject experts work with you to create a
custom presentation that gets your employees up to speed on topics spanning
the full spectrum of prepress and publishing technologies covered in our publications. Full-day and half-day seminars are available.

○ **Site Licenses**
Our electronic licensing program keeps everyone in your organization, sales
force, or marketing department up to date at a fraction of the cost of buying
individual subscriptions. One hard copy of *The Seybold Report* is included with
each electronic license.

For more information on **CUSTOM CORPORATE SERVICES,**
please visit **seyboldreports.com**.

SEYBOLD SEMINARS

EVENTS

Seybold Seminars facilitates exchange and discussion within the high-tech publishing community several times a year. A hard-hitting lineup of conferences, an opportunity to meet leading media technology vendors, and special events bring innovators and leaders together to share ideas and experiences.

Conferences

Our diverse educational programs are designed to tackle the full range of the latest developments in publishing technology. Topics include:

- ○ Print publishing
- ○ Web publishing
- ○ Design
- ○ Creative tools and standards
- ○ Best practices

- ○ Multimedia
- ○ Content management
- ○ Technology standards
- ○ Security
- ○ Digital rights management

In addition to the conferences, you'll have the opportunity to meet representatives from companies that bring you the newest products and technologies in the publishing marketplace. Test tools, evaluate products, and take free classes from the experts.

For more information on **SEYBOLD SEMINARS EVENTS,** please visit **seyboldseminars.com.**

Wiley Publishing, Inc.
End-User License Agreement

READ THIS. You should carefully read these terms and conditions before opening the software packet(s) included with this book "Book". This is a license agreement "Agreement" between you and Wiley Publishing, Inc. "WPI". By opening the accompanying software packet(s), you acknowledge that you have read and accept the following terms and conditions. If you do not agree and do not want to be bound by such terms and conditions, promptly return the Book and the unopened software packet(s) to the place you obtained them for a full refund.

1. **License Grant.** WPI grants to you (either an individual or entity) a nonexclusive license to use one copy of the enclosed software program(s) (collectively, the "Software") solely for your own personal or business purposes on a single computer (whether a standard computer or a workstation component of a multi-user network). The Software is in use on a computer when it is loaded into temporary memory (RAM) or installed into permanent memory (hard disk, CD-ROM, or other storage device). WPI reserves all rights not expressly granted herein.

2. **Ownership.** WPI is the owner of all right, title, and interest, including copyright, in and to the compilation of the Software recorded on the disk(s) or CD-ROM "Software Media". Copyright to the individual programs recorded on the Software Media is owned by the author or other authorized copyright owner of each program. Ownership of the Software and all proprietary rights relating thereto remain with WPI and its licensers.

3. **Restrictions on Use and Transfer.**

   (a) You may only (i) make one copy of the Software for backup or archival purposes, or (ii) transfer the Software to a single hard disk, provided that you keep the original for backup or archival purposes. You may not (i) rent or lease the Software, (ii) copy or reproduce the Software through a LAN or other network system or through any computer subscriber system or bulletin-board system, or (iii) modify, adapt, or create derivative works based on the Software.

   (b) You may not reverse engineer, decompile, or disassemble the Software. You may transfer the Software and user documentation on a permanent basis, provided that the transferee agrees to accept the terms and conditions of this Agreement and you retain no copies. If the Software is an update or has been updated, any transfer must include the most recent update and all prior versions.

4. **Restrictions on Use of Individual Programs.** You must follow the individual requirements and restrictions detailed for each individual program in the About the CD-ROM appendix of this Book. These limitations are also contained in the individual license agreements recorded on the Software Media. These limitations may include a requirement that after using the program for a specified period of time, the user must pay a registration fee or discontinue use. By opening the Software packet(s), you will be agreeing to abide by the licenses and restrictions for these individual programs that are detailed in the About the CD-ROM appendix and on the Software Media. None of the material on this Software Media or listed in this Book may ever be redistributed, in original or modified form, for commercial purposes.

5. **Limited Warranty.**

   (a) WPI warrants that the Software and Software Media are free from defects in materials and workmanship under normal use for a period of sixty (60) days from the date of purchase of this Book. If WPI receives notification within the warranty period of defects in materials or workmanship, WPI will replace the defective Software Media.

   (b) WPI AND THE AUTHOR(S) OF THE BOOK DISCLAIM ALL OTHER WARRANTIES, EXPRESS OR IMPLIED, INCLUDING WITHOUT LIMITATION IMPLIED WARRANTIES OF MERCHANTABILITY AND FITNESS FOR A PARTICULAR PURPOSE, WITH RESPECT TO THE SOFTWARE, THE PROGRAMS, THE SOURCE CODE CONTAINED THEREIN, AND/OR THE TECHNIQUES DESCRIBED IN THIS BOOK. WPI DOES NOT WARRANT THAT THE FUNCTIONS CONTAINED IN THE SOFTWARE WILL MEET YOUR REQUIREMENTS OR THAT THE OPERATION OF THE SOFTWARE WILL BE ERROR FREE.

   (c) This limited warranty gives you specific legal rights, and you may have other rights that vary from jurisdiction to jurisdiction.

6. **Remedies.**

   (a) WPI's entire liability and your exclusive remedy for defects in materials and workmanship shall be limited to replacement of the Software Media, which may be returned to WPI with a copy of your receipt at the following address: Software Media Fulfillment Department, Attn.: *Dreamweaver MX 2004 Complete Course,* Wiley Publishing, Inc., 10475 Crosspoint Blvd., Indianapolis, IN 46256, or call 1-800-762-2974. Please allow four to six weeks for delivery. This Limited Warranty is void if failure of the Software Media has resulted from accident, abuse, or misapplication. Any replacement Software Media will be warranted for the remainder of the original warranty period or thirty (30) days, whichever is longer.

   (b) In no event shall WPI or the author be liable for any damages whatsoever (including without limitation damages for loss of business profits, business interruption, loss of business information, or any other pecuniary loss) arising from the use of or inability to use the Book or the Software, even if WPI has been advised of the possibility of such damages.

   (c) Because some jurisdictions do not allow the exclusion or limitation of liability for consequential or incidental damages, the above limitation or exclusion may not apply to you.

7. **U.S. Government Restricted Rights.** Use, duplication, or disclosure of the Software for or on behalf of the United States of America, its agencies and/or instrumentalities "U.S. Government" is subject to restrictions as stated in paragraph (c)(1)(ii) of the Rights in Technical Data and Computer Software clause of DFARS 252.227-7013, or subparagraphs (c) (1) and (2) of the Commercial Computer Software - Restricted Rights clause at FAR 52.227-19, and in similar clauses in the NASA FAR supplement, as applicable.

8. **General.** This Agreement constitutes the entire understanding of the parties and revokes and supersedes all prior agreements, oral or written, between them and may not be modified or amended except in a writing signed by both parties hereto that specifically refers to this Agreement. This Agreement shall take precedence over any other documents that may be in conflict herewith. If any one or more provisions contained in this Agreement are held by any court or tribunal to be invalid, illegal, or otherwise unenforceable, each and every other provision shall remain in full force and effect.